even
more
of the
world's
very best
e-mails

even more

of the

world's

very best

e-mails

>>> compiled by
Geoff Young

Hodder Moa Beckett

National Library of New Zealand Cataloguing-in-Publication Data
Even more of the world's very best e-mails / compiled by Geoff Young.
ISBN 1-86958-962-9
1. English wit and humour. 2. Electronic mail systems—Humour.
I. Young, Geoff.
827.008—dc 21

Published by Hodder Moa Beckett Publishers Ltd
[a member of the Hodder Headline Group]
4 Whetu Place, Mairangi Bay
Auckland, New Zealand

Designed and produced by Hodder Moa Beckett Publishers Ltd
Printed by Griffin Press, Australia

Geoff Young

is a journalist living in Auckland. After returning from 14 years working on British newspapers, including the *Daily Telegraph*, he did stints on the *New Zealand Herald* and the *Sunday Star-Times* before returning to freelance work, chiefly with Reuters. His book credits include Gerarda Bossard's *P.O.W. — One Girl's Experience in a Japanese P.O.W. Camp*, *Inside the Taxi: Tales from Kiwi Cab Drivers*, Bernice Mene's *Mene Confessions*, *The World's Very Best E-mails* and *More of the World's Best E-mails*.

For those of nervous disposition, beware of the following pages. The complete lack of taste puts you at grave risk of getting a life. Be warned!

contents

intro

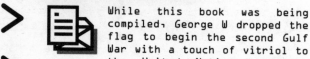

While this book was being compiled, George W dropped the flag to begin the second Gulf War with a touch of vitriol to the United Nations and the world who wouldn't go along with his desire to play the world's policeman. George W wanted to give Saddam a thrashing with a rubber truncheon, thinly disguised as the Mother of All Bombs, and to hell with all the niceties of waiting for a UN sanction.

The war drums had been beating for a long time during the making of this tome; the America's Cup was raced and lost; the Super 12 competition began and the cricket World Cup was going on in South Africa. Now, all of those are serious enough and some more serious than others — depending on your priorities — but of course the event that drew the most jokes out of that lot was the pending war.

The hawkish George W is generally made out to be a dimwit in the missives that have made the book. But George W isn't the only one who gets it in the neck. Saddam Hussein, a butcher from Baghdad, naturally cops a bit of stick in the 'The Good, the Bad and the Ugly' chapter, and our boat boy Russell Coutts is mentioned in the same joke — the reason for which, funnily enough, escapes us!

Even Bill Clinton manages to make it, although Monica Lewinsky has finally managed to get 'that' dress to the drycleaners. The randy grey-haired bugger is a great friend of ours, and a publication without him in it would not be complete.

The chapters in this edition have been changed slightly, but they all contain roughly the same sort of ditties. There is no section taking the piss out of the royals, for the simple reason that they seem to be behaving themselves and not giving rise to any of the British jokesters to let us in on the odd story. We would have thought Charles and Camilla's comings and goings still had a bit of mileage, but their lives have become so dull and unsensational they only make it into 'Hello!' magazine.

And then there was the alleged homosexual hows-yer-father in one of the royal palaces. Someone could have made a joke involving Edward, but it was not to be. And what of the butler whom the Queen let off the hook when she 'remembered' him telling her he was taking some of Princess Di's possessions for safe-keeping.

Now, we all know of historical cases of 'what the butler saw' and we could have been let in on the odd bit of gossip regarding the late princess. But then, we know most of that, so perhaps it would only have made the also-ran file after all.

A new chapter is 'The Animal Kingdom'. This was well overdue, because so many good jokes revolve around animals, and the cuddly bear seems to be the star of this section. There is a lovely list of ways in which dogs are different from our partners and a tale involving the Lone Ranger's horse, Silver.

Talking about our partners, there is never a shortage of piss-taking nasties about either sex, presumably written by members of the opposite sex (although there could be any number of traitorous renegades among the authors).

Blonde jokes survive and get all the more ridiculous, even though they are still very funny, and workplace practices get a going over in the 'Earning a Crust' chapter, which makes one miss the interaction of an office — almost.

Speaking of the America's Cup, there is the odd mention of Signor Bertarelli. A home-made raft race down the Whanganui River recently had a craft named 'Adinghi' after Bertarelli's victorious

Swiss yacht 'Alinghi', which we thought was rather good. Shame Bertarelli's vessel did not sail like a dinghy in the real thing, but we aren't bitter at all.

Having a poke at our neighbours is good old-fashioned sport and 'Across the Seas' is the medium for a fair bit of that, while 'The Boozers' gives us a laugh at the expense of the lovers of alcohol out there, although most of the time we didn't have a clue what they were going on about!

The 'Naughty but Nice' chapter is a bit saucy and may well offend. The dirty joke, like life we suppose, has grown in smuttiness over the years, but we also suppose our eyes and ears have become more immune to them. What we get away with these days is really quite disgusting, but it would be interesting to be a fly on the wall when someone picks up this book to see what chapter they turn to first.

On the other hand, we ditched all the puke-inducing 'feel-good' stuff that floats around cyberspace. Do we really want to think of someone who did us a favour or influenced us along life's rocky road, with the odd fork in the track, towards the University of Life? Tell the truth, there may not be many of us who can pinpoint any one particular angel of mercy that gave us a kick-start in life, apart from our dear old mums — and that was their job, wasn't it?

And an important warning. Do not attempt to read this in one sitting. It will drive you potty and, take it from us, numb your sense of humour. Let's face it, in these days of war and pestilence, if you can't laugh, you might as well hop off to Hebron, join the Hezbollah and volunteer for a suicide sortie across to the West Bank, or go and join Saddam and his mad sons, where having a sense of humour would be decidedly dodgy.

bending the genders

This chapter is devoted to the ones we love to hate — members of the opposite sex. The put-downs in this chapter follow a familiar theme of the women insulting the men, men insulting them back and plenty of those lovely lists where members of both sexes tell us all about OUR good bits and THEIR rotten bits.

As we know, or as were always told, hell hath no fury like a woman scorned and they continue to get their own back. We discover that the word can be just as sharp as the sword — or blunt — as the case may be.

So settle down, turn down the page of the particularly delicious ones that perfectly sum up the partner in your life and remember, no one takes the repetitive taunts in this chapter seriously — unless they were copied into a blank birthday card!

These are entries to a competition asking for a rhyme with the most romantic first line, but least romantic second line:

Love may be beautiful, love may be bliss
But I only slept with you, 'cause I was pissed.

Roses are red, violets are blue, sugar is sweet, and so are you
But the roses are wilting, the violets are dead, the sugar bowl's empty and so is your head.

Of loving beauty you float with grace
If only you could hide your face.

I thought that I could love no other
Until, that is, I met your brother.

Kind, intelligent, loving and hot
This describes everything you are not.

I want to feel your sweet embrace
But don't take that paper bag off your face.

I love your smile, your face and your eyes
Damn, I'm good at telling lies!

Every time I see your face
I wish I were in outer space.

I saw your face as you walked by
But then I saw a better guy.

My darling, my lover, my beautiful wife
Marrying you screwed up my life.

I see your face when I am dreaming
That's why I always wake up screaming.

My love, you take my breath away
What have you stepped in to smell this way?

My feelings for you no words can tell
Except for maybe 'Go to hell'.

What inspired this amorous rhyme?
Two parts vodka, one part lime.

HEAVY CONTACT >>>

Name of Boyfriend/Fiancé/Husband:

I request permission for a leave of absence from the highest
authority in my life for the following period:

Date: **Time of departure:**   **Time of return:**

Should permission be granted, I do solemnly swear to only visit the
locations stated below, at the stated times. I agree to refrain from
hitting on or flirting with other women. I shall not even speak to
another female, except as expressly permitted in writing below. I will
not turn off my cellphone after two pints, nor shall I consume above
the allowed volume of alcohol without first phoning for a taxi and
calling you. My girlfriend/fiancé/wife — you, my sweetest — retain
the right to be pissed off with me the following week for no valid
reason whatsoever — be generous, oh gorgeous one.
Amount of alcohol allowed (units): **Beer**   **Wine**   **Liquor**
Total:
Locations to be visited:
Females with whom conversation is permitted:

IMPORTANT — STRIPPER CLAUSE: Notwithstanding the
female contact permitted above, I promise to refrain from coming
within 30 metres of a stripper or exotic dancer. Violation of this
Stripper Clause shall be grounds for immediate termination of the
relationship.
    I acknowledge my position in life. I know who wears the trousers
in our relationship and I agree it's not me. I promise to abide by

your rules and regulations. I understand that this is going to cost me a fortune in chocolates and flowers. You reserve the right to obtain and use my credit cards whenever you wish to do so. I hereby promise to take you to a Robbie Williams concert, should I not return home by the approved time. On my way home, I will not pick a fight with any stranger, nor shall I conduct in-depth discussions with the said entity. Upon my return home, I promise not to urinate anywhere other than in the toilet. In addition, I will refrain from waking you up, breathing my vile breath in your face, and attempting to breed like a (drunken) rabbit.

I declare that to the best of my knowledge (of which I have none compared to my **BETTER** half), the above information is correct.
Signed (Boyfriend/Fiancé/Husband):

Request is: **APPROVED / DENIED**

This decision is not negotiable. If approved, cut permission slip below and carry at all times.

✂ ....

....

Permission for my boyfriend/fiancé/husband to be away for the following period of time:
Date: Time of departure: Time of return:

Signed (Girlfriend/Fiancée/Wife):

On the other hand ...
Name of Girlfriend/Fiancée/Partner/Wife:

I'M GOING OUT, OK.

Signed (me):

✉ BUMPER STICKERS FOR THE SISTERS >>>

- So many men, but so few can afford me.
- God made us sisters, Prozac made us friends.
- Coffee, chocolate, men ... some things are just better rich.
- Don't treat me any differently than you would the Queen.
- I'm out of oestrogen and I have a gun.
- Warning: I have an attitude and I know how to use it.
- Of course I don't look busy ... I did it right the first time.
- Do not start with me. You will not win.
- All stressed out and no one to choke.
- How can I miss you if you won't go away?
- Don't upset me! I'm running out of places to hide the bodies.
- If you want breakfast in bed, sleep in the kitchen.

✉ BRAIN BREAKERS >>>

New evening classes for men. All are welcome.
Open to men only

Note: Due to the complexity and level of difficulty of their content, each course will accept a maximum of eight participants each.

Topic 1. How to fill ice-cube trays. Step by step with slide presentation.

Topic 2. Lavatory paper rolls: do they grow on the holders? Round-table discussion.

Topic 3. Differences between the laundry basket and the floor. Pictures and explanatory graphics.

Topic 4. The after-dinner dishes and silverware: can they levitate and fly into the kitchen sink? Examples on video.

Topic 5. Loss of identity: losing the TV remote to your significant other. Helpline and support groups.

Topic 6. Learning how to find things, starting with looking in the right place instead of turning the house upside down while screaming. Open forum.

Topic 7. Health watch: bringing her flowers is not harmful to your health. Graphics and audiotape.

Topic 8. Real men ask for directions when lost. Real-life testimonials.

Topic 9. Is it genetically impossible to sit quietly as she parallel parks? Driving simulation.

Topic 10. Learning to live: basic differences between mother and wife. Online class and role-playing.

Topic 11. How to be the ideal shopping companion. Relaxation exercises, meditation and breathing techniques.

Topic 12. How to fight cerebral atrophy: remembering birthdays, anniversaries, other important dates and calling when you're going to be late. Cerebral shock therapy sessions and full lobotomies offered.

Extracurricular courses for men

Pub a: It will still be there if you wait 30 minutes.

Pub b: It will not fall down if you leave before closing time.

Pub c: It will not go out of business if you don't spend every penny you brought with you.

Note: Only one course is currently available for men due to inability to multi-task/leave pub.

 FIGURES OF EIGHT >>>

A man asked his wife what she'd like for her birthday. 'I'd love to be eight again,' she replied. So on the morning of her birthday, he got her up bright and early and off they went to a local theme park. What a day! He put her on every ride in the park: the Death Slide, the Screaming Loop, the Wall of Fear — everything there was! Wow!

Five hours later she staggered out of the theme park, her head reeling and her stomach upside down and went to a McDonald's, where her husband ordered her a Big Mac along with extra fries and a refreshing chocolate shake.

Then it was off to a movie — the latest *Star Wars* epic, and hot dogs, popcorn, Pepsi Cola and M&Ms.

What a fabulous adventure! Finally she wobbled home with her husband and collapsed into bed. He leaned over and lovingly asked, 'Well, dear, what was it like being eight again?'

One eye slowly opened, and the wife said, 'You idiot, I meant my dress size.'

The moral of this story: Even when the man is listening, he's still going to get it wrong.

✉ THE BLOKES' CREED >>>

- Under no circumstances may two men share an umbrella.
- It is OK for a man to cry under the following circumstances: a) when a heroic dog dies to save its master; b) the moment Angelina Jolie starts unbuttoning her blouse; c) after wrecking your boss's car; d) one hour, 12 minutes, 37 seconds into *The Crying Game*.
- Unless he murdered someone in your family, you must bail a friend out of jail within 12 hours.
- If you've known a bloke for more than 24 hours, his sister is off limits forever, unless you actually marry her.
- Moaning about the brand of free beer in a mate's fridge is forbidden. Complain at will if the temperature is unsuitable.
- No man shall ever be required to buy a birthday present for another man. In fact, even remembering your mate's birthday is strictly optional.
- On a road trip, the strongest bladder determines pit stops, not the weakest.
- When stumbling upon other blokes watching a sporting event, you may ask the score of the game in progress, but you may never ask who's playing.
- You may flatulate in front of a woman only after you have brought her to climax. If you trap her head under the covers for the purpose of flatulent entertainment, you are obliged to marry her.
- It is permissible to quaff a fruity alcopop drink only when you're sunning on a tropical beach … and it's delivered by a topless supermodel … and it's free.
- Only in situations of moral and/or physical peril are you allowed to kick another bloke in the nuts.
- Unless you're in prison, never fight naked.
- Friends don't let friends wear Speedos. Ever. Issue closed.

bending the genders

- If a man's fly is down, that's his problem, you didn't see anything.
- Women who claim they 'love to watch sports' must be treated as spies until they demonstrate knowledge of the game and the ability to drink as much as the other sports watchers.
- You must offer heartfelt and public condolences over the death of a girlfriend's cat, even if it was you who secretly set it on fire and threw it into a ceiling fan.
- Never hesitate to reach for the last beer or the last slice of pizza, but not both — that's just mean.
- If you compliment a bloke on his six-pack, you'd better be talking about his choice of beer.
- Never join your girlfriend or wife in kissing a mate of yours, except if she's withholding sex pending your response.
- Phrases that may not be uttered to another man while lifting weights: a) yeah, baby, push it; b) c'mon, give me one more! Harder!; c) another set and we can hit the showers.
- Never talk to a man in a public toilet unless you are on equal footing, both urinating, both waiting in line, etc. For all other situations, an almost imperceptible nod is all the conversation you need.
- You cannot grass on a colleague who shows up at work with a massive hangover. You may, however, hide the aspirin, smear his chair with cheese, turn the brightness dial all the way down so he thinks his monitor is broken, and have him paged over the loudspeaker every seven minutes.
- It is acceptable for you to drive her car. It is not acceptable for her to drive yours.
- Never buy a car in the colours of brown, pink, lime green, orange or sky blue.
- The girl who replies to the question 'What do you want for Christmas?' with 'If you loved me, you'd know what I want!' gets a PlayStation 2.

OOH, PAINFUL >>>

Fresh from her shower, a woman stands in front of the mirror, complaining to her husband that her breasts are too small. Instead of his standard response of reassuring her that her breasts are fine, her husband uncharacteristically comes up with a suggestion.

'If you want your breasts to grow, then take a piece of toilet paper and rub it between your breasts for a few seconds every day.'

Willing to try anything, the wife fetches a piece of toilet paper, and stands in front of the mirror, rubbing it between her breasts.

'How long will this take?' she asks.

'They'll grow larger over a period of years,' he replies.

The wife stops. 'Why do you think rubbing a piece of toilet paper between my breasts every day will make my breasts grow over the years?'

He shrugged and said, 'Worked for your bum, didn't it?'

He lived, and with extensive therapy, may even walk again.

ARTHUR'S HORNY DILEMMA >>>

Young King Arthur was ambushed and imprisoned by the monarch of a neighbouring kingdom. The monarch could have killed him, but was moved by Arthur's youth and ideals. So the monarch offered him freedom, as long as he could answer a very difficult question.

Arthur would have a year to figure out the answer; and if, after a year, he still had no answer, he would be put to death.

The question was: What do women really want?

Such a question would perplex even the most knowledgeable man, and, to young Arthur, it seemed an impossible query. But, since it was better than death, he accepted the monarch's proposition to have an answer by year's end.

He returned to his kingdom and began to poll everybody — the princess, the prostitutes, the priests, the wise men, the court jester. He spoke with everyone, but no one could give him a satisfactory answer. Many people advised him to consult the old witch — only she would know the answer. The price would be high, as the witch was famous throughout the kingdom for the exorbitant prices she exacted.

The last day of the year arrived and Arthur had no alternative but to talk to the witch. She agreed to answer his question, but he'd have to accept her price first. The old witch wanted to marry Gawain, the most noble of the Knights of the Round Table and Arthur's closest friend.

Young Arthur was horrified. She was hunchbacked and hideous, had only one tooth, smelled like sewage and made obscene noises. He had never encountered such a repugnant creature. He refused to force his friend to marry her and have to endure such a burden.

But Gawain, upon learning of the proposal, spoke with Arthur. He told him that nothing was too big a sacrifice compared to Arthur's life and the preservation of the Round Table.

Hence, their wedding was proclaimed, and the witch answered Arthur's question: 'What a woman really wants is to be in charge of her own life.'

Everyone instantly knew that the witch had uttered a great truth and that Arthur's life would be spared. And so it was. The neighbouring monarch granted Arthur total freedom.

What a wedding Gawain and the witch had! Arthur was torn between relief and anguish. Gawain was proper and, as always, gentle and courteous. The old witch put her worst manners on display, and generally made everyone very uncomfortable.

The honeymoon hour approached. Gawain, steeling himself for a horrific experience, entered the bedroom. But what a sight awaited him! The most beautiful woman he'd ever seen lay before him!

The astounded Gawain asked what had happened. The beauty replied that since he had been so kind to her when she'd appeared as a witch, she would henceforth be her horrible, deformed self half the time, and the other half, she would be her beautiful maiden self. Which would he want her to be during the day, and which during the night?

What a cruel question! Gawain pondered his predicament. During the day, a beautiful woman to show off to his friends, but at night, in the privacy of his home, an old witch? Or would he prefer having by day a hideous witch, but by night a beautiful woman with whom to enjoy many intimate moments?

What would you do?

What Gawain chose follows below, but don't read until you've made your own choice.

WAIT!
THINK!

Noble Gawain replied that he would let her choose for herself. Upon hearing this, she announced that she would be beautiful all the time, because he had respected her enough to let her be in charge of her own life.

What is the moral of this story?

WAIT!
THINK!

The moral of the story: If a woman doesn't get her own way, things are going to get ugly!

 ## CHEEKY BASTARD >>>

A man came home from work, sat down in his favourite chair, turned on the TV and said to his wife, 'Quick, bring me a beer before it starts.'

She looked a little puzzled, but brought him a beer. When he finished it, he said, 'Quick, bring me another beer. It's gonna start.'

This time she looked a little angry, but brought him a beer. When it was gone, he said, 'Quick, another beer before it starts.'

'That's it!' She blows her top. 'You bastard! You waltz in here, flop your fat arse down, don't even say hello to me and then expect me to run around like your slave. Don't you realise that I cook and clean and wash and iron all day long?'

The husband gives a big heavy sigh. 'It's started!'

MOTHER-IN-LAW TROUBLES >>>

I was happy. My girlfriend and I were dating for over a year, and so we decided to get married. My parents helped us in every way, my friends encouraged me, and my girlfriend? She was a dream!

There was only one thing bothering me, quite a lot indeed, and that was my mother-in-law to be. She was a career woman, smart, but most of all beautiful and sexy, who sometimes flirted with me, and this made me feel uncomfortable.

One day she called me and asked me to come over to check the wedding invitations. So I went. She was alone, and when I arrived, she whispered to me, that soon I was to be married, and she had feelings and desires for me that she couldn't overcome. So before I got married and committed my life to her daughter, she wanted to make love to me just once.

What could I say? I was in total shock, and couldn't say a word. So, she said, 'I'll go to the bedroom, and if you are up for it, just come and get me.' I stood there for a moment, and then turned around and went to the front door. I opened it, and stepped out of the house. Her husband was standing outside, and with tears in his eyes, hugged me and said, 'We are very happy and pleased, you have passed our little test. We couldn't have asked for a better man for our daughter. Welcome to the family.'

Moral of the story: Always keep your condoms in your car.

 ## LES DAWSON WOULD BE SPINNING IN HIS GRAVE >>>

Yo Mama's So Fat ... when she was diagnosed with that flesh-eating disease, the doctor gave her 13 years to live.

Yo Mama's So Fat ... when she dances she makes the band skip.

Yo Mama's So Fat ... she puts mayonnaise on aspirin.

Yo Mama's So Fat ... her cereal bowl came with a lifeguard.

Yo Mama's So Fat ... when she goes to the zoo the elephants throw her peanuts.

Yo Mama's So Fat ... her driver's licence says 'Picture continued on other side'.

Yo Mama's So Fat ... the back of her neck looks like a pack of hot dogs.

Yo Mama's So Fat ... all the restaurants in town have signs that say 'Maximum Occupancy: 240 Patrons OR Yo Mama'.

Yo Mama's So Fat ... when she gets in a lift, it HAS to go down.

Yo Mama's So Fat ... she was born with a silver shovel in her mouth.

Yo Mama's So Fat ... she's got smaller fat women orbiting around her.

Yo **Mama's So Fat** ... I had to take a train and two buses just to get on her good side.

Yo **Mama's So Fat** ... she has to iron her pants on the driveway.

Yo **Mama's So Fat** ... she's on BOTH sides of the family.

Yo **Mama's So Fat** ... she could sell shade.

Yo **Mama's So Fat** ... when she crosses the street, cars look out for her.

Yo **Mama's So Fat** ... people jog around her for exercise.

Yo **Mama's So Fat** ... when she goes to a restaurant, she doesn't get a menu, she gets an estimate.

Yo **Mama's So Fat** ... if she got her shoes shined, she'd have to take his word for it!

Yo **Mama's So Fat** ... she has to put her belt on with a boomerang.

Yo **Mama's So Fat** ... when she turns around, people throw her a welcome back party.

Yo **Mama's So Fat** ... she can't even jump to a conclusion.

Yo **Mama's So Fat** ... she went to the movies and sat next to everyone.

Yo **Mama's So Fat** ... her belly button doesn't have lint, it has sweaters.

Yo **Mama's So Fat** ... she was walking down the street, I swerved to miss her and ran out of petrol.

 TOUCH >>>

A woman was at home happily jumping on her bed and squealing with delight. Her husband watches her for a while, before asking, 'Do you have any idea how ridiculous you look? What's the matter with you?'

The woman continues to bounce on the bed and says, 'I don't care. I just got back from the doctor's and he says I have the breasts of an 18-year-old!'

The husband says, 'What did he say about your 43-year-old arse?'

'Your name never came up,' she replied.

bending the genders

NAKED TRUTH >>>

A woman stopped by unannounced at her recently married son's house. She rang the doorbell and walked in. She was shocked to see her daughter-in-law lying on the couch, totally naked. Soft music was playing, and the aroma of perfume filled the room.

'What are you doing?' she asked.

'I'm waiting for my husband to come home from work,' the daughter-in-law answered.

'But you're naked!' the mother-in-law exclaimed.

'This is my love dress,' the daughter-in-law explained.

'Love dress? But you're naked!' the mother-in-law said.

'My husband loves me to wear this dress,' she explained. 'It excites him no end. Every time he sees me in this dress, he instantly becomes romantic and ravages me for hours on end. He can't get enough of me.'

The mother-in-law left. When she got home, she undressed, showered, put on her best perfume, dimmed the lights, put on a romantic CD and lay on the couch waiting for her husband to arrive. Finally, her husband came home.

He walked in and saw her lying there provocatively.

'What are you doing?' he asked.

'This is my love dress,' she whispered, sensually.

'Needs ironing,' he said. 'What's for dinner?'

TRADING STANDARDS >>>

A saleswoman is driving toward home in Northern Arizona when she sees a Navajo woman hitchhiking. Because the trip had been long and quiet, she stops the car and the Navajo woman climbs in. During their small talk, the Navajo woman glances surreptitiously at a brown bag on the front seat between them.

If you're wondering what's in the bag,' offers the saleswoman, 'it's a bottle of wine. I got it for my husband.'

The Navajo woman is silent for a while, nods several times and says, 'Good trade.'

✉ RELATIONSHIP SECRETS >>>

1. It is important to find a man who works around the house, occasionally cooks and cleans, and who has a job.
2. It is important to find a man who makes you laugh.
3. It is important to find a man who is dependable and doesn't lie.
4. It is important to find a man who's good in bed and who loves to have sex with you.
5. It is important that these four men never meet.

✉ THE OLD CUT AND TUCK >>>

Dear Sir,

I wish to apply for an operation to make me sterile. My reasons are numerous. After being married for seven years and having seven children I have come to the conclusion that contraceptives are totally useless.

After getting married I was advised to use the rhythm method. Despite trying the tango and the rumba my wife fell pregnant and I ruptured myself doing the chacha.

A doctor suggested we use the safe period. At the time we were living with the in-laws and we had to wait three weeks for a safe period when the house was empty. Needless to say, this didn't work.

A lady of several years' experience informed us that if we made love whilst breast-feeding it would be alright. It's hardly XXX but I did finish up with clear skin, silky hair and felt very healthy, but once again my wife became pregnant.

Another old wives' tale we heard was that if my wife jumped up and down after sex this would prevent pregnancy. After constant breast-feeding, including my earlier attempts, the size of my wife's breasts were such that if she jumped up and down too many times, she would finish up with two black eyes and eventually knock herself unconscious.

I asked the chemist about the sheath. He demonstrated how easy it was to use, so I got a packet. My wife fell pregnant again, which really didn't surprise me as I fail to see how a sheath stretched over a thumb can prevent babies.

A coil was then supplied but after several unsuccessful attempts to fit it we realised we had got a left-hand thread and my wife is definitely a right-hand screw.

A Dutch cap came next. We were very hopeful of this as it didn't interfere with our sex life at all. But alas, it gave my wife severe headaches for although we were given the largest size available, it was still too tight across her forehead.

Finally we tried the pill. At first it kept falling out until we realised we were doing it wrong. My wife then started holding the pill between her knees, thus preventing me from getting anywhere near her. This did work for a while until the night she forgot her pill.

You must appreciate my problem. If this operation is unsuccessful I don't know what we will do. I guess we will have to revert to oral sex, although just talking about it can never be a substitute for the real thing.

 ## DIVORCEIFICATION >>>

A hillbilly farmer who wanted to get a divorce paid a visit to a lawyer. The lawyer said, 'How can I help you?' The farmer said, 'I want to get one of them thar dayvorces.' The lawyer said, 'Do you have any grounds?' The farmer said, 'Yes, I got 40 acres.' The lawyer said, 'No, you don't understand … do you have a suit?' The farmer said, 'Yes, I got a suit, I wears it to church on Sundays.' The lawyer said, 'No, no, I mean, do you have a case?' The farmer said, 'No, I ain't got a case, but I got a John Deere.' The lawyer said, 'No, I mean, do you have a grudge?' The farmer said, 'Sure, I got a grudge … that's where I parks the John Deere.' The lawyer said, 'Does your wife beat you up or something?' The farmer said, 'No, we both get up at 4.30.' The lawyer said, 'Is your wife a nagger?' The farmer said, 'No, she's a little white gal, but our last child was a nagger and that's why I wants a dayvorce.'

 ## MALE POINTS SCORING >>>

- Your arse is never a factor in a job interview.
- Your orgasms are real. Always.
- Your last name stays put.
- The garage is all yours.

- Wedding plans take care of themselves.
- You never feel compelled to stop a friend from getting laid.
- Car mechanics tell you the truth.
- You don't give a rat's arse if someone notices your new haircut.
- Hot wax never comes near your pubic area.
- Wrinkles add character.
- A few well-placed one-night stands gain credibility, not leave you tarnished.
- You don't have to leave the room to make emergency crotch adjustments.
- People never glance at your chest when you're talking to them.
- The occasional well-rendered belch is practically expected.
- Porn movies are designed with you in mind.
- Your pals can be trusted never to trap you with 'So, notice anything different?'
- You can throw a ball more than two metres.
- One mood, ALL the damn time.
- You can open all your own jars.
- Drycleaners and hairdressers don't rob you blind.
- You can go to a public toilet without a support group.
- You can leave a hotel bed unmade.
- You can kill your own food.
- You get extra credit for the slightest act of thoughtfulness.
- If someone forgets to invite you to something, he or she can still be your friend.
- If you are 30 and single, nobody notices.
- Everything on your face stays its original colour.
- You can quietly enjoy a car ride from the passenger's seat.
- Three pairs of shoes are more than enough.
- You don't have to clean your house if the meter reader is coming.
- You can sit in silence watching a football game with your mate for hours without ever thinking 'He must be mad at me.'
- You can drop by to see a friend without having to bring a little gift.
- If another guy shows up at the party in the same outfit, you just might become lifelong friends.
- The same hairstyle lasts for years, maybe decades.
- You don't have to shave below your neck.
- One wallet and one pair of shoes, one colour, all seasons.

- You can 'do' your nails with a pocket-knife.
- You have freedom of choice concerning growing a moustache.
- Christmas shopping can be accomplished for 25 relatives, on December 24, in 45 minutes.
- The world is your urinal.

 LIFE'S A LOTTERY >>>

A woman rushes home, bursts through the front door of her house and yells to her husband: 'Pack your bags, honey, I just won the lottery! All $10 million of it ... Woooohoooo!'

'That's great, darling!' he replies. 'Do I pack for the beach or for the mountains?'

'Who cares?' she replies. 'Just fuck off!'

 LABOUR SAVING >>>

A married couple went to the hospital to have their baby delivered. Upon arrival, the doctor said the hospital was testing an amazing new hi-tech machine that would transfer a portion of the mother's labour pain to the baby's father. He asked if they were willing to try it out.

Both said they were very much in favour of it.

The doctor set the pain transfer to 10 percent for starters, explaining that even 10 percent was probably more pain than the father had ever experienced before.

But, as the labour progressed, the father felt fine and suggested the doctor go ahead and kick it up a notch. The doctor then adjusted the machine to 20 percent pain transfer.

The husband was still feeling fine. The doctor then checked the husband's blood pressure and was amazed at how well he was doing. At this point they decided to try for 50 percent. The husband continued to feel quite well.

Since the pain transfer was obviously helping the wife considerably, the husband encouraged the doctor to transfer all the pain to him. The wife delivered a healthy baby with virtually no pain, and the husband had also experienced none. She and her husband were ecstatic.

When the husband got home after saying goodnight to his wife and newborn baby, he found the postman dead on the porch.

✉ CYCLE SCIENCE >>>

A study in Wisconsin showed that the kind of male face a woman finds attractive can differ depending on where she is in her menstrual cycle.

For instance, if she is ovulating she is attracted to men with rugged and masculine features. And if she is menstruating, she is more prone to be attracted to a man with scissors shoved in his temple and a bat jammed up his arse while he is on fire.

No further studies are expected.

✉ 007 TIMES IT WRONG >>>

James Bond walks into a bar and takes a seat next to a very attractive woman. He gives her a quick glance, then casually looks at his watch for a moment and presses a button on the side. The woman notices this and asks, 'Is your date running late?'

'No,' he replies. 'Q has just given me this state-of-the-art tele-watch. I was just testing it.'

The intrigued woman says, 'A state-of-the-art tele-watch? What's so special about it?'

Bond explains, 'It uses alpha waves to talk to me telepathically.'

The woman crosses her legs seductively, runs her tongue across her upper lip and says, 'And what's it telling you now?'

'Well, it says you're not wearing any knickers ...' Bond replies.

The woman giggles and says, 'Well, it must be broken because I am wearing knickers!'

Bond smirks, taps his watch and says, 'Bloody thing's an hour fast again.'

✉ DOG OF A THOUGHT >>>

A man was leaving a café with his morning coffee when he noticed a most unusual funeral procession approaching the nearby cemetery.

A long black hearse was followed by a second long black hearse about 50 metres behind the first. Behind the second hearse was a solitary man walking a pitbull on a leash. Behind him was a queue of 200 men walking in single file.

The man was curious. He respectfully approached the man walking the dog. 'I am so sorry for your loss, and I know now is a bad time to disturb you, but I've never seen a funeral like this with so many of you walking in single file. Whose funeral is it?'

The man replied, 'Well, that first hearse is my wife.'

'What happened to her?'

The man replied, 'My dog attacked and killed her.'

He inquired further, 'Well, who is in the second hearse?'

The man answered, 'My mother-in-law. She was trying to help my wife when the dog turned on her.'

A poignant and thoughtful moment of silence passes between the two men.

'Can I borrow the dog?'

'Join the queue.'

 DRIVING YOU MAD >>>

Driving to the office this morning on the motorway, I looked over to my left and there was a woman in a brand-new Falcon doing 120km/h with her face up next to her rear-view mirror putting on her eyeliner.

I looked away for a couple of seconds and when I looked back she was halfway over in my lane, still working on that make-up. It scared me (I'm a man) so badly, I dropped my electric shaver, which knocked the donut out of my other hand.

In all the confusion of trying to straighten out the car using my knees against the steering wheel, it knocked my cellphone away from my ear which fell into the coffee between my legs, splashed and burned big Jim and the twins, causing me to scream, which made me drop the cigarette out of my mouth, ruined the damn phone and disconnected an important call.

F***ing women drivers!

Q. *What's the fastest way to a man's heart?*
A. Through his chest with a sharp knife.

Q. *Why are men and parking spaces alike?*
A. Because all the good ones are gone and the only ones left are disabled.

Q. *Why do men want to marry virgins?*
A. They can't stand criticism.

Q. *Why is it so hard for women to find men that are sensitive, caring and good-looking?*
A. Because those men already have boyfriends.

Q. *How do men sort their laundry?*
A. 'Filthy' and 'Filthy but wearable.'

Q. *Do you know why women fake orgasm?*
A. Because men fake foreplay.

Q. *What's the difference between a new husband and a new dog?*
A. After a year, the dog is still excited to see you.

Q. *What makes men chase women they have no intention of marrying?*
A. The same urge that makes dogs chase cars they have no intention of driving.

Q. *What should you do if you see your ex-husband rolling around in pain on the ground?*
A. Shoot him again.

Q. *How can you tell when a man is well hung?*
A. When you can just barely slip your finger in between his neck and the noose.

Q. Why do little boys whine?
A. Because they're practising to be men.

Q. How many men does it take to screw in a light bulb?
A. One — he just holds it up there and waits for the world to revolve around him.
or
Three — one to screw in the bulb, and two to listen to him brag about the screwing part.

Q. What do you call a handcuffed man?
A. Trustworthy.

Q. What does it mean when a man is in your bed gasping for breath and calling your name?
A. You didn't hold the pillow down long enough.

Q. Why does it take 100,000,000 sperm to fertilise one egg?
A. Because not one will stop and ask directions.

Q. Why do female black widow spiders kill their males after mating?
A. To stop the snoring before it starts.

Q. Why do men whistle when they're sitting on the toilet?
A. Because it helps them remember which end they need to wipe.

Q. What is the difference between men and women?
A. A woman wants one man to satisfy her every need. A man wants every woman to satisfy his one need.

Q. How does a man keep his youth?
A. By giving her money, furs and diamonds.

Q: How do you keep your husband from reading your e-mail?
A: Rename the mail folder 'Instruction Manuals'.

Send this to five bright, funny women you know and make their day!! And send this to five bright men who have the sense of humour to find this funny!

P.S. At least finding five bright women is probable.

✉ A WAY WITH WORDS >>>

A girl walks into a supermarket and buys the following:

1 bar of soap	1 toothbrush	1 tube of toothpaste
1 loaf of bread	1 litre of milk	1 apple
1 banana	1 orange	1 plum
1 peach	1 grapefruit	1 tomato
1 lettuce	1 cabbage	1 baking potato
1 cheese segment	1 samosa	1 vegetable pakora
1 muesli bar	1 pie	1 single serving of cereal
1 single frozen dinner	1 single frozen pizza	

The checkout guy looks at her, smiles, and says, 'Single, huh?'
The girl smiles sheepishly and replies, 'How'd you guess?'
He says, 'Because you're f***ing ugly!'

✉ BEWARE OF THAT KNOB >>>

A woman in her late forties went to a plastic surgeon for a face-lift. The surgeon told her about a new procedure called 'The Knob', where a small knob is placed on the back of a woman's head and can be turned to tighten up her skin to produce the effect of a brand-new face-lift.

Of course, the woman wanted 'The Knob'.

Fifteen years later, the woman returned to the surgeon with two problems. 'All these years, everything has been working just fine. I've had to turn the knob many times and I've always loved the results. But now I've developed two annoying problems. First, I have these terrible bags under my eyes and the knob won't get rid of them.'

The doctor looked at her closely and said, 'Those aren't bags, those are your breasts.'

She said, 'Well, I guess that explains the goatee.'

bending the genders

Hers

He was in an odd mood Sunday night. We planned to meet at a bar for a drink. I spent the afternoon shopping with the girls and I thought it might have been my fault because I was a bit later than I promised, but he didn't say anything much about it.

The conversation was very slow going, so I thought we should go off somewhere more intimate so we could talk more privately. We went to this restaurant and he was still acting a bit funny. I tried to cheer him up and started to wonder whether it was me or something else. I asked him, and he said no. But I wasn't really sure.

So anyway, in the car on the way back home, I said that I loved him deeply and he just put his arm around me. I didn't know what the hell that meant because you know he didn't say it back or anything. We finally got back home and I was wondering if he was going to leave me! So I tried to get him to talk but he just switched on the TV.

Reluctantly, I said I was going to go to bed. Then after about 10 minutes, he joined me and to my surprise, we made love. But, he still seemed really distracted, so afterwards I just wanted to confront him but instead I just cried myself to sleep. I just don't know what to do any more. I mean, I really think he's seeing someone else.

His

The Blues lost again. Had a shag though.

HOSTAGE TO THE HORMONES >>>

Every hormone hostage knows there are days in the month when all a man has to do is open his mouth and he takes his life in his hands. This is a handy guide that should be as common as a driver's licence in the wallet of every husband, boyfriend or significant other.

DANGEROUS: What's for dinner?
SAFER: Can I help you with dinner?

SAFEST: Where would you like to go for dinner?

DANGEROUS: Are you wearing that?
SAFER: Gee, you look good in brown.
SAFEST: Wow! Look at you!

DANGEROUS: What are you so worked up about?
SAFER: Could we be overreacting?
SAFEST: Here's $50.

DANGEROUS: Should you be eating that?
SAFER: You know, there are a lot of apples left.
SAFEST: Can I get you a glass of wine with that?

DANGEROUS: What did you do all day?
SAFER: I hope you didn't overdo it today.
SAFEST: I've always loved you in that robe.

... and then there are plenty of things that PMS stands for — so be warned.

Pass My Shotgun
Psychotic Mood Shift
Perpetual Munching Spree
Puffy Mid Section
People Make Me Sick
Provide Me with Sweets
Pardon My Sobbing
Pimples May Surface
Pass My Sweatpants
Pissy Mood Syndrome
Plainly, Men Suck
Pack My Stuff
Permanent Menstrual Syndrome

And finally, an often-asked question designed to get you a damn good kick in the bollocks after the tirade ...

Q: How many women with PMS does it take to change a light bulb?

A: One. Only ONE!! And do you know WHY? Because no one else in this house knows HOW to change a light bulb! They don't even know that the bulb is BURNED OUT! They would sit in the dark for THREE DAYS before they figured it out. And, once they figured it out, they wouldn't be able to find the light bulbs, despite the fact that they've been in the SAME CUPBOARD for the past 17 YEARS! But if they did, by some miracle, actually find them TWO DAYS LATER, the chair they dragged to stand on to change the STUPID light bulb would STILL BE IN THE SAME SPOT!! AND UNDERNEATH IT WOULD BE THE BOX THE STUPID F***ING LIGHT BULBS CAME IN! WHY? BECAUSE NO ONE EVER TAKES OUT THE RUBBISH!! IT'S A WONDER WE HAVEN'T ALL SUFFOCATED FROM THE PILES OF RUBBISH THAT ARE 12M DEEP THROUGHOUT THE ENTIRE HOUSE. THE HOUSE!! — IT WOULD TAKE AN ARMY TO CLEAN THIS F***ING HOUSE! I'm sorry … what did you ask me?

 THE GIRL'S PRAYER >>>

Our Cash
Which art on plastic
Hallowed be thy name
Thy Cartier watch
Thy Prada bag
In Myer
As it is in David Jones
Give us each day our Platinum Visa
And forgive us our overdraft
As we forgive those who stop our Mastercard
And lead us not into Minnie Cooper
And deliver us from High Street
For thine is the Dinnigan, the Esprit and the Armani
For Chanel No 5 and Eternity
Amex

 THE BOY'S PRAYER >>>

Our beer
Which art in bottles
Hallowed be thy sport

Thy will be drunk
I will be drunk
At home as I am in the pub
Give us each day our daily pints
And forgive us our spillage
As we forgive those who spillest against us
And lead us not into the practice of poofy wine tasting
And deliver us from Tequila
For mine is the bitter
The chicks and the footy
Forever and ever
Barmen

 ## THE LANGUAGE BARRIER >>>

Women's English

No = Yes

Maybe = No

'It's your decision' = The correct decision should be obvious by now!

'Do what you want' = You'll pay for this later!

'We need to talk' = I need to bitch.

'Sure ... go ahead' = I don't want you to.

'I'm not upset' = Of course I'm upset, you stupid moron!

'How much do you love me?' = I did something today you're not going to like.

'Is my bum fat?' = Tell me I'm beautiful.

'You have to learn to communicate!' = Just agree with me.

'Are you listening to me?' = Too late, you're dead!

Guy's English

'I'm hungry' = I'm hungry.

'I'm sleepy' = I'm sleepy.

'I'm tired' = I'm tired.

'Do you want to go to a movie?' = I'd eventually like to have sex with you.

'Can I take you to dinner?' = I'd eventually like to have sex with you.

'Can I call you sometime?' = I'd eventually like to have sex with you.

'May I have this dance?' = I'd eventually like to have sex with you.

'Nice dress' = Nice cleavage.

'You look tense, let me give you a massage' = I want to fondle you.

'What's wrong?' = What meaningless self-inflicted psychological trauma are you going through now?

'What's wrong?' = I guess sex tonight is out of the question?

'I'm bored' = Do you want to have sex?

'I love you' = Let's have sex right now.

'I love you too' = OK I said it, we'd better have sex now!

'Let's talk' = I am trying to impress you by showing that I'm a deep person and maybe then you'd like to have sex with me!

'Will you marry me?' = I want to make it illegal for you to have sex with other guys.

 ## FEMALE POINTS SCORING >>>

- Free dinners.
- You can cry without pretending there's something in your eye.
- Speeding ticket? What's that?
- You actually get extra points for sitting on your bum, watching sports.
- If you're a lousy athlete, you don't have to question your worth as a human being.
- A new lipstick gives you a whole new lease on life.
- In high school, you never had to walk down the hall with your binder strategically positioned.
- If you have to be home in time for *Ally McBeal,* you can say so, out loud.
- If you're not making enough money, you can blame the glass ceiling.
- If you're not very attractive, you can fool 'em with make-up.
- If you use self-tanner, it doesn't necessarily mean you're a big loser.
- You could possibly live your whole life without ever taking a group shower.
- Brad Pitt.
- You don't have to fart to amuse yourself.
- You'll never have to decide where to hide your nose-hair clippers.

- When you take off your shoes, nobody passes out.
- If the person you're in a relationship with is much better at something than you are, you don't have to break up with him.
- If you think the person you're going out with really likes you, you don't have to break up with him.
- If you don't shave, no one will know.
- If you're dumb, some people will find it cute.
- You don't have to memorise lines from old movies to fit in.
- You can dress yourself.
- Your hair is yours to keep.
- If you are bald, people will think you did it on purpose, and you're really chic.
- You don't have to pretend to like cigars.
- You'll never have to blow two months' salary on anything.
- If you marry someone 20 years younger, you know you look like an idiot.
- You're rarely compelled to scream at the TV.
- You and your friends don't have to get pissed in order to share your feelings.
- If you pick up the bill once in a while, that's plenty.
- Sitting and watching people is all the entertainment you need.
- Your friend won't think you're weird when you ask if there's spinach in your teeth.
- When you get a million catalogues in the mail, it's a good thing.
- Sometimes, chocolate truly can solve all your problems.
- You'll never regret piercing your ears.
- You can fully assess someone just by looking at his or her shoes.
- You'll never discover you've been fooled by a Wonderbra.
- You don't have hair on your back.
- If anything on your body isn't as big as it should be, you can get implants.
- You can tell which glass was yours by the lipstick mark.
- If you have big ears, no one has to know.
- You can be attracted to someone just because they're really funny.
- You can borrow your spouse's clothes and it doesn't mean you have a problem.

Dear Diary

For my 50th birthday this year, my husband (the dear) purchased a week of personal training at the local health club for me. Although I am still in great shape since playing on my high school hockey team, I decided it would be a good idea to go ahead and give it a try. I called the club and was connected with a man who identified himself as a 26-year-old aerobics instructor and model for athletic clothing and swimwear. My husband seemed pleased with my enthusiasm to get started. The club encouraged me to keep a diary to chart my progress.

Monday

Started my day at 6am. Tough to get out of bed, but found it was well worth it when I arrived at the health club to find Bruce waiting for me. He is something of a Greek god with blond hair, dancing eyes and a dazzling white smile. Woohoo!! Bruce gave me a tour and showed me the machines. He took my pulse after five minutes on the treadmill. He was alarmed that my pulse was so fast, but I attribute it to standing next to him in his Lycra aerobic outfit. I enjoyed watching the skilful way in which he conducted his aerobics class after my workout today. Very inspiring. Bruce was encouraging as I did my sit-ups, although my gut was already aching from holding it in the whole time he was around. This is going to be a FANTASTIC week!

Tuesday

I drank a whole pot of coffee, but I finally made it out the door. Bruce made me lie on my back and push a heavy iron bar into the air — then he put weights on it! My legs were a little wobbly on the treadmill, but I made the full mile. Bruce's rewarding smile made it all worthwhile. I feel GREAT! It's a whole new life for me.

Wednesday

The only way I can brush my teeth is by lying the toothbrush on the bench and moving my mouth back and forth over it. I believe I have a hernia in both pectorals. Driving was OK as long as I didn't try to steer or stop. I parked on a wheelchair user's space in the carpark. Bruce was impatient with me, insisting that my screams bothered other club members. His voice is a little too perky for early in the morning and when he scolds, he gets this nasally whine that is VERY annoying. My chest hurt when I got on the treadmill, so Bruce put me on the stair monster. Why the hell would anyone invent a machine to simulate an activity rendered obsolete by lifts? Bruce told me it would help me get in shape and enjoy life. He said some other shit too.

Thursday
Bruce was waiting for me with his vampire-like teeth exposed as his thin, cruel lips were pulled back in a full snarl. I couldn't help being a half-an-hour late, it took me that long to tie my shoes. Bruce took me to work out with dumb-bells. When he was not looking, I ran and hid in the men's room. He sent Lars to find me, then, as punishment, put me on the rowing machine — which I sank.

Friday
I hate that bastard Bruce more than any human being has ever hated any other human being in the history of the world. Stupid, skinny, anaemic little cheerleader wanna-be bastard. If there was a part of my body I could move without unbearable pain, I would beat him with it. Bruce wanted me to work on my triceps. I don't have any triceps! And if you don't want dents in the floor, don't hand me the f***ing barbells or anything that weighs more than a sandwich (which I am sure you learned in the sadist school you attended and graduated *magna cum laude* from, you Nazi bastard). The treadmill flung me off and I landed on a health and nutrition teacher. Why couldn't it have been someone softer, like the drama coach or the choir director?

Saturday
Bruce left a message on my answering machine in his grating, shrill voice wondering why I did not show up today. Just hearing him made me want to smash the machine with my planner. However, I lacked the strength to even use the TV remote and ended up catching 11 straight hours of the damn weather channel.

Sunday
I'm having the church van pick me up for services today so I can

go and thank God that this week is over. I will also pray that next year my husband (the bastard) will choose a gift for me that is fun — like a root canal, a mammogram, a pelvic exam, or even a hysterectomy.

MODERN PHRASEOLOGY >>>

- You see a gorgeous girl at a party. You go up to her and say, 'I'm fantastic in bed.' That's Direct Marketing.
- You're at a party with a bunch of friends and see a gorgeous girl. One of your friends goes up to her and pointing at you says, 'He's fantastic in bed.' That's Advertising.
- You're at a party and see a gorgeous girl. You get up and straighten your tie, you walk up to her and pour her a drink. You open the door for her, pick up her bag after she drops it, offer her a ride, and then say, 'By the way, I'm fantastic in bed.' That's Public Relations.
- You're at a party and see a gorgeous girl. She walks up to you and says, 'I hear you're fantastic in bed.' That's Brand Recognition.

THAT'S A TOUGH ONE >>>

There was a couple that had been married for 20 years. Every time they made love the husband always insisted on turning the lights off.

Well, after 20 years the wife felt this was ridiculous. She thought she would break him out of this stupid habit. So one night, while they were in the middle of a wild, screaming, romantic session, she turned the lights on.

She looked down … and saw her husband was holding a battery-operated pleasure device … a vibrator … soft, wonderful and larger than a real one. She went completely ballistic.

'You impotent bastard,' she screamed at him. 'How could you be lying to me all these years? You better explain yourself!'

The husband looked her straight in the eye and said calmly, 'I'll explain the toy — if you explain the kids.'

✉ BREAKING THE CHAIN >>>

This chain letter was started in the hope of bringing relief to other tired and discouraged men. Unlike most chain letters, this one does not cost anything. Just send a copy of this letter to five of your friends who are equally tired and discontented. Then bundle up your wife or girlfriend and send her to the man whose name appears at the top of the list, and add your name to the bottom of the list.

When your turn comes, you will receive 15,625 women. One of them is bound to be better than the one you already have. At the time of the writing of this letter, a friend of mine had already received 184 women, of whom four were worth keeping.

REMEMBER this chain brings luck. One man's pitbull died, and the next day he received a Playboy swimsuit model. An unmarried Jewish man living with his widowed mother was able to choose between a topless waitress and a Hollywood supermodel.

You can be lucky too, but DO NOT BREAK THE CHAIN! One man broke the chain, and got his own wife back again.

✉ SAYING IT IN RHYME >>>

John woke up one morning immensely aroused, so he turned over to his wife's side of the bed. His wife, Heather, had already awakened though, and she was downstairs preparing breakfast in the kitchen. Afraid that he might spoil things by getting up, John called his little boy into the room and said, 'Take this note to your beautiful mummy.'
The note read:
The tent pole is up,
The canvas is spread,
To hell with breakfast,
Come back to bed.

Heather, grinning, answered the note and then said to her son, 'Take this to your silly daddy.'
The note read:
Take the tent pole down,
Put the canvas away,

The monkey had a haemorrhage,
No circus today.

John read the note and quickly scribbled a reply and asked his son
to take it back to 'the lady in the kitchen'.
The note read:
The tent pole's still up,
And the canvas still spread,
So drop what you're doing,
And come give me some head.

Laughing, Heather answered the note and then said to her son,
'Take this to the poor man upstairs.'
The note read:
I'm sure that your pole's
The best in the land.
But I'm busy right now,
So do it by hand!

 A WOMAN'S RANDOM THOUGHTS >>>

- Insanity is my only means of relaxation.
- Every seven minutes of every day, someone in an aerobics class
  pulls a hamstring and that makes me smile.
- Women over 50 don't have babies because they would put them
  down and forget where they left them.
- One of life's mysteries is how a two-kilogram box of chocolates
  can make a woman gain five kilograms.
- My mind not only wanders, it sometimes leaves completely.
- The best way to forget all your troubles is to wear tight shoes.
- The nice part about living in a small town is that when you
  don't know what you're doing, someone else does.
- The older you get, the tougher it is to lose weight because by
  then, your body and your fat are really good friends.
- Just when I was getting used to yesterday, along came today.
- Sometimes I think I understand everything, then I regain
  consciousness.
- I gave up jogging for my health when my thighs kept rubbing
  together and setting my pantyhose on fire.

- Amazing! You hang something in your closet for a while and it shrinks two sizes!
- Skinny people irritate me! Especially when they say things like, 'You know sometimes I just forget to eat.' Now I've forgotten my address, my mother's maiden name, and my keys. But I've never forgotten to eat. You have to be a special kind of stupid to forget to eat.
- A friend of mine confused her Valium with her birth-control pills. She had 14 kids, but she doesn't really care.
- They keep telling us to get in touch with our bodies. Mine isn't all that communicative but I heard from it the other day after I said, 'Body, how'd you like to go to the six o'clock class in vigorous toning?' Clear as a bell, my body said, 'Listen bitch, do it and die.'
- The trouble with some women is that they get all excited about nothing — and then they marry him.
- I read this article that said the typical symptoms of stress are eating too much, impulse buying and driving too fast. Are they kidding? That is my idea of a perfect day.
- I know what Victoria's Secret is. The secret is that nobody older than 30 can fit into their stuff.
- If men can run the world, why can't they stop wearing neckties? How intelligent is it to start the day by tying a noose around your neck?

✉ HARD DRIVE OR SOFT DRIVE! >>>

A language instructor was explaining to her class that French nouns, unlike their English counterparts, are grammatically designated as masculine or feminine.

'House,' in French, is feminine: 'la maison.' 'Pencil,' in French, is masculine: 'le crayon.'

One puzzled student asked, 'What gender is a computer?' The teacher did not know, and the word wasn't in her French dictionary, so for fun she split the class into two groups, appropriately enough, by gender, and asked them to decide whether 'computer' should be a masculine or feminine noun.

Both groups were required to give four reasons for their recommendation.

The men's group decided that computers should definitely be of the feminine gender ('la computer'), because:

1. No one but their creator understands their internal logic.
2. The native language they use to communicate with other computers is incomprehensible to everyone else.
3. Even the smallest mistakes are stored in long-term memory for possible later retrieval.
4. As soon as you make a commitment to one, you find yourself spending half your pay on accessories for it.

The women's group, however, concluded that computers should be masculine ('le computer'), because:

1. In order to get their attention, you have to turn them on.
2. They have a lot of data but they are still clueless.
3. They are supposed to help you solve problems, but half the time they are the problem.
4. As soon as you commit to one, you realise that if you'd waited a little longer, you could have got a better model.

✉ ON WOMEN, AGAIN >>>

Women have strengths that amaze men. They carry children, they carry hardships, they carry burdens, but they hold happiness, love and joy.

They smile when they want to scream. They sing when they want to cry. They cry when they are happy and laugh when they are nervous.

Women wait by the phone for a 'safe-at-home call' from a friend after a snowy drive home.

They are childcare workers, executives, attorneys, stay-at-home mums, bikers, babes and your neighbours. They wear suits, jeans and they wear uniforms.

They fight for what they believe in. They stand up for injustice. They walk and talk the extra mile to get their children to the right schools and their family the right healthcare. They go to the doctor with a frightened friend.

Women are honest, loyal and forgiving. They are smart, knowing that knowledge is power. But they still know to use their softer side to make a point.

Women want to be the best for their family, their friends and themselves.

Their hearts break when a friend dies.

They have sorrow for the loss of a family member, yet they are strong when they think there is no strength left.

A woman can make a romantic evening unforgettable.

Women come in all sizes, in all colours and shapes. They live in homes, apartments and cabins. They drive, fly, walk, run or e-mail you to show how much they care about you.

The heart of a woman is what makes the world spin!

Women do more than just give birth, they bring joy and hope. They give compassion and ideals.

They give moral support to their family and friends, and all they want back is a hug, a smile and for you to do the same with who you come in contact with.

 AND MEN, AGAIN >>>

Men are good at lifting stuff.

 SONY ABOUT THAT >>>

A woman came home to find her husband in the kitchen shaking frantically, almost in a dancing frenzy, with some kind of wire running from his waist towards the electric kettle. Intending to jolt him away from the deadly current, she whacked him with a handy plank of wood, breaking his arm in two places. Up to that moment, he had been happily listening to his Walkman.

 ## HELICOPTER HORRORS >>>

Eleven people were hanging on a rope under a helicopter, 10 men and one woman. The rope was not strong enough to carry them all, so they decided that one had to leave, otherwise they all would fall and die.

They were not able to name that person, until the woman made a very touching speech.

She said that she would voluntarily let go of the rope, because as a woman she was used to giving up everything for her husband and kids, or for men in general, without ever getting anything in return.

As soon as she finished her speech, all the men started clapping.

 ## GETTING SOME BALLS >>>

A mild-mannered man was tired of being bossed around by his wife, so he went to a psychiatrist. The psychiatrist said he needed to build his self-esteem, and so gave him a book on assertiveness, which he read on the way home. He had finished the book by the time he reached his house.

The man stormed into the house and walked up to his wife. Pointing a finger in her face, he said, 'From now on, I want you to know that I am the man of this house, and my word is law. I want you to prepare me a gourmet meal tonight, and when I'm finished eating my meal, I expect a sumptuous dessert afterward. Then, after dinner, you're going to run me my bath so I can relax. And, when I'm finished with my bath, guess who's going to dress me and comb my hair?'

'The funeral director,' said his wife.

He does not have a **BEER GUT** — he has developed a **LIQUID GRAIN STORAGE FACILITY**.
He is not a **BAD DANCER** — he is **OVERLY CAUCASIAN**.
He does not **GET LOST ALL THE TIME** — he **INVESTIGATES ALTERNATIVE DESTINATIONS**.
He is not **BALDING** — he is in **FOLLICLE REGRESSION**.
He is not a **CRADLE SNATCHER** — he prefers **GENERATIONALLY DIFFERENTIAL RELATIONSHIPS**.
He does not get **FALLING-DOWN DRUNK** — he becomes **ACCIDENTALLY HORIZONTAL**.
He does not act like a **TOTAL ARSE** — he develops a case of **RECTAL-CRANIAL INVERSION**.
He is not a **MALE CHAUVINIST PIG** — he has **SWINE EMPATHY**.
He is not afraid of **COMMITMENT** — he is **MONOGAMOUSLY CHALLENGED**.

THE PC HE ON HER >>>

She is not a **BABE** or a **CHICK** — she is a **BREASTED HUMAN**.
She is not a **SCREAMER** or **MOANER** — she is **VOCALLY APPRECIATIVE**.
She is not **EASY** — she is **HORIZONTALLY ACCESSIBLE**.
She is not **DUMB** — she is a **DETOUR OFF THE INFORMATION SUPERHIGHWAY**.
She has not **BEEN AROUND** — she is a **PREVIOUSLY ENJOYED COMPANION**.
She is not an **AIRHEAD** — she is **REALITY IMPAIRED**.
She does not get **DRUNK** or **TIPSY** — she gets **CHEMICALLY INCONVENIENCED**.
She is not **HORNY** — she is **SEXUALLY FOCUSED**.
She does not have **BREAST IMPLANTS** — she is **MEDICALLY ENHANCED**.
She does not **NAG YOU** — she becomes **VERBALLY REPETITIVE**.
She is not a **SLUT** — she is **SEXUALLY EXTROVERTED**.
She does not have **MAJOR LEAGUE HOOTERS** — she is **PECTORALLY SUPERIOR**.
She is not a **TWO-BIT WHORE** — she is a **LOW COST PROVIDER**.

✉ STEP RIGHT UP >>>

A woman meets a gorgeous man in a bar. They talk, they connect, they end up leaving together.

They get back to his place, and as he shows her around his apartment, she notices that his bedroom is completely packed with sweet cuddly teddy bears. Hundreds of cute small bears on a shelf all the way along the floor, cuddly medium-sized ones on a shelf a little higher, and enormous bears on the top shelf along the wall.

The woman is surprised that this guy would have a collection of teddy bears, especially one that's so extensive, but she decides not to mention this to him, and is actually quite impressed by his sensitive side.

She turns to him … they kiss … and then they rip each other's clothes off and make hot, steamy love.

After an intense night of passion with this sensitive guy, they are lying there together in the afterglow, and the woman rolls over and asks, smiling, 'Well, how was it?'

The guy says, 'Help yourself to any prize from the bottom shelf.'

✉ ANOTHER GIRL'S PRAYER >>>

Lord, before I lay me down to sleep
I pray for a man who's not a creep
One who's handsome, smart and strong
One who's willy's thick and long
One who thinks before he speaks
When he promises to call, he won't wait weeks
I pray that he is gainfully employed
And when I spend his cash, won't be annoyed
Pulls out my chair and opens my door
Massages my back and begs to do more
Oh, send me a man who will make love to my mind
Knows just what to say, when I ask 'How big's my behind?'
One who'll make love till my body's a twitchin'
In the hall, the loo, the garden and kitchen!
I pray that this man will love me no end
And never attempt to shag my best friend

*And as I kneel and pray by my bed
I look at the dickhead you sent me instead.
Amen.*

AND ANOTHER BOY'S PRAYER
*Lord, I pray for a girl with nice tits.
Amen*

 WOMEN-ONLY WORDS >>>

FINE — This is the word we use at the end of any argument that
we feel we are right about but need to shut you up. NEVER use **FINE**
to describe how a woman looks. This will cause you to have one of
those arguments.

FIVE MINUTES — This is half-an-hour. It is equivalent to the
FIVE MINUTES that your football game is going to last before you
take out the rubbish, so it's an even trade.

NOTHING — If you ask her what is wrong and she says
NOTHING, this means 'something' and you should be on your toes.
NOTHING is usually used to describe the feeling a woman has of
wanting to turn you inside out, upside down, and backwards.
NOTHING usually signifies an argument that will last **FIVE
MINUTES** and end with the word **FINE**.

GO AHEAD (with raised eyebrows) — This is a dare. One that
will result in a woman getting upset over **NOTHING** and will end
with the word **FINE**.

GO AHEAD (normal eyebrows) — This means 'I give up' or 'Do
what you want because I don't care'. You will get a raised eyebrow
GO AHEAD in just a few minutes, followed by **NOTHING** and **FINE**
and she will talk to you in about **FIVE MINUTES** when she cools
off.

LOUD SIGH — This is not actually a word, but is still often a
verbal statement often misunderstood by men. A **LOUD SIGH**
means she thinks you are an idiot at that moment and wonders why

she is wasting her time standing here and arguing with you over **NOTHING**.

SOFT SIGH — Again, not a word, but a verbal statement. SOFT SIGHS are one of the few things that some men actually understand. She is content. Your best bet is to not move or breathe and she will stay content.

THAT'S OK — This is one of the most dangerous statements that a woman can say to a man. **THAT'S OK** means that she wants to think long and hard before paying you retributions for whatever it is that you have done. **THAT'S OK** is often used with the word **FINE** and used in conjunction with a raised eyebrow **GO AHEAD**. At some point in the near future when she has plotted and planned, you are going to be in some mighty big trouble.

PLEASE DO — This is not a statement, it is an offer. A woman is giving you the chance to come up with whatever excuse or reason you have for doing whatever it is that you have done. You have a fair chance to tell the truth, so be careful and you shouldn't get a **THAT'S OK**.

THANKS — A woman is thanking you. Do not faint; just say 'You're welcome'.

THANKS A LOT — This is much different from **THANKS**. A woman will say **THANKS A LOT** when she is really ticked off at you. It signifies that you have hurt her in some callous way, and will be followed by the **LOUD SIGH**. Be careful not to ask what is wrong after the **LOUD SIGH**, as she will only tell you **NOTHING**.

 DREAMS ARE FREE >>>

What women want in a man:

Age 16
1. Cute
2. Has a car
3. Likes me

Age 21

1. Handsome
2. Charming and polite
3. Financially successful
4. Caring and sympathetic
5. Witty
6. Athletic
7. Stylish dresser
8. Appreciates finer things in life
9. Full of thoughtful surprises
10. An imaginative, romantic lover

Age 32

1. Decent looking, preferably with hair
2. Opens car doors, holds chairs
3. Has enough money for a nice dinner
4. Laughs at my jokes
5. Carries bags of groceries with ease
6. Owns at least one suit
7. Appreciates a good home-cooked meal
8. Remembers birthdays and anniversaries
9. Wants romance at least once a week
10. Bathes

Age 40

1. Not too ugly, balding is OK
2. Steady job
3. Takes me out to dinner occasionally
4. Nods head when I'm talking
5. Usually remembers punchlines of jokes
6. Is in good enough shape to rearrange the furniture
7. Wears a shirt that covers his stomach
8. Knows not to buy champagne with screw-top lids
9. Remembers to put the toilet seat down
10. Shaves most weekends

Age 55

1. Keeps nose and ear hair trimmed
2. Doesn't belch or scratch in public
3. Has at least a little money saved

4. Doesn't nod off to sleep when I'm venting
5. Doesn't retell the same joke too many times
6. Is in good enough shape to get off couch on weekends
7. Usually wears matching socks and fairly clean underwear
8. Appreciates a good TV dinner
9. Usually remembers names
10. Shaves occasionally

Age 65
1. Doesn't scare small children
2. Remembers where bathroom is
3. Doesn't require much money for upkeep
4. Does not snore too loudly
5. Remembers why he's laughing
6. Is in good enough shape to stand up by himself
7. Usually wears some clothes
8. Remembers where he left his teeth
10. Remembers who I am

Age 75
1. Breathing
2. Doesn't miss the toilet

 LOUD AND PROUD >>>

This is a story about a couple who had been happily married for years. The only friction in their marriage was the husband's habit of farting loudly every morning when he awoke. The noise would wake his wife and the smell would make her eyes water and make her gasp for air.

Every morning she would plead with him to stop ripping them off because it was making her sick. He told her he couldn't stop it and that it was perfectly natural. She told him to see a doctor; she was concerned that one day he would blow his guts out. The years went by and he continued to rip them out.

Then one Christmas morning as she was preparing the turkey for dinner and he was upstairs sound asleep, she looked at the bowl where she had put the turkey innards and neck, gizzard, liver — all the spare parts — and a malicious thought came to her. She took the bowl and went upstairs where her husband was sound asleep and, gently pulling back the bed covers, she pulled back the elastic waistband of his underpants and emptied the bowl of turkey guts into them.

Some time later she heard her husband waken with his usual trumpeting which was followed by a blood-curdling scream and the sound of frantic footsteps as he ran into the bathroom. The wife could hardly control herself as she rolled about laughing, tears in her eyes. After years of torture she reckoned she had got him back pretty good.

About 20 minutes later, her husband came downstairs in his blood-stained underpants with a look of horror on his face. She bit her lip as she asked him what was the matter. He said, 'Honey, you were right. All these years you have warned me and I didn't listen to you.'

'What do you mean?' asked his wife.

'Well, you always told me that one day I would end up farting my guts out, and today it finally happened. But by the grace of God, some Vaseline, and these two fingers, I think I got most of them back in.'

 ## ART OF LISTENING >>>

A man is driving down a road. A woman is driving down the same road from the opposite direction and as they pass each other, the woman leans out the window and yells, PIG!

The man immediately leans out his window and yells, SLUT! They each continue on their way, and as the man rounds the next curve, he crashes into a huge pig in the middle of the road and dies.

Thought for the day: if only men would listen.

 ## KEVIN AND REBECCA >>>

Kevin decided to propose to Rebecca, but prior to her acceptance, Rebecca had to confess to him about her childhood illness.

She informed Kevin that she had suffered a growth disease that left her breasts with the maturity of a 12-year-old girl. He stated that it was OK because he loved her so much.

bending the genders

However, Kevin felt this was also the time for him to open up and admit that he had a deformity too. Kevin looked Rebecca in the eyes and said, 'I too have a problem. My penis is the same size as an infant and I hope you can deal with that once we are married.'

She said, 'Yes, I would marry you and learn to live with your infant-sized penis.'

Rebecca and Kevin got married and Kevin whisked Rebecca off to their hotel suite and they started touching, teasing, holding one another.

Shortly thereafter, as Rebecca put her hands in Kevin's pants, she suddenly began to scream and then ran out of the room.

Kevin ran after her to find out what was wrong. When Kevin caught up with her, Rebecca said to him, 'You told me that your penis was the size of an infant!'

Kevin said, 'It is … it's 8 pounds, 7 ounces and 19 inches long.'

 ## DADDY'S NOT COMING HOME >>>

The following are all replies that women have put on British Child Support Agency forms in the section for listing the father's details:

Regarding the identity of the father of my twins, child A was fathered by [name removed]. I am unsure as to the identity of the father of child B, but I believe that he was conceived on the same night.

I am unsure as to the identity of the father of my child as I was being sick out of a window when taken unexpectedly from behind. I can provide you with a list of names of men that I think were at the party if this helps.

I do not know the name of the father of my little girl. She was conceived at a party [address and date given] where I had unprotected sex with a man I met that night. I do remember that the sex was so good that I fainted. If you do manage to track down the father can you send me his phone number? Thanks.

I don't know the identity of the father of my daughter. He drives a BMW that now has a hole made by my stiletto in one of the door panels. Perhaps you can contact BMW service stations in this area and see if he's had it replaced.

I have never had sex with a man. I am awaiting a letter from the Pope confirming that my son's conception was immaculate and that he is Christ risen again.

I cannot tell you the name of child A's dad as he informs me that to do so would blow his cover and that would have cataclysmic implications for the British economy. I am torn between doing right by you and right by my country. Please advise.

I do not know who the father of my child was as all squaddies look the same to me. I can confirm that he was a Royal Green Jacket.

[Name given] is the father of child A. If you do catch up with him can you ask him what he did with my AC/DC CDs?

From the dates it seems that my daughter was conceived at EuroDisney. Maybe it really is the Magic Kingdom.

So much about that night is a blur. The only thing that I remember for sure is Delia Smith did a programme about eggs earlier in the evening. If I'd have stayed in and watched more TV rather than going to the party at [address given] mine might have remained unfertilised.

WOMEN ON A
POINT-TO-POINT BASIS >>>

For thousands of years, men have tried to understand the rules when dealing with women. Finally, this merit/demerit guide will help you to understand just how it works. Remember, in the world of romance, one single rule applies: make the woman happy. Do something she likes and you get points. Do something she dislikes and points are subtracted. You don't get any points for doing something she expects. Sorry, that's the way the game is played. Here is a guide to the points system:

Simple duties

You make the bed	+1
You make the bed, but forget to add the decorative pillows	0
You throw the bedspread over rumpled sheets	-1
You leave the toilet seat up	-5
You replace the toilet paper roll when it is empty	0
When the toilet paper roll is barren, you resort to Kleenex	-1
When the Kleenex runs out you use the other bathroom	-2
You go out to buy her tampons	+5
in the snow	+8
but return with beer	-5
and no tampons	-25
You check out a suspicious noise at night	0
You check out a suspicious noise and it is nothing	0
You check out a suspicious noise and it is something	+5
You pummel it with a six iron	+10
It's her dog	-40

At the party

You stay by her side the entire party	0
You stay by her side for a while, then leave to chat with a drinking buddy	-2
Named Stephanie	-4
Stephanie is a dancer	-10
With breast implants	-18

Her birthday

You remember her birthday	0
You buy a card and flowers	0
You take her out to dinner	0
You take her out to dinner and it's not a sports bar	+1
OK, it is a sports bar	-2
And it's all-you-can-eat night	-3
It's a sports bar, it's all-you-can-eat night, and your face is painted the colours of your favourite team	-10

A night out with the boys

Go with a pal	0
The pal is happily married	+1

The pal is single   -7
He drives a Ferrari   -10
With a personalised licence plate (GR8 NBED)   -15

A night out with her
You take her to a movie   +2
You take her to a movie she likes   +4
You take her to a movie you hate   +6
You take her to a movie you like   -2
It's called Death Cop III   -3
Which features Cyborgs that eat humans   -9
You lied and said it was a foreign film about orphans   -15

Your physique
You develop a noticeable pot-belly   -15
You develop a noticeable pot-belly and exercise to get
  rid of it   +10
You develop a noticeable pot-belly and resort to loose jeans
  and baggy Hawaiian shirts   -30
You say, 'It doesn't matter, you have one too.'   -800

The big question
She asks, 'Does this dress make me look fat?'
You hesitate in responding   -10
You reply, 'Where?'   -35
You reply, 'No, I think it's your bottom.'   -100
Any other response   -20

Communication
When she wants to talk about a problem:
You listen, displaying a concerned expression   0
You listen, for over 30 minutes   +5
You relate to her problem and share a similar experience   +50
Your mind wanders to sports and you suddenly hear her
  saying, 'Well, what do you think I should do?'   -100
You have fallen asleep   -200

It's that time of the month
You talk   -100
You don't talk   -150

You spend time with her   -200
You don't spend time with her   -500
You are seen to be enjoying yourself: GAME OVER — YOU LOSE

YOU LOSE (PART 2) >>>

The 10 things men know (for sure) about women:

1.	2.	3.
4.	5.	6.
7.	8.	9.

10. They have boobs!

HAPPINESS IS? >>>

How to make a man happy
  1. Let him have sex with you.

How to make a woman happy
  All you have to do is be...

  1. a friend   2. a companion   3. a lover
  4. a brother   5. a father figure   6. a teacher
  7. an educator   8. a cook   9. a gardener
  10. a carpenter   11. a driver   12. an engineer
  13. a mechanic   14. an interior decorator
  15. a stylist   16. a sex therapist
  17. a gynaecologist/obstetrician   18. a psychologist
  19. a psychiatrist   20. a therapist   21. a good father
  22. a gentleman   23. well organised   24. tidy
  25. very clean   27. athletic   28. affectionate
  29. affable   30. attentive   31. ambitious
  32. amenable   33. articulate   34. bold
  35. brave   36. creative   37. courageous
  38. complimentary   39. capable   40. decisive
  41. intelligent   42. imaginative   43. interesting
  44. prudent   45. patient   46. polite
  47. passionate   48. respectful   49. sweet
  50. strong   51. skilful   52. supportive
  53. sympathetic   54. tolerant   55. understanding
  56. someone who loves shopping

57. someone who doesn't make problems
58. someone who never looks at other women
59. very rich

At the same time you must pay attention to make sure you
60. are neither jealous nor disinterested
61. get on well with her family, but don't spend more time with them than with her
62. give her space, but show interest and concern in where she goes

Above all it is very important to
63. Not forget the dates of
● anniversaries (wedding, engagement, first date …)
● graduation
● birthday
● menstruation.

However, even if you observe the above instructions perfectly, you are not 100 percent guaranteed that she will be happy, as she could one day feel overcome with the suffocating perfection of her life with you and run off with the first wild bastard-bohemian-drunk-bon vivant she meets.

 FOLLOW THAT CAR >>>

Yet more clever bumper stickers:
● Behind every successful woman is herself.
● Ginger Rogers did everything Fred Astaire did, but she did it backwards and in high heels.
● A woman is like a tea-bag — you don't know how strong she is until you put her in hot water.
● I have yet to hear a man ask for advice on how to combine marriage and a career.

 SHOPPING FOR A MAN >>>

Recently a 'Husband Shopping Centre' opened, where women could go to choose a husband from among many men. It was laid out in

bending the genders

five floors, with the men increasing in positive attributes as you ascended up the floors.

There were two rules. Once you opened the door to any floor, you must choose a man from that floor. Secondly, if you went up a floor, you couldn't go back down except to leave the place never to return.

A couple of girlfriends went to the place looking for a partner. On the first floor, the door had a sign saying: 'These men have jobs and love kids.' The women read the sign and said, 'Well, that's better than not having jobs, or not loving kids but I wonder what's further up?' So up they went.

The second-floor door says: 'These men have high-paying jobs, love kids, and are extremely good-looking,'

'Hmmm,' say the girls. 'But, I wonder what's further up?'

Third-floor door reads: 'These men have high-paying jobs, are extremely good-looking, love kids and help with the housework.'

'Wow!' say the women. 'Very tempting, BUT there's more further up!' And up they went.

Fourth-floor door: 'These men have high-paying jobs, love kids, are extremely good-looking, help with the housework, and have a strong romantic streak.'

'Oh, mercy me. But just think! What must be awaiting us further on!' So up to the fifth floor they went.

The sign on the door read: 'This floor is empty and exists only to prove that women are bloody impossible to please.'

the

generation

game

Most people will have some empathy with this chapter — it has both ends of the age spectrum covered. Little Johnny is in here, naturally, plus a number of other smart-arse — or cute, depending on your point of view and mood at the time — kids.

It's the poor parents who bear the brunt of the piss-taking, including a marvellous one about what our mothers taught us, which may bring back memories — fond or otherwise.

And the old folks don't get off lightly either. Although it's kinder to taunt them as they probably won't remember the insults tomorrow — no harm done.

SWEET LITTLE MISS >>>

A little girl walks into a pet shop and asks in the sweetest little lisp, 'Excuthe me, mithter, do you keep wittle wabbiths?'

And the shopkeeper gets down on his knees, so that he's on her level, and asks, 'Do you want a wittle white wabby or a soft and fuwwy bwack wabby?'

She, in turn, puts her hands on her knees, bends forward and says, 'I don't fink my pyfon gives a f***!'

 ### IT'S COOL, MUM! >>>

The mother of a 17-year-old girl was concerned that her daughter was having sex. Worried the girl might become pregnant and adversely impact the family's status, she consulted the family doctor.

The doctor told her that teenagers today were very wilful, and any attempt to stop the girl would probably result in rebellion. He then told her to arrange for her daughter to be put on birth control and, until then, talk to her and give her a box of condoms.

Later that evening, as her daughter was preparing for a date, the woman told her about the situation and her suspicions and handed her a box of condoms.

The girl started to laugh and reached over to hug her mother saying, 'Oh Mum! You don't have to worry about that! I'm dating Susan!'

 ### ICE CREAM, YOU SCREAM >>>

A teacher asks her class, 'If there are five birds sitting on a fence and you shoot one of them, how many will be left?'
She calls on Little Johnny. He replies, 'One. They will all fly away with the first gunshot.'

The teacher replies, 'The correct answer is four, but I like your thinking.'

Then Little Johnny says, 'I have a question for you. There are three women sitting on a bench having ice cream. One is delicately licking the sides of the triple scoop of ice cream, the second is gobbling down the top and sucking the cone and the third is biting off the top of the ice cream. Which one is married?'

The teacher, blushing a great deal, replied, 'Well, I suppose the one that's gobbled down the top and sucked the cone.'

To which Little Johnny replied, 'The correct answer is the one with the wedding ring on but I like your thinking.'

MATHEMATICAL PROBLEM >>>

Little Johnny returns from school and says he got an F in arithmetic. 'Why?' asks his father.

'The teacher asked "How much is two times three", I said six,' replies Johnny.

'But that's right!'

'Yeah, but then she asked, "How much is three times two?"'

'What's the f***ing difference?' asks the father.

'That's what I said!' exclaimed Johnny.

TAKING THE PISS >>>

Little Johnny was sitting in class one day. All of a sudden, he needed to go to the toilet. He yelled out, 'Miss Jones, I need to take a piss!' The teacher replied, 'Now, Johnny, that is not the proper word to use in this situation. The correct word you want to use is urinate. Please use the word urinate in a sentence correctly, and I will allow you to go.'

Little Johnny thinks for a bit, then says, 'You're an eight, but if you had bigger tits, you'd be a 10.'

TO THE POINT >>>

Little Johnny was sitting on a park bench munching on one chocolate bar after another. After the sixth one, a man on the bench across from him said, 'Son, you know eating all that chocolate isn't good for you. It will give you acne, rot your teeth and make you fat.'

Little Johnny replied, 'My grandfather lived to be 107 years old.'

the generation game

The man asked, 'Did your grandfather eat six chocolate bars at a time?'

Little Johnny answered, 'No, he minded his own f***ing business!'

✉ LIFE'S LITTLE UPS AND DOWNS >>>

1. Raising teenagers is like nailing jelly to a tree.
2. Wrinkles don't hurt.
3. Families are like fudge … mostly sweet, with a few nuts.
4. Today's mighty oak is just yesterday's nut that held its ground.
5. Laughing is good exercise. It's like jogging on the inside.
6. Middle age is when you choose your cereal for the fibre, not the toy.

✉ THE FOUR STAGES OF LIFE >>>

1. You believe in Santa Claus.
2. You don't believe in Santa Claus.
3. You are Santa Claus.
4. You look like Santa Claus.

✉ AND 10 STAGES OF SUCCESS >>>

1. At age 4 success is not wetting your pants.
2. At age 12 success is having friends.
3. At age 16 success is having a driver's licence.
4. At age 20 success is having sex.
5. At age 35 success is having money.
6. At age 50 success is having money.
7. At age 60 success is having sex.
8. At age 70 success is having a driver's licence.
9. At age 75 success is having friends.
10. At age 80 success is not wetting your pants.

I was driving with my three young children one warm summer evening when a woman in the convertible in front of us stood up and waved. She was stark naked! As I was reeling from the shock, I heard my five-year-old shout from the back seat, 'Mum! That lady isn't wearing a seat-belt!'

My four-year-old son, Zachary, came screaming out of the bathroom to tell me he'd dropped his toothbrush in the toilet. So I fished it out and threw it in the rubbish. Zachary stood there thinking for a moment, then ran to my bathroom and came out with my toothbrush. He held it up and said with a charming little smile, 'We better throw this one out too then, 'cause it fell in the toilet a few days ago.'

On his first day of school, a new-entrant handed his teacher a note from his mother. The note read, 'The opinions expressed by this child are not necessarily those of his parents.'

A woman was trying hard to get the tomato sauce to come out of the bottle. During her struggle the phone rang, so she asked her four-year-old daughter to answer the phone. 'It's the minister, Mummy,' the child said to her mother. Then she said into the phone, 'Mummy can't come to the phone to talk to you right now. She's hitting the bottle.'

I love the outdoors, and because of my passion for hunting and fishing, my family eats a considerable amount of wild game. So much, in fact, that one evening as I set a platter of broiled venison steaks on the dinner table, my 10-year-old daughter looked up and said, 'Boy, it sure would be nice if pizzas lived in the wild.'

A mother was showing her son how to zip up his coat. 'The secret,' she said, 'is to get the left part of the zipper to fit in the other side before you try to zip it up.' The boy looked at her dizzily. 'Why does it have to be a secret?'

When my daughter was three, we watched *Snow White and the Seven Dwarfs* for the first time. The wicked queen appeared, disguised as an old lady selling apples, and my daughter was spellbound. Then Snow White took a bite of the poisoned apple and fell to the ground unconscious. As the apple rolled away, my daughter spoke up. 'See, Mum. She doesn't like the skin either.'

A little boy got lost at the YMCA and found himself in the women's changing room. When he was spotted, the room burst into shrieks, with ladies grabbing towels and running for cover. The little boy watched in amazement and then asked, 'What's the matter ... haven't you ever seen a little boy before?'

 ## MARRIED BLISS >>>

Kids' opinions on marriage

How do you decide whom to marry?
- You got to find somebody who likes the same stuff. Like, if you like sports, she should like it that you like sports, and she should keep the chips and dip coming. *Alan, age 10*
- No person really decides before they grow up who they're going to marry. God decides it all way before, and you get to find out later who you're stuck with. *Kirsten, age 10*

What is the right age to get married?
- Twenty-three is the best age because you know the person FOREVER by then. *Camille, age 10*
- No age is good to get married at. You got to be a fool to get married. *Freddie, age 6*

How can a stranger tell if two people are married?
- You might have to guess, based on whether they seem to be yelling at the same kids. *Derrick, age 8*

What do you think your mum and dad have in common?
- Both don't want any more kids. *Lori, age 8*

What do most people do on a date?
- Dates are for having fun, and people should use them to get to know each other. Even boys have something to say if you

listen long enough. *Lynnette, age 8*
- On the first date, they just tell each other lies, and that usually gets them interested enough to go for a second date. *Martin, age 10*

What would you do on a first date that was turning sour?
- I'd run home and play dead. The next day I would call all the newspapers and make sure they wrote about me in all the dead columns. *Craig, age 9*

When is it okay to kiss someone?
- When they're rich. *Pam, age 7*
- The law says you have to be eighteen, so I wouldn't want to mess with that. *Curt, age 7*
- The rule goes like this: if you kiss someone, then you should marry them and have kids with them. It's the right thing to do. *Howard, age 8*

Is it better to be single or married?
- I don't know which is better, but I'll tell you one thing. I'm never going to have sex with my wife. I don't want to be all grossed out. *Theodore, age 8*
- It's better for girls to be single but not for boys. Boys need someone to clean up after them. *Anita, age 9*

How would the world be different if people didn't get married?
- There sure would be a lot of kids to explain, wouldn't there? *Kelvin, age 8*

And the favourite is:
How would you make a marriage work?
- Tell your wife that she looks pretty, even if she looks like a truck. *Ricky, age 10*

✉ HOW SWEET >>>

A young family moved into a house next door to a vacant lot. One day a construction crew turned up to start building a house on the empty lot. The young family's six-year-old daughter naturally took an interest in the activity going on next door and started talking with the workers.

She hung around and eventually the construction crew more or less adopted her as a kind of project mascot.

They chatted with her, let her sit with them while they had coffee and lunch breaks, and gave her little jobs to do here and there to make her feel important.

At the end of the first week they even presented her with a pay envelope containing five dollars. The little girl took it home to her mother who said all the appropriate words of admiration and suggested that they take the five dollars pay she had received to the bank the next day to start a savings account.

When they got to the bank the teller was equally impressed with the story and asked the little girl how she had come by her very own pay at such a young age. The little girl proudly replied, 'I've been working with a construction crew building a house.'

'My goodness gracious,' said the teller, 'and will you be working on the house again this week too?'

'I will if those worthless f***ers at the timber yard ever bring us the f****n' fibro we ordered,' replied the little girl.

 GRAMMATICALLY SPEAKING >>>

Little Johnny goes to school, and the teacher says, 'Today we are going to learn multi-syllable words, class. Does anybody have an example of a multi-syllable word?'

Johnny says, 'Masturbate.'

Miss Rogers smiles and says, 'Wow, little Johnny, that's a mouthful.'

Little Johnny says, 'No, Miss Rogers, you're thinking of a blowjob.'

 ANNOYING LITTLE PRICK >>>

Little Mary was not the best student in Sunday school. Usually she slept through class. One day the teacher spoke to her while she was sleeping, 'Tell me, Mary, who created the universe?'

When Mary didn't stir, little Johnny, an altruistic boy seated behind her, took a pin and jabbed her in the backside. 'God Almighty!' shouted Mary.

The teacher said, 'Very good,' and Mary fell asleep again. A while later the teacher asked Mary, 'Who is our Lord and Saviour?'

But Mary didn't even stir from her slumber. Once again, Johnny came to the rescue and pricked her again. 'Jesus Christ!!' shouted Mary.

The teacher said, 'Very good,' and Mary fell asleep again. Then the teacher asked Mary a third question. 'What did Eve say to Adam after she had her twenty-third child?' And again Johnny jabbed her with the pin.

This time Mary jumped up and shouted, 'If you stick that damn thing in me one more time, I'll break it in half!'

GREEN EGGS AND HAM MADE IT >>>

Dr Seuss books that were rejected by his publisher:

How the Grinch Stole Columbus Day
Marvin K Mooney, Get the F*** Out!
The Cat in the Microwave
Herbert the Pervert Likes Sherbert
Your Colon Can Moo — Can You?
The Fox in Detox
The Grinch's Ten Inches
One Bitch, Two Bitch, Dead Bitch, Blue Bitch
Zippy the Gerbil
My Pocket Rocket Needs a Socket
Who Shat in the Hat?
Horton Hires a Ho
Aunts in My Pants
The Flesh-Eating Lorax
Oh, the Places You'll Scratch and Sniff!
Yentl the Lentil

BUTTER WOULDN'T MELT >>>

A kindergarten pupil told his teacher he'd found a cat. She asked him if it was dead or alive. 'Dead,' she was informed.

'How do you know?' she asked her pupil.

'Because I pissed in its ear and it didn't move,' answered the child innocently.

'You did WHAT?!' the teacher exclaimed in surprise.

'You know,' explained the boy, 'I leaned over and said "Pssst!" and it didn't move.'

A small boy is sent to bed by his father. Five minutes later: 'Da-ad.'

'What?'

'I'm thirsty. Can you bring me a drink of water?'

'No. You had your chance. Lights out.'

Five minutes later: 'Da-aaaad.'

'WHAT?'

'I'm THIRSTY. Can I have a drink of water?'

'I told you NO! If you ask again, I'll have to smack you!'

Five minutes later: 'Daaaa-aaaad.'

'WHAT NOW!'

'When you come in to smack me, can you bring a drink of water?'

An exasperated mother, whose son was always getting into mischief, finally asked him, 'How do you expect to get into Heaven?'

The boy thought it over and said, 'Well, I'll run in and out and in and out and keep slamming the door until St Peter says, "For Heaven's sake, Dylan, come in or stay out!"'

One summer evening during a violent thunderstorm a mother was tucking her son into bed. She was about to turn off the light when he asked with a tremor in his voice, 'Mummy, will you sleep with me tonight?'

The mother smiled and gave him a reassuring hug. 'I can't dear,' she said. 'I have to sleep in Daddy's room.'

A long silence was broken at last by his shaky little voice: 'The big sissy.'

It was that time, during the Sunday morning service, for the children's sermon. All the children were invited to come forwards.

One little girl was wearing a particularly pretty dress and, as she sat down, the pastor leaned over and said, 'That is a very pretty dress. Is it your Easter Dress?' The little girl replied, directly into the pastor's clip-on microphone, 'Yes, and my mum says it's a bitch to iron.'

When I was six months pregnant with my third child, my three-year-old came into the room when I was just getting ready to get into the shower. She said, 'Mummy, you are getting fat!'

I replied, 'Yes, honey, remember Mummy has a baby growing in her tummy.'

'I know,' she replied, 'but what's growing in your bum?'

A little boy was doing his maths homework. He said to himself, 'Two plus five, that son of a bitch is seven. Three plus six, that son of a bitch is nine …'

His mother heard what he was saying and gasped, 'What are you doing?'

The little boy answered, 'I'm doing my maths homework, Mum.'

'And this is how your teacher taught you to do it?' the mother asked.

'Yes,' he answered.

Infuriated, the mother asked the teacher the next day, 'What are you teaching my son in maths?'

The teacher replied, 'We're learning addition.'

The mother asked, 'And are you teaching them to say two plus two, that son of a bitch is four?'

After the teacher stopped laughing, she answered, 'What I taught them was, two plus two, THE SUM OF WHICH is four.'

One day a teacher read the story *Chicken Little* to her class. She came to the part of the story where Chicken Little tried to warn the farmer. She read: '… and so Chicken Little went up to the farmer and said, "The sky is falling, the sky is falling!"' The teacher paused then asked the class, 'And what do you think that farmer said?'

One little girl raised her hand and said, 'I think he said, "Holy shit! A talking chicken!"' The teacher was unable to teach for the next 10 minutes.

When I was a child, I loved show-and-tell. So I always have a few sessions with my students. It helps them get over their shyness and experience a little public speaking. And it gives me a break and some guaranteed entertainment. Usually, show-and-tell is pretty tame. Kids bring in pet turtles, model aeroplanes, pictures of fish they catch, stuff like that. And I never, ever place any boundaries or limitations on them. If they want to lug it to school and talk about it, they're welcome. Well, one day a little girl, Erica, a very bright, very out-going kid, takes her turn and waddles up to the front of the class with a pillow stuffed under her sweater. She holds up a snapshot of an infant.

'This is Luke, my baby brother, and I'm going to tell you about his birthday. First, Mummy and Daddy made him as a symbol of their love, and then Daddy put a seed in my mother's stomach, and Luke grew in there. He ate for nine months through an umbrella cord.'

She's standing there with her hands on the pillow, and I'm trying not to laugh and wishing I had a video camera rolling. The kids are watching her in amazement.

'Then, about two Saturdays ago, my mother starts going, "Oh, oh, oh!"' Erica puts a hand behind her back and groans. 'She walked around the house for, like an hour, "Oh, oh, oh!"' Now the kid is doing this hysterical duck-walk, holding her back and groaning.

'My father called the middle wife. She delivers babies, but she doesn't have a sign on the car like the pizza delivery man. They got my mother to lie down in bed like this.' Erica lies down with her back against the wall. 'And then, pop! My mother had this bag of water she kept in there in case he got thirsty, and it just blew up and spilled all over the bed, like psshhheew!' The kid has her legs spread and with her little hands is miming water flowing. It was too much!

'Then the middle wife starts going "push, push" and "breathe, breathe". They start counting, but they never even got past 10. Then, all of a sudden, out comes my brother. He was covered in yucky stuff they said was from the play-centre, so there must be a lot of stuff inside there.'

Then Erica stood up, took a big theatrical bow and returned to her seat. I'm sure I applauded the loudest. Ever since then, if it's show-and-tell day, I bring my camcorder — just in case another Erica comes along.

✉ PAD, PLEASE! >>>

An insurance man visited me at home to talk about our mortgage insurance. He was throwing a lot of facts and figures at me, and I wanted to follow as best I could, so I told my six-year-old son to run and get me a pad. He came back and handed me a pad — a sanitary pad — right in front of our guest.

✉ HO, HO, HO >>>

I was taking a shower when my two-year-old son came into the bathroom and wrapped himself in toilet paper. Although he made a mess, he looked adorable, so I ran for my camera and took a few shots. They came out so well that I had copies made and included one with each of our Christmas cards. Days later, a relative called about the picture, laughing hysterically, and suggesting I take a closer look. Puzzled, I stared at the photo and was shocked to discover that in addition to my son, I had captured my reflection in the mirror — wearing nothing but a camera!

✉ NA-NA NA-NA NA-NAH! >>>

While in line at the bank one afternoon, my toddler decided to release some pent-up energy and ran amok. I was finally able to grab hold of her after receiving looks of disgust and annoyance from other patrons. I told her that if she did not start behaving right now she would be punished. To my horror, she looked me in the eye and said in a voice just as threatening, 'If you don't let me go right now, I will tell Grandma that I saw you kissing Daddy's willy last night!' The silence was deafening after this enlightening exchange. Even the tellers stopped what they were doing. I mustered up the last of my dignity and walked out of the bank with my daughter in tow. The last thing I heard when the door closed behind me were screams of laughter.

the generation game

ASK A CHILD THE SAME QUESTION TOO MANY TIMES ... >>>

Have you ever asked your child a question too many times? My three-year-old son had a lot of problems with potty training and I was on at him constantly. One day we stopped at a cafeteria for a quick lunch in between errands. It was very busy, with a full dining room. While enjoying my lunch, I smelled something funny, so of course I checked my seven-month-old daughter, and she was clean. Then I realised that Danny had not asked to go 'potty' in a while, so I asked him if he needed to go, and he said, 'No.' I kept thinking, Oh no, that child has had an accident, and I don't have any clothes with me. Then I said, 'Danny, are you SURE you didn't have an accident?' 'No,' he replied. I just KNEW that he must have had an accident, because the smell was getting worse. I asked one more time, 'Danny, did you have an accident?' This time he jumped up, pulled down his pants, bent over, spread his cheeks and yelled 'SEE MUM, IT'S ONLY FARTS!!' While 30 people nearly choked to death on their lunch laughing, he calmly pulled up his pants and sat down. An old couple made me feel better by thanking me for the best laugh they'd ever had!

GO GIRL, GO >>>

A woman and a baby were in the doctor's examining room, waiting for the doctor to come in. The doctor arrived, examined the baby and determined that it had a fever and was also hungry.

The doctor inquired as to whether the baby was breast-fed or bottle-fed.

'Breast-fed,' the woman replied.

'Well, strip down to your waist,' the doctor ordered. She did. He pressed, kneaded and pinched both breasts for a while in a detailed examination. After stopping to take some notes, he pressed, kneaded and pinched both breasts some more.

Finally he stopped, took more notes, and told her, 'No wonder this baby is hungry. You don't have any milk.'

'I know,' she said, 'I'm his Grandma, but I'm glad I came!'

Samples culled from some Year 12 English essays:

Her face was a perfect oval, like a circle that had its two sides gently compressed by a Thigh Master.

He spoke with the wisdom that can only come from experience, like a guy who went blind because he looked at a solar eclipse without one of those boxes with a pinhole in it and now goes around the country speaking at high schools about the dangers of looking at a solar eclipse without one of those boxes with a pinhole in it.

She grew on him like she was a colony of E. coli and he was room-temperature prime English beef.

She had a deep, throaty, genuine laugh, like that sound a dog makes just before it throws up.

Her vocabulary was as bad as, like, whatever.

He was as tall as a six-foot-three-inch tree.

The revelation that his marriage of 30 years had disintegrated because of his wife's infidelity came as a rude shock, like a surcharge at a formerly surcharge-free ATM.

The little boat gently drifted across the pond exactly the way a bowling ball wouldn't.

McBride fell 12 storeys, hitting the pavement like a hefty bag filled with vegetable soup.

From the attic came an unearthly howl. The whole scene had an eerie, surreal quality, like when you're on holiday in another city and *Sex in the City* comes on at 7pm instead of 7.30.

Her hair glistened in the rain like a nose hair after a sneeze.

The hailstones leaped from the pavement, just like maggots when you fry them in hot oil.

John and Mary had never met. They were like two hummingbirds who had also never met.

Even in his last years, Granddad had a mind like a steel trap, only one that had been left out so long, it had rusted shut.

The plan was simple, like my brother-in-law Phil. But unlike Phil, this plan just might work.

The young fighter had a hungry look, the kind you get from not eating for a while.

'Oh, Jason, take me!' she panted, her breasts heaving like a Uni student on $1-a-beer night.

He was as lame as a duck. Not the metaphorical lame duck, either, but a real duck that was actually lame. Maybe from stepping on a landmine or something.

The ballerina rose gracefully en pointe and extended one slender leg behind her, like a dog at a fire hydrant.

He was deeply in love. When she spoke, he thought he heard bells, as if she were a rubbish truck reversing.

She was as easy as the *TV Guide* crossword.

She walked into my office like a centipede with nine missing legs.

It hurt the way your tongue hurts after you accidentally staple it to the wall.

 REPORTS HORROR >>>

Actual comments made on student's report cards by teachers in the New York City public school system:

1. Since my last report, your child has reached rock bottom and has started to dig.
2. I would not allow this student to breed.
3. Your child has delusions of adequacy.
4. Your son is depriving a village somewhere of an idiot.
5. Your son sets low personal standards and then consistently fails to achieve them.
6. The student has a 'full six-pack' but lacks the plastic thing to hold it all together.
7. This child has been working with too much glue.
8. When your daughter's IQ reaches 50, she should sell.
9. The gates are down, the lights are flashing, but the train isn't coming.
10. If this student were any more stupid, he'd have to be watered twice a week.
11. It's impossible to believe that the sperm that created this child beat out 1,000,000 others.
12. The wheel is turning but the hamster is definitely dead.

N.B. All teachers were reprimanded.

✉ OH DEAR, OH DEAR >>>

A little boy came down for breakfast one morning and asked his grandma, 'Where's Mum and Dad?'

'They're up in bed,' she replied. The little boy started to giggle and ate his breakfast and went out to play.

When he came back in for lunch he asked his grandma, 'Where's Mum and Dad?' and she replied, 'They're still up in bed.'

Again the little boy started to giggle and he ate his lunch and went out to play. Then the little boy came in for dinner and once again he asked his grandma, 'Where's Mum and Dad?' and his grandmother replied, 'They're still up in bed.'

The little boy started to laugh and his grandmother asked, 'What's the matter with you? Every time I tell you they're still up in bed you start to laugh! What is going on here?'

The little boy replied, 'Well last night Daddy came into my bedroom and asked me for the Vaseline and I gave him super-glue.'

How to write a university essay:

1. Sit in a straight, comfortable chair in a well-lit place in front of your computer.
2. Check your e-mail.
3. Read the assignment carefully, to make sure you understand it.
4. Walk down to the vending machines and buy some chocolate to help you concentrate.
5. Check your e-mail.
6. Phone a friend and ask if he/she wants to go to the caf and grab a hot chocolate. Just to get settled down and ready to work.
7. When you get back to your room, sit in a straight, comfortable chair in a clean, well-lit place.
7a. If your room is not clean, take out the rubbish and vacuum first.
8. Read the assignment again to make absolutely sure you understand it.
9. Check your e-mail.
10. Look at your teeth in the bathroom mirror.
11. Check your e-mail.

ANY OF THIS SOUND FAMILIAR YET?!

12. Computer chat with one of your friends about the future (i.e. your holiday plans).
13. Check your e-mail.
14. Phone your friend and ask if she's started writing yet. Exchange derogatory remarks about your tutor, the course, the university or the world at large.
15. Walk to the shop and buy chewing gum. You've probably run out.
16. While you've got the gum, you may as well buy a magazine and read it.
17. Check your e-mail.
18. Check the newspaper listings to make sure you aren't missing something truly worthwhile on TV.
19. Play some solitaire.

20. Check out bored.com.
21. Wash your hands.
22. Phone another friend to see how much they have done —
    they probably haven't started, either.
23. Look through your flatmate's photo album. Ask who everyone is.
24. Sit down and do some serious thinking about your plans for
    the future.
25. Check to see if bored.com has been updated yet.
26. Check your e-mail.
27. You should be rebooting by now, assuming that Windows is
    crashing on schedule.
28. Read the assignment one more time, just for the hell of it.
29. Scoot your chair across the room to the window and watch the
    sunrise.
30. Lie face down on the floor and moan.
31. Punch the wall and break something.
32. Check your e-mail.
33. Mumble obscenities.
34. At 5am start panic-writing without stopping. At 6am the essay
    is finished.
35. Complain to everyone that you didn't get any sleep because
    you had to write that stupid essay.
36. Go to your lecture, hand in the essay, and leave straight away
    so you can go home and sleep.

 LOOK BACK IN HORROR >>>

If you lived as a child in the 40s, 50s, 60s or 70s (and even the
early 80s), looking back, it's hard to believe that we have lived as
long as we have.

As children, we would ride in cars with no seat-belts or air-bags.
Riding in the back of a ute on a warm day was always a special
treat.

Our cots were covered with brightly coloured lead-based paint. We
had no childproof lids on medicine bottles, doors, or cupboards,
and when we rode our bikes we had no helmets.

We drank water from the garden hose and not from a bottle.
Horrors.

We would spend hours building go-karts out of scraps and then ride
down the hill, only to find out we forgot the brakes. After running
into the bushes a few times we learned to solve the problem.

We would leave home in the morning and play all day, as long as
we were back when the streetlights came on. No one was able to
reach us all day.

No cellphones. Unthinkable.

We got cut and broke bones and broke teeth, and there were no
lawsuits from these accidents. They were accidents. No one was to
blame, but us. Remember accidents?

We had fights and punched each other and got black and blue and
learned to get over it.

We ate pikelets, bread and butter, and drank cordial, but we were
never overweight — we were always outside playing. We shared one
drink with four friends, from one bottle and no one died from this.

We did not have PlayStations, Nintendo 64, X-Boxes, video games,
65 channels on pay TV, videotape movies, surround sound, personal
cellphones, personal computers, Internet chat rooms … we had
friends. We went outside and found them.

We rode bikes or walked to a friend's home and knocked on the
door, or rung the doorbell, or just walked in and talked to them.
    Imagine such a thing. Without asking a parent! By ourselves!
Out there in the cold cruel world! Without a guardian — how did
we do it?

We made up games with sticks and tennis balls, and ate worms, and
although we were told it would happen, we didn't poke out any
eyes, nor did the worms live inside us forever.

Footy and netball had tryouts and not everyone made the team. Those who didn't had to learn to deal with disappointment.

Some students weren't as smart as others, so they failed and were held back to repeat the same year. Tests were not adjusted for any reason.

Our actions were our own. Consequences were expected. No one to hide behind. The idea of a parent bailing us out if we broke a law was unheard of. They actually sided with the law — imagine that!

This generation has produced some of the best risk-takers and problem-solvers and inventors, ever.

The past 50 years has been an explosion of innovation and new ideas. We had freedom, failure, success and responsibility, and we learned how to deal with it all.

And if you're one of them. Congratulations!

✉ GETTING ALL THE ANSWERS >>>

A mum is driving a little girl to her friend's house to play.
'Mummy,' the little girl asks, 'how old are you?'
'Honey, you are not supposed to ask a lady her age,' the mother warns. 'It isn't polite.'
'OK,' the little girl says, 'how much do you weigh?'
'Now really,' the mother says, 'these are personal questions and are really none of your business.'
Undaunted, the little girl asks, 'Why did you and Daddy get a divorce?'
'That is enough questions, honestly!'
The exasperated mother walks away as the two friends begin to play. 'My mum wouldn't tell me anything,' the little girl says to her friend.
'Well,' said the friend, 'all you need to do is look at her driver's licence. It is like a report card, it has everything on it.'
Later that night the little girl says to her mother, 'I know how old you are, you are 32.'

The mother is surprised and asks, 'How did you find that out?'

'I also know that you weigh 140 pounds.'

The mother is past surprise and shock now. 'How in heaven's name did you find that out?'

'And,' the little girl says triumphantly, 'I know why you and daddy got a divorce.'

'Oh really?' the mother asks. 'Why?'

'Because you got an F in sex.'

✉ RHYME TIME >>>

Mary had a little lamb
Her father shot it dead
Now it goes to school with her
between two chunks of bread.

Simple Simon met a pie man, going to the fair
Said Simple Simon to the pie man
'What have you got there?'
Said the pie man unto Simon,
'Pies, you dickhead.'

Humpty Dumpty sat on a wall
Humpty Dumpty had a great fall
All the king's horses and all the king's men
Said, 'Stuff him, he's only an egg.'

Mary had a little lamb
It ran into a pylon
10,000 volts went up its ass
And turned its wool to nylon.

Georgie Porgy pudding and pie
Kissed the girls and made them cry
When the boys came out to play
He kissed them too, 'cause he was gay.

Jack and Jill
Went up the hill

To have some hanky panky
Silly Jill forgot her pill
And now there's little Franky.

My mother taught me **TO APPRECIATE A JOB WELL DONE**.
'If you're going to kill each other, do it outside. I've just finished cleaning.'

My mother taught me **RELIGION**. 'You better pray that will come out of the carpet.'

My mother taught me about **TIME TRAVEL**. 'If you don't straighten up, I'm going to knock you into the middle of next week!'

My mother taught me **LOGIC**. 'Because I said so, that's why.'

My mother taught me **MORE LOGIC**. 'If you fall out of that swing and break your neck, you're not going to the shops with me.'

My mother taught me **FORESIGHT**. 'Make sure you wear clean underwear, in case you're in an accident.'

My mother taught me **IRONY**. 'Keep crying, and I'll give you something to cry about.'

My mother taught me about the science of **OSMOSIS**. 'Shut your mouth and eat your dinner.'

My mother taught me about **CONTORTIONISM**. 'Will you look at that dirt on the back of your neck!'

My mother taught me about **PATIENCE**. 'You'll sit there until all that spinach is gone.'

My mother taught me about **WEATHER**. 'This room of yours looks as if a tornado went through it.'

My mother taught me about **HYPOCRISY**. 'If I told you once, I've told you a million times. Don't exaggerate!'

My mother taught me the **CIRCLE OF LIFE**. 'I brought you into this world, and I can take you out.'

My mother taught me about **BEHAVIOUR MODIFICATION**. 'Stop acting like your father!'

My mother taught me about **ENVY**. 'There are millions of less fortunate children in this world who don't have wonderful parents like you do.'

My mother taught me about **ANTICIPATION**. 'Just wait until we get home.'

My mother taught me about **RECEIVING**. 'You are going to get it when you get home!'

My mother taught me **MEDICAL SCIENCE**. 'If you don't stop crossing your eyes, they are going to freeze that way.'

My mother taught me **ESP**. 'Put your sweater on; don't you think I know when you are cold?'

My mother taught me **HUMOUR**. 'When that lawn mower cuts off your toes, don't come running to me.'

My mother taught me **HOW TO BECOME AN ADULT**. 'If you don't eat your vegetables, you'll never grow up.'

My mother taught me **GENETICS**. 'You're just like your father.'

My mother taught me about my **ROOTS**. 'Shut that door behind you. Do you think you were born in a tent?'

My mother taught me **WISDOM**. 'When you get to be my age, you'll understand.'

And my favourite: my mother taught me about **JUSTICE**. 'One day you'll have kids, and I hope they turn out just like you!'

OBSESSIONS >>>

A psychiatrist was conducting a group therapy session with four young mothers and their small children. He observed, 'You all have obsessions.'

To the first mother, he said, 'You are obsessed with eating. You've even named your daughter Candy.'

He turned to the second mum. 'Your obsession is money. Again, it manifests itself in your child's name, Penny.

He turned to the third mum, 'Your obsession is alcohol. It manifests itself in your child's name, Brandy.'

At this point, the fourth mother got up, took her little boy by the hand and whispered, 'Come on, Dick, we're going home.'

MUM KNOWS BEST >>>

John invited his mother to dinner and during the meal his mother couldn't help noticing how handsome her son's flatmate James was.

She had long been suspicious of a relationship between John and James and over the course of the evening, while watching them interact, she started to wonder if there was more between the two than met the eye.

Reading his mum's thoughts, John volunteered, 'I know what you must be thinking, but I assure you, James and I are just flatmates, and we are not gay.'

About a week later, James came to John and said, 'Ever since your mother came to dinner I've been unable to find the beautiful gravy ladle we had. You don't suppose she took it, do you?'

John said, 'Well, I doubt it, but I'll e-mail her just to be sure.'

So, he got on the computer and wrote, 'Dear Mother, I'm not saying you "did" take the gravy ladle from my house, and I'm not saying you "did not" take a gravy ladle but, the fact remains that one has been missing ever since you were here for dinner.'

An hour later, John received an e-mail from his mother which read, 'Dear Son, I'm not saying that you "do" sleep with James, and

I am not saying you "do not" sleep with James. But the fact remains that if he was sleeping in his own bed, he would have found the gravy ladle by now.

Love Mum

 LIFE BEGINS AT 40 >>>

A woman over 40 will never wake you in the middle of the night to ask, 'What are you thinking?' She doesn't care what you think.

If a woman over 40 doesn't want to watch the game, she doesn't sit around whining about it. She does something she wants to do. And it's usually something more interesting.

A woman over 40 knows herself well enough to be self-assured in who she is, what she is, what she wants and from whom. Few women past the age of 40 give a damn what you might think about her or what she's doing.

Women over 40 are dignified. They seldom have a screaming match with you at the opera or in the middle of an expensive restaurant. Of course, if you deserve it, they won't hesitate to shoot you if they think they can get away with it.

Older women are generous with praise, often undeserved. They know what it's like to be unappreciated.

A woman over 40 has the self-assurance to introduce you to her women friends. A younger woman with a man will often ignore even her best friend because she doesn't trust the guy with other women.

Women over 40 couldn't care less if you're attracted to her friends because she knows her friends won't betray her.

Women get psychic as they age. You never have to confess your sins to a woman over 40. They always know.

A woman over 40 looks good wearing bright-red lipstick. This is not true of younger women or drag queens.

Once you get past a wrinkle or two, a woman over 40 is far sexier than her younger counterpart.

Older women are forthright and honest. They'll tell you straight away you are an idiot if you are acting like one. You don't ever have to wonder where you stand with her.

Yes, we praise women over 40 for a multitude of reasons. Unfortunately, it's not reciprocal. For every stunning, smart, wellcoiffured hot woman of 40+, there is a bald, paunchy relic in yellow pants making a fool of himself with some 22-year-old waitress.

MOTHER'S WARNING >>>

A gay man, finally deciding he could no longer hide his sexuality from his parents, went over to their house and found his mother in the kitchen cooking dinner.

He sat down at the kitchen table, let out a big sigh and said, 'Mum, I have something to tell you — I'm gay.'

His mother made no reply or gave any response and the guy was about to repeat it to make sure she'd heard him, when she turned away from the pot she was stirring and said calmly, 'You're gay. Doesn't that mean you have oral sex with other men?'

The guy said nervously, 'Uh, yeah, Mum, that's right.'

His mother went back to stirring the pot, then suddenly whirled around and hit him over the head with her spoon and said, 'Don't you EVER complain about the taste of my cooking again!'

THE OLDER GENERATION >>>

Three old guys are out walking. First one says, 'Windy, isn't it?'
Second one says, 'No, it's Thursday!'
Third one says, 'So am I. Let's go get a beer.'

A man was telling his neighbour, 'I just bought a new hearing aid. It cost me 4000 dollars, but it's state of the art. It's perfect.'
'Really,' answered the neighbour. 'What kind is it?'
'Twelve-thirty.'

Morris, an 82-year-old man, went to the doctor to get a physical. A few days later the doctor saw Morris walking down the street with a gorgeous young lady on his arm.

A couple of days after that the doctor spoke to Morris and said, 'You're really doing great, aren't you?'

Morris replied, 'Just doing what you said, Doctor, "Get a hot mamma and be cheerful."'

The doctor said, 'I didn't say that! I said you've got a heart murmur and be careful!'

An elderly gent was invited to his old friend's home for dinner one evening. He was impressed by the way his buddy preceded every request to his wife with endearing terms — honey, my love, darling, sweetheart, pumpkin, etc. The couple had been married almost 70 years and, clearly, they were still very much in love.

While the wife was in the kitchen, the man leaned over and said to his host, 'I think it's wonderful that, after all these years, you still call your wife those loving pet names.'

The old man hung his head. 'I have to tell you the truth,' he said, 'I forgot her name about 10 years ago.'

✉ HEAD TURNING >>>

An old lady was very upset because her husband, Albert, had just passed away. She went to the undertakers to have one last look at her dearly departed husband. The instant she saw him she started crying.

As one of the undertakers tried to comfort her, through her tears she explained that she was upset because her dearest Albert was wearing a black suit, and it was his wish to be buried in a blue suit. The undertaker apologised, explaining that it was traditional to put the body of the deceased in black, but he'd see whether he could arrange for a blue suit.

The next day the widow returned to the undertakers to have one last moment with Albert before his funeral the following day. When the undertaker pulled back the curtain, she managed to smile through her tears — she saw that Albert was resplendent in a very smart blue suit.

She said to the undertaker, 'Wonderful! Wonderful! But where did you get that smart blue suit?'

The undertaker replied, 'Well, yesterday afternoon after you had left, a man about your husband's size was brought in and he was wearing that blue suit. His wife explained that she was very upset as he had always wanted to be buried in a black suit, and so I told her that I would see what I could do about a black suit. After that, it was simply a matter of swapping the heads!'

✉ TAKING THE HINT >>>

Old aunts used to come up to me at weddings, poking me in the ribs and cackling, telling me, 'You're next.' They stopped after I started doing the same thing to them at funerals.

✉ GOOD QUESTION >>>

A 75-year-old man goes to his doctor for a check-up.
Doctor: 'You're doing fairly well for your age.'
Patient: 'You think I'll live to be 80?'
D: 'Well, do you smoke tobacco or drink beer?'
P: 'No, I've never done either.'
D: 'Do you eat rib-eye steaks and barbecued ribs?'
P: 'No, red meat is unhealthy!'
D: 'Do you spend a lot of time in the sun, such as playing golf?'
P: 'No, I don't.'
D: 'Do you gamble, drive fast cars or fool around with sexy women?'
P: 'No, never!'
D: 'Then why the hell do you want to live to be 80?'

✉ A ROSE BY ANY OTHER NAME >>>

An elderly couple had dinner at another couple's house, and after eating, the wives left the table and went into the kitchen.

The two elderly gentlemen were talking, and one said, 'Last night we went out to a new restaurant, and it was really great. I would recommend it very highly.'

The other man said, 'What's the name of the restaurant?'

The first man knitted his brow in obvious concentration, and finally said to his companion, 'Aahh, what is the name of that red flower you give to someone you love?'

His friend replies, 'A carnation?'

'No. No. The other one,' the man says.

His friend offers another suggestion, 'The poppy?'

'Nahhhh,' growls the man. 'You know, the one that is red and has thorns.'

His friend said, 'Do you mean a rose?'

'Yes, yes that's it. Thank you!' the first man says.

He then turns toward the kitchen and yells, 'Rose, what's the name of that restaurant we went to last night?'

 ## NEIGH-UP NEDDY! >>>

A little old lady answered a knock on the door one day, only to be confronted by a well-dressed young man carrying a vacuum cleaner.

'Good morning,' said the young man. 'If I could take a couple of minutes of your time, I would like to demonstrate the very latest in high-powered vacuum cleaners.'

'Piss off!' said the old lady. 'I haven't got any money.' And she proceeded to close the door. Quick as a flash, the young man wedged his foot in the door and pushed it wide open.

'Don't be too hasty!' he said. 'Not until you have at least seen my demonstration.' And with that, he emptied a bucket of horse shit all over her hallway carpet. 'If this vacuum cleaner does not remove all traces of this horse shit from your carpet, madam, I will personally eat the remainder.'

'Well,' she said, 'I hope you've got a good appetite, because the electricity was cut off this morning.'

ROAD CODE RULES, OK >>>

At a nursing home in Christchurch, a group of senior citizens were sitting around talking about their aches and pains.

'My arms are so weak I can hardly lift this cup of tea,' said one.

'I know what you mean. My cataracts are so bad I can't even see my tea,' replied another.

'I can't turn my head because of the arthritis in my neck,' said a third.

'My blood pressure pills make me dizzy,' another contributed.

'I guess that's the price we pay for getting old,' winced an old man. Then there was a short moment of silence.

'Thank God we can all still drive,' said one woman cheerfully.

SLEEPING PROBLEM >>>

Three old men are sitting on the porch moaning and groaning about the state of the world and the state of their aged bodies.

One said, 'I wish I could take a decent piss.'

Another said, 'I wish I could take a decent crap.'

The third one said, 'I have no trouble with either. I have a crap at 6am and a piss at 11am. I just wish I could get up before noon.'

ON GROWING OLD >>>

- Growing old is mandatory; growing up is optional.
- Forget the health food. I need all the preservatives I can get.
- When you fall down, you wonder what else you can do while you're down there.
- You're getting old when you get the same sensation from a rocking chair that you once got from a roller coaster.
- It's frustrating when you know all the answers, but nobody bothers to ask you the questions.
- Time may be a great healer, but it's a lousy beautician.
- Wisdom comes with age, but sometimes age comes alone.

a crazy world

> The title of this chapter is apposite. The world is crazy, what with terrorists and threats of war, but luckily, this chapter does not take itself too seriously. Any serious ditties — you know, the ones with halo-hovering morals and asking us to send a message on to someone who made a difference to us in our sad, pathetic lives — got short shrift. If we want to read that stuff, we can cop a load of Matthew, Mark, Luke and John.

> This section is a sort of catch-all of subjects that don't necessarily make it into the other chapters, so the subject matter is varied, with lists galore that make you think — not too hard, we hope — and marvel

> at the people (sick or sad?) out
> there who have the art and wit to
> think outside the square.

✉ MORONS OF THE WORLD UNITE — IN PEACE >>>

The Darwin Awards 2002: the annual honour given to the person who did the gene pool the biggest service by accidentally killing themselves in the most extraordinarily stupid way. Last year's winner was the fellow who was killed by a Coke machine which toppled over on top of him as he was attempting to tip a free Coke out of it. The 2002 nominees are:

Semi-finalist 1. A young Canadian man, searching for a way of getting drunk cheaply because he had no money with which to buy alcohol, mixed gasoline with milk. Not surprisingly, this concoction made him ill, and he vomited into the fireplace in his house. The resulting explosion and fire burned his house down, killing both him and his sister.

Semi-finalist 2. Three Brazilian men were flying in a light aircraft at low altitude when another plane approached. It appears that they decided to moon the occupants of the other plane, but lost control of their own aircraft and crashed. They were all found dead in the wreckage with their pants around their ankles.

Semi-finalist 3. A 22-year-old from Reston, Virginia, was found dead after he tried to use octopus straps to bungee jump off a 70-foot railway trestle. Fairfax County police said Eric Barcia, a fast-food worker, taped a load of these straps together, wrapped an end around one foot, anchored the other end to the trestle at Lake Accotink Park, jumped and hit the pavement. Warren Carmichael, a police spokesman, said investigators think Barcia was alone because his car was found nearby. 'The length of the cord that he had assembled was greater than the distance between the trestle and the ground,' Carmichael said. Police say the apparent cause of death was 'major trauma'.

Semi-finalist 4. A man in Alabama died from rattlesnake bites. It seems that he and a friend were playing a game of catch, using the rattlesnake as a ball. The friend, no doubt a future Darwin Awards candidate — was hospitalised.

Semi-finalist 5. Employees in a medium-sized warehouse in West Texas noticed the smell of a gas leak. Sensibly, management evacuated the building, extinguishing all potential sources of ignition: lights, power, etc. After the building had been evacuated, two technicians from the gas company were dispatched. Upon entering the building, they found they had difficulty navigating in the dark. To their frustration, none of the lights worked. Witnesses later described the sight of one of the technicians reaching into his pocket and retrieving an object that resembled a cigarette lighter. Upon operation of the lighter-like object, the gas in the warehouse exploded, sending pieces of it up to five kilometres away. Nothing was found of the technicians, but the lighter was virtually untouched by the explosion. The technician suspected of causing the blast had never been thought of as 'bright' by his peers.

And the winner is …
The Arizona Highway Patrol came upon a pile of smouldering metal embedded into the side of a cliff rising above the road at the apex of a curve. The wreckage resembled the site of an aeroplane crash, but it was a car. The type of car was unidentifiable at the scene. The lab finally figured out what it was and what had happened. It seems that a guy had somehow got hold of a JATO unit (Jet Assisted Take Off) — a solid fuel rocket that is used to give heavy military transport planes an extra 'push' for taking off from short airfields.

He had driven his Chevy Impala out into the desert and found a long, straight stretch of road. Then he attached the JATO unit to his car, jumped in, got up some speed and fired off the JATO! The facts, as could be determined, are that the operator of the 1967 Impala hit the JATO ignition at a distance of approximately five kilometres from the crash site. This was established by the prominent scorched and melted asphalt at that location.

The JATO, if operating properly, would have reached maximum thrust within five seconds, causing the Chevy to reach speeds well in excess of 350mph and continuing at full power for an additional

20–25 seconds. The driver, and soon to be pilot, most likely would have experienced G-forces usually reserved for dog-fighting F-14 jocks under full afterburners, causing him to become insignificant for the remainder of the event. However, the Impala remained on the straight highway for about four kilometres (15–20 seconds) before the driver applied the brakes and completely melted them — blowing the tyres and leaving thick rubber marks on the road surface, then becoming airborne for an additional two and a half kilometres and impacting the face of the cliff at a height of 38 metres, leaving a blackened crater one metre deep in the rock.

Most of the driver's remains were not recoverable. However, small fragments of bone, teeth and hair were extracted from the crater and fingernail and bone shards were removed from a piece of debris believed to be a portion of the steering wheel.

Epilogue: It has been calculated that this moron nearly reached Mach I, attaining a ground speed of approximately 420mph.

Epitaph (for every single one of these characters): It seemed like a good idea at the time!

✉ FOR F***'S SAKE! >>>

Now the F word is not to be used in polite company and even in this book it is cunningly disguised with the odd ***. But if you forget about the literal sense of one of the oldest slang words in the 'English' speaking world, and use it as a description, there are plenty of times it could have been very acceptable, appropriate, and damn near obligatory like on the 10 occasions listed.

1. What the f*** was that?' — Mayor of Hiroshima, August 1945
2. 'Look at all those f***ing Indians!' — General Custer, 1876
3. 'Any f***ing idiot could understand that!' — Einstein, 1938
7. 'It does so f***ing look like her!' — Picasso, 1926
6. 'How the f*** did you work that out?' — Pythagoras, 126 BC
7. 'You want WHAT on the f***ing ceiling?' — Michelangelo, 1566
8. 'Where the f*** are we?' — Amelia Earhart, 1937
9. 'Scattered f***ing showers … my arse!' — Noah of the ark, 4314 BC
10. 'Aw c'mon. Who the f***'s going to find out?' — Bill Clinton, 1997

PRICELESS >>>

The nobby lady from the poshest of suburbs was shopping for a new carpet. She went, of course, to the most exclusive of the exclusive carpet emporia and viewed the goods on display.

She was most taken by a very elegant imported rug from Upper Vulgastan and bent over to feel the texture. She then broke wind, vastly and explosively.

She stood up and carefully looked around to ensure that no one had heard the event. It appeared her fart had gone unnoticed, so she walked around for another four or five minutes before approaching the sole salesman.

'Could you please give me a price on that carpet over there my good man?'

'Madam, if you farted when you touched it you would certainly shit yourself if I told you the price.'

COMMUNICATION BREAKDOWN >>>

You know you are living in the year 2003 when:

1. Your reason for not staying in touch with family is because they do not have e-mail.
2. You have a list of 15 phone numbers to reach your family of three.
3. Your grandmother asks you to send her a JPEG of your newborn so she can create a screen saver.
4. You pull up in your own driveway and use your cellphone to see if anyone is home.
5. Every commercial on television has a website address at the bottom of the screen.
6. You buy a computer and two months later it's out of date and sells for half the price you paid.
7. Leaving the house without your cellphone, which you didn't have the first 20 or 30 (or 60) years of your life, is now a cause for panic and you turn around to go and get it.
8. Using real money, instead of credit or debit card, to make a purchase would be a hassle and take planning.
9. You just tried to enter your password on the microwave.

a crazy world

10. You consider second-day air delivery painfully slow.
11. Your dining-room table is now your flat filing cabinet.
12. Your idea of being organised is multiple-coloured Post-it notes.
13. You hear most of your jokes via e-mail instead of in person.
14. You get an extra phone line so you can get phone calls.
15. You disconnect from the Internet and get this awful feeling, as if you just pulled the plug on a loved one.
16. You get up in the morning and go online before making your coffee.
17. You wake up at 2am to go to the toilet and check your e-mail on your way back to bed.
18. You start tilting your head sideways to smile. :)
19. You're reading this and nodding and laughing.
20. Even worse, you know exactly who you are going to forward this to …

 WAYS WITH WORDS >>>

The *Washington Post* asked readers to take any word from the dictionary, alter it by adding, subtracting, or changing one letter, and supply a new definition. Here are some winners:

Intaxication: Euphoria at getting a tax refund, which lasts until you realise it was your money to start with.

Bozone (n.): The substance surrounding stupid people that stops bright ideas from penetrating. The bozone layer, unfortunately, shows little sign of breaking down in the near future.

Foreploy: Any misrepresentation about yourself for the purpose of getting laid.

Cashtration (n.): The act of buying a house, which renders the subject financially impotent for an indefinite period.

Giraffiti: Vandalism spray-painted very, very high.

Sarchasm: The gulf between the author of sarcastic wit and the person who doesn't get it.

Inoculatte: To take coffee intravenously when you are running late.

Hipatitis: Terminal coolness.

Osteopornosis: A degenerate disease. (This one got extra credit.)

Karmageddon: It's like, when everybody is sending off all these really bad vibes, right? And then, like, the Earth explodes and it's like, a serious bummer.

Decaflon (n.): The gruelling event of getting through the day consuming only things that are good for you.

Glibido: All talk and no action.

Dopeler effect: The tendency of stupid ideas to seem smarter when they come at you rapidly.

Arachnoleptic fit (n.): The frantic dance performed just after you've accidentally walked through a spider web.

Beelzebug (n.): Satan in the form of a mosquito that gets into your bedroom at three in the morning and cannot be cast out.

Caterpallor (n.): The colour you turn after finding half a grub in the fruit you're eating.

And the pick of the literature is *Ignoranus:* A person who's both stupid AND an asshole.

K-MART BOREDOM >>>

While your partner is taking his or her own sweet time:

1. Pick up condom packets and randomly put them in peoples' trolleys when they aren't looking.
2. Set all the alarm clocks to go off at five-minute intervals.
3. Make a trail of tomato juice on the floor to the toilets.
4. Walk up to an employee and tell him/her in an official tone, 'Code three in homeware' and see what happens.
5. Go to the Service Desk and ask to put a bag of M&Ms on lay-by.
6. Move a 'CAUTION — WET FLOOR' sign to a carpeted area.
7. Set up a tent in the camping department and tell other shoppers you'll only invite them in if they bring pillows from the bedding department.
8. When a shop assistant (if you can find one) asks if they can help you, begin to cry and ask, 'Why can't you people just leave me alone?'
9. Look right into the security camera and use it as a mirror while you pick your nose.
10. While handling a large blunt or sharp instrument ask the shop assistant if he/she knows where the anti-depressants are.

11. Dart around the shop suspiciously, while loudly humming the theme from *Mission Impossible*.
12. In the automotive department practise your Madonna-look using different-size funnels.
13. Hide in the clothes rack and when people browse through say, 'PICK ME! PICK ME!'
14. When an announcement comes over the loudspeaker assume the foetal position and scream 'NO! It's those voices again!'
15. Go into a fitting room and yell real loud, 'We've run out of toilet paper in here!'

✉ BUMPER-STICKER HEAVEN >>>

- Mean people suck, nice people swallow.
- My boss is just like a nappy — always on my arse and always full of shit.
- Cats — the other white meat.
- If you don't like the way I drive, call 0800-EAT-SHIT.
- I still miss my ex — but my aim is improving.
- If I wanted to hear from an arsehole, I'd fart.
- Keep honking — I'm reloading.
- Horn broke — watch for finger.
- Lost your cat? Try looking under my tyres.
- I am trying to see things from your perspective — but I can't get my head that far up my arse.
- Smile if you aren't wearing any underwear.
- Save a tree — eat a beaver.

✉ SHIT HOT >>>

Here's some exciting research you may find interesting about the provenance of a word in common usage today.

In the sixteenth and seventeenth centuries, sailing ships were a major form of transport. As commercial fertiliser had not yet been invented, large shipments of manure were common. It was shipped dry, because in dry form it weighed a lot less than when wet. Usually bagged and stowed in the lower holds, which usually shipped in a lot of water, the manure would get wet and it not only became heavier, but the process of fermentation began again, generating methane gas as a by-product.

You can well envisage what could (and did) happen. Methane began to build up below deck and if someone came below with a lantern the result was explosive! Several ships were destroyed in this manner before the ship owners latched on to just what was happening.

After that, the bags of manure were always stamped with the term 'Ship High In Transit' on them, which meant that the sailors were to stow it high enough off the deck so that any water that came into the hold would not touch this volatile cargo and start the production of methane.

Thus evolved the abbreviation 'S. H. I. T' — which came to be associated with manure and has come down through the centuries to this very day. You probably did not know the true history of this word. Neither did I. I always thought it was a golfing term!

PARDON THE PUNS >>>

Two boll weevils grew up in South Carolina. One went to Hollywood and became a famous actor. The other stayed behind in the cotton fields and never amounted to much. The second one, naturally, became known as the lesser of two weevils.

Two Eskimos sitting in a kayak were chilly. But when they lit a fire in the craft it sank, proving, once again, that you can't have your kayak and heat it too.

A three-legged dog walks into a saloon in the Old West. He slides up to the bar and announces: 'I'm looking for the man who shot my paw.'

Did you hear about the Buddhist who refused Novocaine during a root canal? He wanted to transcend dental medication.

A group of chess enthusiasts checked into a hotel and were standing in the lobby discussing their recent tournament victories. After about an hour, the manager came out of the office and asked them to disperse. 'But why?' they asked, as they moved off.

'Because,' he said, 'I can't stand chess nuts boasting in an open foyer.'

A woman has twins and gives them up for adoption. One of them goes to a family in Egypt and is named 'Ahmal'. The other goes to a family in Spain; they name him 'Juan'. Years later, Juan sends a picture of himself to his birth mother. Upon receiving the picture, she tells her husband that she wishes she also had a picture of Ahmal. Her husband responds, 'They're twins! If you've seen Juan, you've seen Ahmal.'

These friars were behind on their belfry payments, so they opened up a small florist shop to raise funds. Since everyone liked to buy flowers from the men of God, a rival florist across town thought the competition was unfair. He asked the good fathers to close down, but they would not. He went back and begged the friars to close. They ignored him. So, the rival florist hired Hugh MacTaggart, the roughest and most vicious thug in town to 'persuade' them to close. Hugh beat up the friars and trashed their store, saying he'd be back if they didn't close up shop. Terrified, they did so, thereby proving that Hugh, and only Hugh, can prevent florist friars.

Mahatma Gandhi, as you know, walked barefoot most of the time, which produced an impressive set of calluses on his feet. He also ate very little, which made him rather frail, and with his odd diet, he suffered from bad breath. This made him — what? A super-callused fragile mystic hexed by halitosis.

And finally, there was a bloke who sent 10 different puns to friends, with the hope that at least one of the puns would make them laugh. Unfortunately, no pun in 10 did.

✉ DEEP, MEANINGFUL QUESTIONS >>>

- Who was the first person to look at a cow and say, 'I think I'll squeeze these dangly things here, and drink whatever comes out?'
- Who was the first person to say, 'See that chicken there … I'm gonna eat the next thing that comes outta it's butt.'

- Why do toasters always have a setting that burns the toast to a horrible crisp, which no decent human being would eat?
- Why is there a light in the fridge and not in the freezer?
- If the professor on *Gilligan's Island* can make a radio out of a coconut, why can't he fix a hole in a boat?
- Why do people point to their wrist when asking for the time, but don't point to their crotch when they ask where the toilet is?
- Why does your gynaecologist leave the room when you get undressed if they are going to look up there anyway?
- Why does Goofy stand erect while Pluto remains on all fours? They're both dogs!
- What do you call male ballerinas?
- If Wile E Coyote had enough money to buy all that Acme crap, why didn't he just buy dinner?
- If quizzes are quizzical, what are tests?
- If corn oil is made from corn, and vegetable oil is made from vegetables, then what is baby oil made from?
- If electricity comes from electrons, does morality come from morons?
- Is Disney World the only people-trap operated by a mouse?
- Why do the Alphabet Song and Twinkle, Twinkle Little Star have the same tune?
- Do illiterate people get the full effect of Alphabet Soup?
- Why do they call it an asteroid when it's outside the hemisphere, but call it a haemorrhoid when it's in your arse?
- Did you ever notice that when you blow in a dog's face, he gets mad at you, but when you take him on a car ride, he sticks his head out the window?
- Does pushing the lift button more than once make it arrive faster?
- Do you ever wonder why you gave me your e-mail address in the first place?

 TRUTHFUL ADVERTISING >>>

For Stella Artois: Makes you talk shite, then fall over.
For Marmite: Smells bloody horrible (tastes OK, though).
For the Army: Have some twat shout at you all day and get paid

stuff-all for it, then blow up some poor defenceless country before being shot in the stomach and dying cold and alone in the middle of nowhere.

For the new Aston Martin: The fanny magnet — because you have a tiny penis.

For BMW Convertible: The best penis extension money can buy.

For Slimfast: You need it because you are FAT and you sweat and stink, and when you run the Earth shakes.

HAIL ALL ABSCONDERS FROM THE BRAIN POOL >>>

When his 38-calibre revolver failed to fire at its intended victim during a hold-up in Long Beach, California, would-be robber James Elliot did something that can only inspire wonder: he peered down the barrel and tried the trigger again. This time it worked.

The chef at a hotel in Switzerland lost a finger in a meat-cutting machine and, after a little hopping around, submitted a claim to his insurance company. The company, suspecting negligence, sent out one of its men to have a look for himself. He tried the machine out and lost a finger. The chef's claim was approved.

A man who shovelled snow for an hour to clear a space for his car during a blizzard in Chicago, returned with his vehicle to find a woman had taken the space. Understandably, he shot her.

After stopping for drinks at an illegal bar, a Zimbabwean bus driver found that the 20 mental patients he was supposed to be transporting from Harare to Bulawayo had escaped. Not wanting to admit his incompetence, the driver went to a nearby bus stop and offered everyone waiting there a free ride. He then delivered the passengers to the mental hospital, telling the staff that the patients were very excitable and prone to bizarre fantasies. The deception wasn't discovered for three days.

MODERN NATIVITY >>>

A mother took her daughter to the doctor and asked him to give her an examination to determine the cause of her daughter's swollen abdomen. It only took the doctor about two seconds to say, 'Your daughter is pregnant.'

The mother turned red with fury and she argued with the doctor that her daughter was a good girl and would never compromise her reputation by having sex with a boy. The doctor faced the window and silently watched the horizon.

The mother became enraged and screamed, 'Quit looking out the window! Aren't you paying attention to me?'

'Yes, of course I am paying attention ma'am. It's just that the last time this happened, a star appeared in the East, and three wise men came. And I was hoping that they would show up again.'

HEY YOU, ARE YOU THICK? >>>

In case you needed further proof that the human race is doomed through stupidity, here are some actual label instructions on consumer goods.

1. *On a Sears hairdryer:* 'Do not use while sleeping.' (But that's the only time I have to do my hair.)
2. *On a bag of Fritos:* You could be a winner! No purchase necessary. Details inside.' (Evidently the shoplifter special.)
3. *On a bar of Dial soap:* 'Directions: Use like regular soap.' (And that would be how?)
4. *On some Swanson frozen dinners:* 'Serving suggestions: Defrost.' (But it's just a suggestion.)
5. *On Tesco's Tiramisu dessert (printed on bottom of box):* 'Do not turn upside down.' (DOH! Too late!)
6. *On Marks & Spencer Bread Pudding:* 'Product will be hot after heating.' (As night follows day …)
7. *On packaging for a Rowenta iron:* 'Do not iron clothes on body.' (But wouldn't this save even more time?)
8. *On Boot's Children's Cough Medicine:* 'Do not drive a car or operate machinery after taking this medication.' (We could do a lot to reduce the rate of construction accidents if we

could just get those five-year-olds with head colds off those forklifts.)

9. *On Nytol Sleep Aid:* 'Warning: May cause drowsiness.' (One would hope.)

10. *On most brands of Christmas lights:* 'For indoor or outdoor use only.' (As opposed to what?)

11. *On a Japanese food processor:* 'Not to be used for the other use.' (I've got to admit I'm curious.)

12. *On Sainsbury's peanuts:* 'Warning: Contains nuts.' (NEWS FLASH.)

13. *On an American Airlines packet of nuts:* 'Instructions: Open packet, eat nuts.' (Step 3: Fly Delta.)

14. *On a child's Superman costume:* 'Wearing of this garment does not enable you to fly.' (I don't blame the company, I blame parents for this one.)

15. *On a Swedish chainsaw:* 'Do not attempt to stop chain with your hands or genitals.' (Was there a chance of this happening somewhere? Good grief.)

16. *On a bottle of Palmolive dishwashing liquid:* 'Do not use on food.' (Hey, Mum, we've run out of syrup! It's OK honey, just grab the Palmolive!)

17. *On a tube of Crest Toothpaste:* 'If swallowed contact poison control.' (Oh please. Have you ever heard about someone dying from swallowing a little toothpaste?)

18. *On a bottle of ALL laundry detergent:* 'Remove clothing before distributing in washing machine.' (No more swimming in the washing machine, kids.)

✉ THE WRIGHT STUFF >>>

If you're not familiar with the work of Steven Wright, he's the guy who once said: 'I woke up one morning and all of my stuff had been stolen ... and replaced by exact duplicates.' Here are some more of his gems.

● I'd kill for a Nobel Peace Prize.
● Borrow money from pessimists — they don't expect it back.
● Half the people you know are below average.
● 99 percent of lawyers give the rest a bad name.
● 42.7 percent of all statistics are made up on the spot.

- A clear conscience is usually the sign of a bad memory.
- If you want the rainbow, you gotta put up with the rain.
- All those who believe in psychokinesis, raise my hand.
- The early bird may get the worm, but the second mouse gets the cheese.
- I almost had a psychic girlfriend but she left me before we met.
- OK, so what's the speed of dark?
- How do you know when you've run out of invisible ink?
- If everything seems to be going well, you have obviously overlooked something.
- Depression is merely anger without enthusiasm.
- When everything is coming your way, you're in the wrong lane.
- Ambition is a poor excuse for not having enough sense to be lazy.
- Hard work pays off in the future, laziness pays off now.
- I intend to live forever — so far, so good.
- If Barbie is so popular, why do you have to buy her friends?
- What happens if you get scared half to death twice?
- My mechanic told me, 'I couldn't repair your brakes, so I made your horn louder.'
- Why do psychics have to ask you for your name?
- If at first you don't succeed, destroy all evidence that you tried.
- A conclusion is the place where you got tired of thinking.
- Experience is something you don't get until just after you need it.
- The hardness of the butter is proportional to the softness of the bread.
- To steal ideas from one person is plagiarism; to steal from many is research.
- The problem with the gene pool is that there is no lifeguard.
- The sooner you fall behind, the more time you'll have to catch up.
- The colder the X-ray table, the more of your body is required to be on it.
- Everyone has a photographic memory, some just don't have film.

Some questions to ponder:

- Do infants enjoy infancy as much as adults enjoy adultery?
- If one synchronised swimmer drowns, do the rest have to drown too?
- If you ate pasta and antipasti, would you still be hungry?
- If a pig loses its voice, is it disgruntled?
- Why do women wear evening gowns to night-clubs? Shouldn't they be wearing night-gowns?
- If love is blind, why is lingerie so popular?
- Why is it that when we bounce a cheque, the bank charges us more of what they already know we don't have any of?
- When someone says, 'A penny for your thoughts' and you put your two cents in, what happens to the other penny?
- Why is the man who invests all your money called a broker?
- Why do croutons come in airtight packages? It's just stale bread to begin with.
- When cheese gets its picture taken, what does it say?
- If you mixed vodka with orange juice and milk of magnesia, would you get a Phillip's Screwdriver?
- Why is a person who plays the piano called a pianist, but a person who drives a race car not called a racist?
- Why can't you make another word using all the letters in 'anagram'?
- Why is it that no word in the English language rhymes with month, orange, silver, or purple?
- Why, when I wind up my watch, I start it; but when I wind up a project, I end it?
- Why is it that we recite at a play and play at a recital?
- Why are a wise man and a wise guy opposites?
- Why don't tomb, comb, and bomb sound alike?
- Why do overlook and oversee mean opposite things?
- If horrific means to make horrible, does terrific mean to make terrible?
- Why isn't 11 pronounced onety one?
- If the singular of geese is goose, shouldn't a Portuguese person be called a Portugoose?
- Why is a procrastinator's work never done?

- If lawyers are disbarred and clergymen defrocked, doesn't it follow that electricians can be delighted, musicians denoted, cowboys deranged, models deposed, tree surgeons debarked and drycleaners depressed?
- Do Roman paramedics refer to IVs as 4s?
- Are people more violently opposed to fur than leather because it's much easier to harass rich women than biker gangs?
- If you take an Oriental person and spin him around several times, does he become disoriented?
- If people from Poland are called Poles, why aren't people from Holland called Holes?

 CLEVER DICKS >>>

Quotes from the Montreal Comedy Festival:

- 'I found my wife in bed naked one day, next to a Vietnamese guy and a black guy. I took a picture and sent it to Benetton. You never know.'
- 'I got kicked out of Riverdance for using my arms.'
- 'Luge strategy? Lie flat and try not to die.'
- 'Clinton lied. A man might forget where he parks or where he lives, but he never forgets oral sex, no matter how bad it is.'

NOT A LOT OF PEOPLE
KNOW THIS >>>

Does the statement, 'We've always done it that way' ring any bells? The US standard railway gauge (distance between the rails) is 4 feet, 8.5 inches. That's an exceedingly odd number.

Why was that gauge used? Because that's the way they built them in Britain, and British expatriates built the US railways.

Why did the English build them like that? Because the first rail lines were built by the same people who built the pre-railway tramways, and that's the gauge they used.

Why did 'they' use that gauge then? Because the people who built the tramways used the same jigs and tools that they used for building wagons, which used that wheel spacing.

a crazy world

OK. Why did the wagons have that particular odd wheel spacing? Well, if they tried to use any other spacing, the wagon wheels would break on some of the old, long-distance roads in Britain, because that's the spacing of the wheel ruts.

So who built those old rutted roads? Imperial Rome built the first long-distance roads in Britain for their legions. The roads have been used ever since.

And the ruts in the roads? Roman war chariots formed the initial ruts, which everyone else had to match for fear of destroying their wagon wheels. Since the chariots were made for Imperial Rome, they were all alike in the matter of wheel spacing.

The United States standard railway gauge of 4 feet, 8.5 inches is derived from the original specifications for an Imperial Roman war chariot. And bureaucracies live forever. So the next time you are handed a specification and wonder what horse's arse came up with it, you may be exactly right, because the Imperial Roman war chariots were made just wide enough to accommodate the back ends of two warhorses.

But there's a twist to this story. When you see a Space Shuttle sitting on its launch pad, there are two big booster rockets attached to the sides of the main fuel tank.

These are solid rocket boosters, or SRBs. The SRBs are made by Thiokol at their factory in Utah. The engineers who designed the SRBs would have preferred to make them a bit fatter, but the SRBs had to be shipped by train from the factory to the launch site.

The railway line from the factory happens to run through a tunnel in the mountains. The SRBs had to fit through that tunnel.

The tunnel is slightly wider than the railway track, and the railway track, as you now know, is about as wide as two horses' behinds.

So, a major Space Shuttle design feature of what is arguably the world's most advanced transportation system was determined over 2000 years ago by the width of a horse's arse.

And you thought being a horse's arse wasn't important?

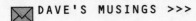

Sixteen Things That it Took Me 50 Years to Learn
by Dave Barry

1. You will never find anybody who can give you a clear and compelling reason why we observe daylight-saving.
2. You should never say anything to a woman that even remotely suggests you think she's pregnant unless you can see an actual baby emerging from her at that moment.
3. The most powerful force in the universe is gossip.
4. The one thing that unites all human beings, regardless of age, gender, religion, economic status or ethnic background, is that, deep down inside, we ALL believe that we are above-average drivers.
5. There comes a time when you should stop expecting other people to make a big deal about your birthday. That time is age 11.
6. There is a very fine line between 'hobby' and 'mental illness'.
7. People who want to share their religious views with you almost never want you to share yours with them.
8. If you had to identify, in one word, the reason why the human race has not achieved, and never will achieve, its full potential, that word would be 'meetings'.
9. The main accomplishment of almost all organised protests is to annoy people who are not in them.
10. If there really is a God who created the entire universe with all of its glories, and He decides to deliver a message to humanity, he WILL NOT use, as His messenger, a person on cable TV with a bad hairstyle.
11. You should not confuse your career with your life.
12. A person who is nice to you, but rude to the waiter, is not a nice person.
13. No matter what happens, somebody will find a way to take it too seriously.
14. When trouble arises and things look bad, there is always one individual who perceives a solution and is willing to take command. Very often, that individual is crazy.
15. Your friends love you, anyway.
16. Nobody cares if you can't dance well. Just get up and dance.

Things you don't want to hear during surgery:

- Better save that. We'll need it for the autopsy.
- Someone call the orderly — we're going to need a mop.
- Accept this sacrifice, O Great Lord of Darkness.
- Bo! Bo! Come back with that! Bad Dog!
- Wait a minute, if this is his spleen, then what's that?
- Hand me that … uh … that, uh … thingie.
- Oh no! I just lost my Rolex.
- Oops! Hey, has anyone ever survived 500ml of this stuff before?
- Rats! There go the lights again.
- You know, there's big money in kidneys. Hey, the guy's got two of 'em.
- Everybody stand back! I lost my contact lens!
- Could you stop that thing from beating; it's throwing my concentration off.
- What's this doing here?
- I hate it when they're missing stuff in here.
- That's cool, now can you make his leg twitch?!
- I wish I hadn't forgotten my glasses.
- Well folks, this will be an experiment for all of us.
- Sterile, schmerile. The floor's clean, right?
- What do you mean he wasn't in for a sex change …!
- Did anyone see where I left that scalpel?
- And now we remove the subject's brain and place it in the body of the ape.
- OK, now take a picture from this angle. This is truly a freak of nature.
- This patient has already had some kids, am I correct?
- Nurse, did this patient sign the organ donation card?
- Don't worry. I think it is sharp enough.
- She's gonna blow! Everyone take cover!
- FIRE! FIRE! Everyone get out!
- Uh oh! Page 47 of the manual is missing!

Things you would never know without the movies:

- If being chased through town, you can usually take cover in a passing St Patrick's Day parade — at any time of the year.
- All shopping bags contain at least one stick of French Bread.
- It's easy for anyone to land a plane providing there is someone to talk you down.
- The Eiffel Tower can be seen from any window in Paris.
- If you need to reload your gun, you will always have more ammunition, even if you haven't been carrying any before now.
- You are very likely to survive any battle in any war unless you make the mistake of showing someone a picture of your sweetheart back home.
- If your town is threatened by an imminent natural disaster or killer beast, the mayor's first concern will be the tourist trade or his forthcoming art exhibition.
- When paying for a taxi, don't look at your wallet as you take out the money — just grab a note at random and hand it over. It will always be the exact fare.
- Kitchens don't have light switches. When entering a kitchen at night, you should open the fridge door and use that light instead.
- Mothers routinely cook eggs, bacon and waffles for their family every morning even though their husband and children never have time to eat it.
- Cars that crash will almost always burst into flames.
- All telephone numbers in America begin with the digits 555.
- A single match will be sufficient to light up a room the size of a stadium.
- It is not necessary to say hello or goodbye when beginning or ending phone conversations.
- Even when driving down a perfectly straight road, it is necessary to turn the wheel vigorously from left to right every few moments.
- It does not matter if you are heavily outnumbered in a fight involving martial arts — your enemies will patiently attack you one by one by dancing around in a threatening manner until you have knocked out their predecessors.

- Once applied, lipstick will never rub off — even while scuba diving.
- You can always find a chainsaw when you need one.

✉ YOU CAN QUOTE ME ON THAT >>>

'When I die, I want to die like my grandmother, who died peacefully in her sleep. Not screaming like all the passengers in her car.'
— Author unknown

'It's so long since I've had sex, I've forgotten who ties up whom.'
— Joan Rivers

'If it wasn't for pick-pockets and frisking at airports I'd have no sex life at all.'
— Rodney Dangerfield

'Sex is one of the most wholesome, beautiful and natural experiences that money can buy.'
— Steve Martin

'My girlfriend said to me in bed last night, "You're a pervert." I said, "That's a big word for a girl of 15."'
— Emo Philips

'My wife is a sex object. Every time I ask for sex, she objects.'
— Les Dawson

'I'm such a good lover because I practise a lot on my own.'
— Woody Allen

'My love life is terrible. The last time I was inside a woman was when I visited the Statue of Liberty.'
— Woody Allen

'I believe that sex is a beautiful thing between two people. Between five, it's fantastic.'
— Woody Allen

'There are a number of mechanical devices that increase sexual arousal, particularly in women. Chief amongst these is the Mercedes-Benz 300SL convertible.'
— Unknown

'You don't appreciate a lot of stuff that happened in school until you get older. Little things like being smacked every day by a middle-aged woman; stuff you pay good money for in later life.'
— Emo Philips

'Instead of getting married again, I'm going to find a woman I don't like and just give her a house.'
— Steven Seagal

'See, the problem is that God gives men a brain and a penis, and only enough blood to run one at a time.'
— Robin Williams

'What do people mean when they say the computer went down on them?'
— Marilyn Pittman

'The day I worry about cleaning my house is the day Harrods comes out with a ride-on vacuum cleaner.'
— Roseanne

'If life was fair, Elvis would be alive and all the impersonators would be dead.'
— Johnny Carson

'Sometimes I think war is God's way of teaching us geography.'
— Paul Rodriguez

'My parents didn't want to move to Florida, but they turned 60, and that's the law.'
— Jerry Seinfeld

'Bigamy is having one wife/husband too many. Monogamy is the same.'
— Oscar Wilde

'Advice for the day: if you have a lot of tension and you get a headache, do what it says on the aspirin packet — "Take two aspirin" and "Keep away from children".'
— A mum

Finally, one of the all-time best quotes. In a recent interview, General Norman Schwarzkopf was asked if he didn't think there was room for forgiveness toward the people who have harboured and abetted the terrorists who perpetrated the September 11 attacks on America. His answer was a classic. Schwarzkopf said, 'I believe that forgiving them is God's function. Our job is simply to arrange the meeting.'

✉ SHORT AND SWEET >>>

A dyslexic armed robber walks into a bank and says, 'Air in hands you motherstickers, this is a f*** up.'

✉ AWARD TIME >>>

It's time once again to consider the candidates for the annual Stella Awards. The Stellas are named after 81-year-old Stella Liebeck who spilled coffee on herself and successfully sued McDonald's. That case inspired the Stella Awards for the most frivolous successful lawsuits in the United States. The following are this year's candidates.

1. Kathleen Robertson of Austin, Texas, was awarded $780,000 by a jury of her peers after breaking her ankle tripping over a toddler who was running inside a furniture store. The owners of the shop were understandably surprised at the verdict, considering the misbehaving little toddler was Ms Robertson's son.
2. A 19-year-old, Carl Truman of Los Angeles, won $74,000 and medical expenses when his neighbour ran over his hand with a Honda Accord. Mr Truman apparently didn't notice there was someone at the wheel of the car when he was trying to steal his neighbour's hubcaps.

3. Terrence Dickson of Bristol, Pennsylvania, was leaving a house he had just finished robbing by way of the garage. He was not able to get the garage door to go up since the automatic door opener was malfunctioning. He couldn't re-enter the house because the door connecting the house and garage locked when he pulled it shut. The family was on holiday, and Mr Dickson found himself locked in the garage for eight days. He existed on a case of Pepsi he found, and a large bag of dry dog food. He sued the homeowner's insurance, claiming the situation caused him undue mental anguish. The jury agreed to the tune of $500,000.

4. Jerry Williams of Little Rock, Arkansas, was awarded $14,500 and medical expenses after being bitten on the buttocks by his next-door neighbour's beagle. The beagle was on a chain in its owner's fenced yard. The award was less than sought because the jury felt the dog might have been just a little provoked at the time by Mr Williams, who was shooting it repeatedly with a pellet gun.

5. A Philadelphia restaurant was ordered to pay Amber Carson of Lancaster, Pennsylvania $113,500 after she slipped on a soft drink and broke her coccyx (tailbone). The beverage was on the floor because Ms Carson had thrown it at her boyfriend 30 seconds earlier during an argument.

6. Kara Walton of Claymont, Delaware, successfully sued the owner of a night-club in a neighbouring city when she fell from the bathroom window to the floor and knocked out her two front teeth. This occurred while Ms Walton was trying to sneak through the window in the ladies room to avoid paying the $3.50 cover charge. She was awarded $12,000 and dental expenses.

7. This year's favourite could easily be Mr Merv Grazinski of Oklahoma City, Oklahoma. Mr Grazinski purchased a brand-new 32-foot Winnebago motor-home. On his first trip home, having driven onto the freeway, he set the cruise control at 70mph and calmly left the driver's seat to go into the back and make himself a cup of coffee. Not surprisingly, the R.V. left the freeway, crashed and overturned. Mr Grazinski sued Winnebago for not advising him in the owner's manual that he couldn't actually do this. The jury awarded him $1,750,000 plus a new motor-home. The company actually changed their

manuals on the basis of this suit, just in case there were any other complete morons buying their recreation vehicles. ONLY IN AMERICA!

✉ IN A TRANCE >>>

It was opening night at the Orpheum and the Amazing Claude was topping the bill. People came from miles around to see the famed hypnotist do his stuff.

As Claude took to the stage, he announced, 'Unlike most stage hypnotists who invite two or three people up onto the stage to be put into a trance, I intend to hypnotise each and every member of this audience.'

The excitement was almost electric as Claude withdrew a beautiful antique pocket watch from his coat and said, 'I want you each to keep your eyes on this antique watch. It's a very special watch. It's been in my family for six generations.'

He began to swing the watch gently back and forth while quietly chanting, 'Watch the watch, watch the watch, watch the watch ...' The crowd became mesmerised as the watch swayed back and forth, light gleaming off its polished surface. Hundreds of pairs of eyes followed the swaying watch, until suddenly it slipped from the hypnotist's fingers and fell to the floor, breaking into 100 pieces.

'SHIT!' said the hypnotist.

And it took three weeks to clean up the theatre.

✉ DID YOU EVER WONDER... >>>

- Why the sun lightens our hair, but darkens our skin?
- Why women can't put on mascara with their mouth closed?
- Why you don't ever see the headline 'Psychic Wins Lottery'?
- Why abbreviated is such a long word?
- Why doctors call what they do 'practice'?
- Why you have to click on 'Start' to stop Windows 98?
- Why bottled lemon juice is made with artificial flavour, while dishwashing liquid is made with real lemons?
- Why there isn't mouse-flavoured cat food?

- Who tastes dog food when it has a 'new and improved' flavour?
- Why they sterilise the needle for lethal injections?
- Why they don't make the whole plane out of the material used for the indestructible black box?
- Why sheep don't shrink when it rains?
- Why they are called apartments when they are all stuck together?
- Why if con is the opposite of pro, is Congress the opposite of progress?
- Why they call the airport 'the terminal' if flying is so safe?

✉ DANCE OF DEATH >>>

Two men, sentenced to die in the electric chair on the same day, were led down to the room in which they would meet their maker. The priest had given them the last rites, the formal speech had been given by the warden and a final prayer had been said among the participants.

The Warden, turning to the first man, solemnly asked, 'Son, do you have a last request?'

To which the man replied, 'Yes sir, I do. I love music. Could you please play the "Macarena" for me one last time?'

'Certainly,' replied the Warden. He turned to the other man and asked, 'Well, what about you son? What is your final request?'

'Please,' said the condemned man, 'kill me first!'

✉ MAJOR THOUGHT FOR THE DAY >>>

There is more money being spent on breast implants and Viagra than Alzheimer's research. So, by 2020, there should be a large elderly population with perky boobs and erections and no recollection of what to do with them.

✉ LITERALLY SPEAKING >>>

- Phone answering-machine message: 'If you want to buy marijuana, press the hash key ...'

- I went to buy some camouflage trousers the other day but I couldn't find any.
- My friend drowned in a bowl of muesli. He was pulled in by a strong currant.
- I went to a seafood disco last week — and pulled a muscle.
- Our ice-cream man was found lying on the floor of his van covered with hundreds and thousands. Police say that he topped himself.
- Man goes to the doctor with a strawberry growing out of his head. Doc says, 'I'll give you some cream to put on it.'
- 'Doc, I can't stop singing "The Green, Green Grass of Home".'
  'That sounds like Tom Jones syndrome.'
  'Is it common?'
  'It's not unusual.'
- Police arrested two kids yesterday. One was drinking battery acid, the other was eating fireworks. They charged one and let the other one off.
- 'You know, somebody actually complimented me on my driving today. They left a little note on the windscreen. It said, "Parking Fine". So that was nice.'
- A man walked into the doctor's and said, 'I've hurt my arm in several places.' The doctor said, 'Well don't go there any more.'

✉ A LITTLE EGG YOKE >>>

How would you like to be an egg? You only get laid once. You only get eaten once. It takes four minutes to get hard and only two minutes to get soft.

You share your box with 11 other guys. But worst of all, the only chick that ever sat on your face was your mother!

✉ LIFE'S MOST IMPORTANT FACTS >>>

- The first couple to be shown in bed together on primetime TV were Fred and Wilma Flintstone.
- Every day more money is printed for Monopoly than the US Treasury.

- Men can read smaller print than women can; women can hear better.
- Coca-Cola was originally green.
- It is impossible to lick your elbow.
- The American state with the highest percentage of people who walk to work is Alaska.
- The percentage of Africa that is wilderness: 28 percent. The percentage of North America that is wilderness: 38 percent.
- In the US, the cost of raising a medium-sized dog to the age of 11 is $6400.
- The average number of people airborne over the US any given hour: 61,000.
- Intelligent people have more zinc and copper in their hair.
- The world's youngest parents were aged eight and nine and lived in China in 1910.
- The youngest Pope was 11 years old.
- The first novel ever written on a typewriter: *Tom Sawyer*.
- Each king in a deck of playing cards represents a great king from history: spades is King David, hearts is Charlemagne, clubs is Alexander and diamonds is Julius Caesar.
- If a statue in the park of a person on a horse has both front legs in the air, the person died in battle. If the horse has one front leg in the air, the person died as a result of wounds received in battle. If the horse has all four legs on the ground, the person died of natural causes.
- Only two people signed the Declaration of Independence on 4 July 1776: John Hancock and Charles Thomson. Most of the rest signed on 2 August, but the last signature wasn't added until five years later.
- Hershey's Kisses are called that because the machine that makes them looks like it's kissing the conveyor belt.
- And finally, at least 75 percent of people who read this will try to lick their elbow!

Q. What occurs more often in December than any other month?
A. Conception.

Q. Half of all Americans live within 80 kilometres of what?
A. Their birthplace.

Q. Most boat owners name their boats. What is the most popular boat name requested?

A. Obsession.

Q. What do bullet-proof vests, fire escapes, windscreen wipers, and laser printers all have in common?

A. They were all invented by women.

Q. What is the only food that doesn't spoil?

A. Honey.

Q. There are more collect calls on what day than any other day of the year?

A. Father's Day.

Q. What trivia fact about Mel Blanc (voice of Bugs Bunny) is the most ironic?

A. He was allergic to carrots.

Q. What is an activity performed by 40 percent of all people at a party?

A. Looking in the host's medicine cabinet.

✉ LONG AGO >>>

In Shakespeare's time, mattresses were secured on bed frames by ropes. When you pulled on the ropes the mattress tightened, making the bed firmer to sleep on. Hence the phrase 'goodnight, sleep tight'.

It was the accepted practice in Babylon 4000 years ago that for a month after the wedding, the bride's father would supply his son-in-law with all the mead he could drink. Mead is a honey beer and because their calendar was lunar-based, this period was called the honey month we know today as the honeymoon.

In English pubs, ale is ordered by pints and quarts. So in old England, when customers got unruly, the bartender would yell at them to mind their own pints and quarts and settle down. It's where we get the phrase 'Mind your Ps and Qs'.

Many years ago in England, pub frequenters had a whistle baked into the rim or candle of their ceramic cups. When they needed a refill, they used the whistle to get some service. 'Wet your whistle' is the phrase inspired by this practice.

In Scotland, a new game was invented. It was entitled Gentlemen Only, Ladies Forbidden — and thus the word GOLF entered into the English language.

✉ WORDS OF WISDOM >>>

- Before attempting to remove stubborn stains from a garment, always circle the stain in permanent pen so that when you remove the garment from the washing machine you can easily locate the area of the stain and check that it has gone.
- High blood pressure sufferers, simply cut yourself and bleed for a while, thus reducing the pressure in your veins.
- Olympic athletes, conceal the fact that you have taken performance-enhancing drugs by simply running a little slower and letting someone else win.
- Heavy smokers, don't throw away those filters from the end of your cigarettes. Save them up and within a few years you'll have enough to insulate your loft.
- Motorists, enjoy the freedom of cycling by removing your windscreen, sticking half a melon skin on your head, then jumping red lights and driving the wrong way up one-way streets.
- Create instant designer stubble by sucking a magnet and dipping your chin in a bowl of iron filings.
- *X File* fans, create the effect of being abducted by aliens by drinking two bottles of vodka. You'll invariably wake up in a strange place the following morning, having had your memory mysteriously 'erased'.
- A sheet of sandpaper makes a cheap and effective substitute for costly maps when visiting the Sahara Desert.
- Toblerone chocolate bars make ideal 'toast racks' for crackers.
- Convince neighbours that you have invented a 'shrinking' device by ruffling your hair, wearing a white laboratory coat and parking a JCB digger outside your house for a few days.

Then dim and flicker the lights in your house during the night and replace the JCB unseen, with a Tonka toy of the same description. Watch their faces in the morning!

- Open your bowels at work. Not only will you save money on toilet paper, but you'll also be getting paid for it.
- Feed bees oranges. Hey presto! They make marmalade instead of honey.
- Nissan Micra drivers, attach a lighted sparkler to the roof of your car before starting a long journey. You drive the things like dodgem cars anyway, so it may as well look like one.
- Tape a chocolate bar to the outside of your microwave. If the chocolate melts you will know that the microwaves are escaping and it is time to have the oven serviced.
- A mousetrap placed on top of your alarm clock will prevent you from rolling over and going back to sleep.

 SELLING CONDOMS >>>

Imagine if all major retailers started making their own condoms but kept the same sales tag line ...

- Sainsbury's condoms — making life taste better.
- Tesco condoms — every little helps.
- Nike condoms — just do it.
- Peugeot condoms — the ride of your life.
- Galaxy condoms — why have rubber when you can have silk.
- KFC condoms — finger-licking good.
- Minstrels condoms — melt in your mouth, not in your hands.
- Safeway condoms — lighten the load.
- Coca-Cola condoms — the real thing.
- Eveready condoms — keeps going and going.
- Pringles condoms — once you pop, you can't stop.
- Burger King condoms — home of the whopper.
- Goodyear condoms — for a longer ride go wide.
- FCUK condoms — no comment required.

- Muller light condoms — so much pleasure, but where's the pain?
- Halford condoms — we go the extra mile.
- On Digital condoms — plug and play.
- Royal Mail condoms — I saw this and thought of you.
- Andrex condoms — soft, strong and very, very long.
- Renault condoms — size matters!

MORE MOVIE 'FACTS' >>>

- In New York City large, loft-style apartments are well within the price range of most people — whether they are employed or not.
- At least one of a pair of identical twins is born evil.
- Should you decide to defuse a bomb, don't worry which wire to cut. You will always choose the right one.
- Most laptop computers are powerful enough to override the communications system of any invading alien society, and run an applications system that everyone is very familiar with.
- When you turn out the light to go to bed, everything in your bedroom will still be clearly visible, just slightly bluish.
- If you are blonde and pretty, it is possible to become a world expert on nuclear fission, or anything else, at the age of 22.
- Honest and hard-working policemen are traditionally gunned down days before their retirement.
- Rather than wasting bullets, megalomaniacs prefer to kill their arch-enemies using complicated machinery involving fuses, pulley systems, deadly gases, lasers, and man-eating sharks, all of which will give their captives at least 20 minutes to escape.
- During all police investigations, it is necessary to visit a strip club at least once.
- All beds have special L-shaped cover sheets that reach up to the armpit level on a woman but only to waist level on the man lying beside her.
- The ventilation system of any building is the perfect hiding place. No one will ever think of looking for you in there and you can travel to any other part of the building you want without difficulty.

- Should you wish to pass yourself off as a German officer, it is not necessary to speak the language. A German accent will do.
- A man will show no pain while taking the most ferocious beating, but will wince when a woman tries to clean his wounds.
- If a large pane of glass is visible, someone will be thrown through it before long.
- If staying in a haunted house, women must investigate any strange noises in their most diaphanous underwear, which is just what they happened to be carrying with them at the time the car broke down.
- All women who are not virgins, have large breasts, and/or display them, will be killed in a gruesome manner.
- If someone says, 'I'll be right back,' they won't.
- Computer monitors never display a cursor on screen but always say: Enter Password Now.
- All bombs are fitted with electronic timing devices with large red read-outs so you know exactly when they're going to go off.
- A detective can only solve a case once he has been suspended from duty.
- If you decide to start dancing in the street, everyone around you will automatically be able to mirror all the steps you come up with and hear the music in your head.
- Police departments give their officers personality tests to make sure they are deliberately assigned a partner who is their total opposite.
- When they are alone, all foreigners prefer to speak English to each other.

THIS PERSON IS SICK! >>>

1. Don't sweat the petty things and don't pet the sweaty things.
2. One tequila, two tequila, three tequila, floor.
3. Atheism is a non-prophet organisation.
4. If man evolved from monkeys and apes, why do we still have monkeys and apes?
5. The main reason Santa is so jolly is because he knows where all the bad girls live.

6. I went to a bookshop and asked the saleswoman, 'Where's the self-help section?' She said if she told me, it would defeat the purpose.

7. What if there were no hypothetical questions?

8. If a deaf person swears, does his mother wash his hands with soap?

9. If a man is standing in the middle of the forest speaking and there is no woman around to hear him — is he still wrong?

10. If someone with multiple personalities threatens to kill himself, is it considered a hostage situation?

11. Is there another word for synonym?

12. Where do forest rangers go to 'get away from it all'?

13. What do you do when you see an endangered animal eating an endangered plant?

14. If a parsley farmer is sued, can they garnish his wages?

15. Would a fly without wings be called a walk?

16. Why do they lock gas-station bathrooms? Are they afraid someone will clean them?

17. If a turtle doesn't have a shell, is he homeless or naked?

18. Can vegetarians eat animal crackers?

19. If the police arrest a mime, do they tell him he has the right to remain silent?

20. How do they get the deer to cross at that yellow road sign?

21. Is it true that cannibals don't eat clowns because they taste funny?

22. What was the best thing before sliced bread?

23. One nice thing about egotists: they don't talk about other people.

24. Does the Little Mermaid wear an algebra?

25. How is it possible to have a civil war?

26. If you try to fail, and succeed, which have you done?

27. Why is it called tourist season if we can't shoot at them?

28. Why is the alphabet in that order? Is it because of that song?

29. Why is there an expiration date on sour cream?

 DRIP DRY >>>

Joe and Helen were both patients in a mental hospital. One day while they were walking past the hospital swimming pool, Joe suddenly jumped into the deep end. He sank to the bottom and stayed there. Helen promptly jumped in to save him, swimming to the bottom and pulling him out.

When the medical director became aware of Helen's heroic act, he immediately ordered her to be discharged from the hospital, as he now considered her to be mentally stable.

When he went to tell Helen the news, he said, 'Helen, I have good news and bad news. The good news is you're being discharged because since you were able to jump in and save the life of another patient, I think you've regained your senses. The bad news is that Joe, the patient you saved, hung himself with his bathrobe belt in the bathroom. I am so sorry but he is dead.'

Helen replied, 'He didn't hang himself. I put him there to dry.'

 ## CAN I HELP YOU? >>>

General Motors doesn't have a 'helpline' for people who don't know how to drive, because people don't buy cars like they buy computers — but imagine if they did …

HELPLINE: 'General Motors Helpline, how can I help you?'
CUSTOMER: 'I got in my car and closed the door, and nothing happened!'
HELPLINE: 'Did you put the key in the ignition and turn it?'
CUSTOMER: 'What's an ignition?'
HELPLINE: 'It's a starter motor that draws current from your battery and turns over the engine.'
CUSTOMER: 'Ignition? Motor? Battery? Engine? How come I have to know all of these technical terms just to use my car?'

HELPLINE: 'General Motors Helpline, how can I help you?'
CUSTOMER: 'My car ran well for a week, and now it won't go anywhere!'
HELPLINE: 'Is the petrol tank empty?'
CUSTOMER: 'Huh? How do I know!?'
HELPLINE: 'There's a little gauge on the front panel, with a needle, and markings from 'E' to 'F'. Where is the needle pointing?'
CUSTOMER: 'It's pointing to 'E'. What does that mean?'
HELPLINE: 'It means that you have to visit a petrol vendor, and

purchase some more petrol. You can install it yourself, or the vendor can install it for you.'

CUSTOMER: 'What!?' I paid $12,000 for this car! Now you tell me that I have to keep buying more components? I want a car that comes with everything built in!'

 ## GO AWAY, YOU BASTARD! >>>

I shall seek and find you.
I shall take you to bed and control you.
I will make you ache, shake and sweat until you grunt and groan.
I will make you beg for mercy.
I will exhaust you to the point that you will be relieved when I
   leave you — and you will be weak for days.

All my love
The flu

IS THIS OFF? >>>

Food spoilage tests for students:

THE GAG TEST: Anything that makes you gag is 'off' (except for leftovers from what you cooked for yourself last night).

EGGS: When something starts pecking its way out of the shell, the egg is probably past its prime.

DAIRY PRODUCTS: Milk is off when it starts to look like yoghurt. Yoghurt is off when it starts to look like cottage cheese. Cottage cheese is off when it starts to look like regular cheese. Regular cheese is nothing but rotten milk anyway and can't get any more rotten than it is already. Cheddar cheese is off when you think it is blue cheese but you realise you've never purchased that kind.

MAYONNAISE: If it makes you violently ill after you eat it, the mayonnaise is off.

FROZEN FOODS: Frozen foods that have become an integral part of the defrosting problem in your freezer compartment will probably be rotten — (or wrecked anyway) by the time you pry them out with a kitchen knife.

(a crazy world)

EXPIRATION DATES: This is NOT a marketing ploy to encourage you to throw away perfectly good food so that you'll spend more on groceries. Perhaps you'd benefit by having a calendar in your kitchen.

SALT: It never goes off.

LETTUCE: Lettuce is rotten when you can't get it off the bottom of the vegetable crisper without Jif or when it turns to liquid.

CANNED GOODS: Any canned goods that have become the size or shape of a softball should be disposed of. Carefully.

EMPTY CONTAINERS: Putting empty containers back into the fridge is an old trick, but it only works if you live with someone or have a maid.

UNMARKED ITEMS: You know it is well beyond prime when you're tempted to discard the Tupperware along with the food. Generally speaking, Tupperware containers should not burp when you open them.

GENERAL RULE OF THUMB: Most food cannot be kept longer than the average life span of a hamster. Keep a hamster in or nearby your fridge to gauge this.

 ## ABSOLUTELY NUTS >>>

I was at the golf shop comparing different kinds of golf balls. I was unhappy with the women's type I had been using. After browsing for several minutes, I was approached by a good-looking gentleman who works at the shop. He asked if he could help me. Without thinking, I looked at him and said, 'I think I like playing with men's balls.'

My sister and I were at the mall and passed by a store that sold a variety of nuts. As we were looking at the display case, the boy behind the counter asked if we needed any help. I replied, 'No, I'm just looking at your nuts.' My sister started to laugh hysterically, the boy grinned, and I turned beetroot-red and walked away. To this day, my sister has never let me forget.

Frank Lingua, president and chief executive of Dissembling Associates, is the United States' leading purveyor of buzzwords, catch phrases and clichés for people too busy to speak in plain English. *Business Finance* contributing editor Dan Danbom interviewed Lingua in his New York City office.

Danbom: Is being a cliché expert a full-time job?

Lingua: Bottom line is I have a full plate 24/7.

D: Is it hard to keep up with the seemingly endless supply of clichés that spew from business?

L: Some days, I don't have the bandwidth. It's like drinking from a fire hydrant.

D: So it's difficult?

L: Harder than nailing Jell-O to the wall.

D: Where do most clichés come from?

L: Stakeholders push the envelope until it's outside the box.

D: How do you track them once they've been coined?

L: It's like herding cats.

D: Can you predict whether a phrase is going to become a cliché?

L: Yes. I skate to where the puck's going to be. Because if you aren't the lead dog, you're not providing a customer-centric proactive solution.

D: Give us a new buzzword that we'll be hearing ad nauseam.

L: 'Enronitis' could be a next-generation player.

D: Do people understand your role as a cliché expert?

L: No, they can't get their arms around that.

D: How do people know you're a cliché expert?

L: I walk the walk and talk the talk.

D: Did incomprehensibility come naturally to you?

L: I wasn't wired that way, but it became mission-critical as I strategically focused on my go-forward plan.

D: What did you do to develop this talent?

L: It's not rocket science. It's not brain surgery. When you drill down to the granular level, it's just basic blocking and tackling.

D: How do you know if you're successful in your work?

L: At the end of the day, it's all about robust, world-class language solutions.

D: How do you stay ahead of others in the buzzword industry?
L: Net-net, my value proposition is based on maximising synergies and being first to market with a leveraged, value-added deliverable. That's the opportunity space on a level playing field.
D: Does everyone in business eventually devolve into the sort of mindless drivel you spout?
L: If you walk like a duck and talk like a duck, you're a duck. They all drink the Kool-Aid.
D: Do you read Dilbert in the newspaper?
L: My knowledge base is deselective of fibre media.
D: Does that mean 'no'?
L: Negative.
D: Does THAT mean 'no'?
L: Let's take your issues offline.
D: No, we are not going to take them 'offline'.
L: You have a result-driven mind-set that isn't a strategic fit with my game plan.
D: I want to push your face in.
L: Your call is very important to me.
D: How can you live with yourself?
L: I eat my own dog food. My vision is to monetise scalable supply chains.
D: When are you going to stop this?
L: I may eventually exit the business to pursue other career opportunities.
D: I hate you.
L: Take it and run with it.

 ## NO PRICE FOR THIS >>>

A woman went to buy several items at a discount shop. When she finally got to the checkout, she learned that one of her items had no price sticker. Imagine her embarrassment when the checkout operator got on the intercom and boomed out for all the shop to hear, 'PRICE CHECK ON LANE 13, TAMPAX SUPER SIZE.' That was bad enough, but somebody at the back of the shop heard 'Tampax' as 'thumbtacks'. In a businesslike tone, a voice boomed back over the intercom: 'DO YOU WANT THE KIND YOU PUSH IN WITH YOUR THUMB OR THE KIND YOU POUND IN WITH A HAMMER?'

ARMLESS ENOUGH >>>

A man came round in hospital after a serious accident. He shouted, 'Doctor, doctor, I can't feel my legs!'

The doctor replied, 'I know you can't, I've cut your arms off.'

PEACE, BROTHER! >>>

People who should've won this year's Nobel prize:

1. Britney Spears and Eminem, who, combined, have written more books than they've read.
2. Dr Phil McGraw, who has managed to convince millions of women to buy his self-help books, despite the fact that his most high-profile patient, Oprah Winfrey, is an overweight woman with serious commitment issues.
3. America's Oil Companies — for a lifetime body of work proving that oil and water don't mix.
4. Yasser Arafat and Ariel Sharon — for those two consecutive days last March when no Israelis or Palestinians killed each other.
5. Bill Gates — for creating the X-Box and convincing Americans that their children need a $200 video-game system during a recession.
6. The editors of *Maxim* — for managing to create 300 magazine pages a month using no other subjects besides beer and models.
7. Jared of Subway Sandwich fame, whose claim of losing hundreds of pounds and achieving optimum health by eating nothing but oversized, greasy Heroes was questioned by no one.
8. Jennifer Lopez, who, in conjunction with DuPont, developed a synthetic fabric capable of containing her arse.
9. That 150kg guy, who always manages to jam himself into the seat right next to yours on domestic flights.
10. Glaxo, who has managed to make 'loose stools' a side effect of every one of the drugs it produces.

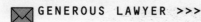 GENEROUS LAWYER >>>

A lawyer was getting driven home by his chauffeur in his stretch limo when he saw a guy on the side of the road eating handfuls of grass.

He asked his driver to stop the car and wound down his window and said to the man, 'My good man, why are you eating grass?'

'Because I am so poor I can't afford a thing to eat.'

The lawyer says, 'Oh, you poor man. Get in the car and come back to my house and I'll fix you up.'

'But I've got a wife and three kids.'

'Well, we'll stop by and pick them up too.'

On the way to the lawyer's house the man thanked his benefactor. 'It's so kind of you to ask us back to your house,' he said.

The lawyer said, 'It's nothing, my good man. You're going to love it there, the grass is at least 30cm tall.'

earning a crust

Most of us spend so much time at work and, unless you are unlucky enough to work with a bunch of charisma bypass-type morons, there should be ample ammunition for a good laugh other than the daily paperclip fight.

This section has traditionally been one of the biggest chapters, which convinces us that there are thousands of workshy jokesters out there who do a bit of extra-curricular thinking and e-mailing. The airline employees are particularly adept at keeping note of all the weird and wonderful events that liven up their drudgery and sending them on for us to enjoy, and the London Underground employs some workers with a particularly good sense of humour — and you'd need one if you've ever experienced the tube in rush hour.

'To the gentleman wearing the long grey coat trying to get on the second carriage, what part of "Stand clear of the doors" don't you understand?'

At Camden Town station (on a crowded Saturday afternoon): 'Please let the passengers off the train first. Please let the passengers off the train first. Please let the passengers off the train first. Let the passengers off the train FIRST! Oh go on then, stuff yourselves in like sardines. See if I care, I'm going home.'

'Ladies and gentleman, upon departing the train may I remind you to take your rubbish with you. Despite the fact that you are in something that is metal, fairly round, filthy and smells, this is a tube train for public transport and not a bin on wheels.'

Driver: 'I apologise for the delay leaving the station, ladies and gentlemen, this is due to a passenger masturbating on the train at Edgware Road. Someone has activated the alarm and he is being removed from the train.'

'Ladies and gentlemen, do you want the good news first or the bad news? The good news is that last Friday was my birthday and I hit the town and had a great time. I felt sadly let down by the fact that none of you sent me a card! I drive you to work and home every day and not even a card.

'The bad news is that there is a points failure somewhere between Stratford and East Ham, which means that we probably won't reach our destination. We may have to stop and return. I won't reverse back up the line — simply get out and walk and go back to where we started. In the meantime if you get bored you can simply talk to the man in front or beside you or opposite you. Let me start you off: 'Hi, my name's Gary, how do you do?'

'Your delay this evening is caused by the line controller suffering from elbow and backside syndrome, not knowing his elbow from his backside. I'll let you know any further information as soon as I'm given any.'

'Please mind the closing doors … the doors close, the doors reopen. Passengers are reminded that the big red slidy things on the side of the train are called the doors. Let's try it again. Please stand clear of the doors. Thank you.'

'I am sorry about the delay, apparently some nutter has just wandered into the tunnel at Euston. We don't know when we'll be moving again, but these people tend to come out pretty quickly … usually in bits.'

✉ THEY'RE QUACKERS >>>

A duck walks into a bar and orders a beer and a sandwich. The barman looks at him and says, 'But you're a duck.'

'I see your eyes are working,' replies the duck.

'And you talk!' exclaims the barman.

'I see your ears are working,' says the duck. 'Now can I have my beer and my sandwich, please?'

'Certainly,' says the barman. 'Sorry about that, it's just we don't get many ducks in this pub. What are you doing round this way?'

'I'm working on the building site across the road', explains the duck. So the duck drinks his beer, eats his sandwich, pays and leaves. This continues for two weeks. One day the circus comes to town. The ringleader of the circus comes into the pub and the barman tells him about the incredible talking duck. 'Marvellous!' says the ringleader. 'Get him to come see me.'

So the next day, the duck comes into the pub. The barman says, 'Hey, Mr Duck, I lined you up with a top job paying really good money!'

'Yeah?' says the duck, 'Sounds great, where is it?'

'At the circus,' says the barman.

'The circus?' the duck enquires.

'That's right,' replies the barman.

'The circus? That place with the big tent? With all the animals? With the big canvas roof with the hole in the middle?' asks the duck.

'That's right!' says the barman.

The duck looks confused and asks, 'What the hell do they want with a plasterer?'

✉ A SIGH OF RELIEF >>>

I am passing this on to you … it's definitely working for me. I think I have found inner peace. I read an article that said the way to achieve inner peace was to finish things I had started. Today I started and finished two bags of potato chips, I started and finished a bacon and egg pie, I started and finished a small box of chocolates and strangled the living crap out of someone I didn't like. I feel better already … I have inner peace … and I pass this on to those who really need it.

✉ DOCTOR, DOCTOR, CAN'T YOU SEE I'M BURNING, BURNING... >>>

Actual 'reports' on hospital charts by doctors:

- She has no rigors or shaking chills, but her husband states she was very hot in bed last night.
- Patient has chest pain if she lies on her left side for over a year.
- On the second day the knee was better, and on the third day it disappeared.
- The patient is tearful and crying constantly. She also appears to be depressed.
- The patient has been depressed since she began seeing me in 1993.
- Discharge status: Alive but without my permission.
- Healthy appearing, decrepit 69-year-old male, mentally alert but forgetful.
- The patient refused autopsy.
- The patient has no previous history of suicides.
- Patient has left white blood cells at another hospital.
- Patient's medical history has been remarkably insignificant with only a 20kg weight gain in the past three days.
- Patient had waffles for breakfast and anorexia for lunch.
- She is numb from her toes down.
- While in ER she was examined, X-rated and sent home.
- The skin was moist and dry.
- Occasional, constant, infrequent headaches.
- Patient was alert and unresponsive.

- Rectal examination revealed a normal-sized thyroid.
- She stated that she had been constipated for most of her life until she got a divorce.
- I saw your patient today, who is still under our car for physical therapy.
- Both breasts are equal and reactive to light and accommodation.
- Examination of genitalia reveals that he is circus sized.
- The lab test indicated abnormal lover function.
- The patient was to have a bowel resection. However, he took a job as a stockbroker instead.
- Skin: somewhat pale but present.
- The pelvic exam will be done later on the floor.
- Patient was seen in consultation by Dr Blank, who felt we should sit on the abdomen and I agree.
- Large brown stool ambulating in the hall.
- Patient has two teenage children, but no other abnormalities.

✉ CHRISTMAS PARTY,
21ST-CENTURY STYLE >>>

FROM: Patty Lewis, Human Resources Director
To: All Employees
DATE: 1 December
RE: Christmas Party

I'm happy to inform you that the company Christmas Party will take place on 23 December, starting at noon in the private function room at the Grill House.

There will be a cash bar and plenty of drinks! We'll have a small band playing traditional carols — feel free to sing along. And don't be surprised if our CEO shows up dressed as Santa Claus!

A Christmas tree will be lit at 1pm. Exchange of gifts among employees can be done at that time, however, no gift should be over $10, to make the giving of gifts easy for everyone's pockets. This gathering is only for employees! A special announcement will be made by our CEO at that time! Merry Christmas to you and your family.

Patty

FROM: Patty Lewis, Human Resources Director
TO: All Employees
DATE: 2 December
RE: Holiday Party

In no way was yesterday's memo intended to exclude our Jewish employees. We recognise that Chanukah is an important holiday which often coincides with Christmas, though unfortunately not this year. However, from now on we're calling it our 'Holiday Party'.

The same policy applies to any other employees who are not Christians or those still celebrating Reconciliation Day.

There will be no Christmas tree present. No Christmas carols sung. We will have other types of music for your enjoyment. Happy Holidays to you and your family.

Patty

FROM: Patty Lewis, Human Resources Director
TO: All Employees
DATE: 3 December
RE: Holiday Party

Regarding the note I received from a member of Alcoholics Anonymous requesting a non-drinking table: you didn't sign your name. I'm happy to accommodate this request, but if I put a sign on a table that reads 'AA Only', you wouldn't be anonymous any more. How am I supposed to handle this? Somebody?

Forget about the gifts exchange, no gift exchanges are allowed since the union members feel that $10 is too much money and executives believe $10 is very little for a gift. NO GIFT EXCHANGES ARE ALLOWED.

FROM: Patty Lewis, Human Resources Director
To: All Employees
DATE: 7 December
RE: Holiday Party

What a diverse group we are! I had no idea that 20 December begins the Muslim holy month of Ramadan, which forbids eating and drinking during daylight hours. There goes the party!

Seriously, we can appreciate how a luncheon at this time of year does not accommodate our Muslim employees' beliefs. Perhaps the Grill House can hold off on serving your meal until the end of the party — or else package everything for you to take it home in a little foil doggy bag. Will that work?

Meanwhile, I've arranged for members of Weight Watchers to sit furthest from the dessert buffet and pregnant women will get the table closest to the toilets. Gays are allowed to sit with each other. Lesbians do not have to sit with gay men, each will have their own table. Yes, there will be a flower arrangement for the gay men's table. No cross-dressing allowed though.

We will have booster seats for short people. Low-fat food will be available for those on a diet. We cannot control the salt used in the food, so we suggest for those people with high blood pressure to taste first.

There will be fresh fruit as dessert for diabetics, as the restaurant cannot supply 'No Sugar' desserts. Sorry! Did I miss anything?!

Patty

FROM:
Patty Lewis, Human Resources Director
TO: All #$%^&*! Employees
DATE: 10 December
RE: The #$%^&*! Holiday Party

Vegetarians! I've had it with you people! We're going to keep this party at the Grill House whether you like it or not, so you can sit quietly at the table furthest from the 'grill of death' and you'll get your #$%^&*! salad bar, including hydroponic tomatoes.

But you know, they have feelings, too. Tomatoes scream when you slice them. I've heard them scream. I'm hearing them scream right now!

HA! I hope you all have a rotten holiday! Drive drunk and die, you hear me?

The Bitch from HELL!

FROM: Joan Bishop, Acting Human Resources Director
DATE: 14 December
RE: Patty Lewis and Holiday Party

I'm sure I speak for all of us in wishing Patty Lewis a speedy recovery from her stress-related illness and I'll continue to forward your cards to her at the hospital. In the meantime, management has decided to cancel our Holiday Party and give everyone the afternoon of the 23rd off with full pay.

QUIDS IN! >>>

I went to the butchers the other day and I bet him 50 quid that he couldn't reach the meat off the top shelf. And he said, 'No, the steaks are too high.'

MONEY: THE ROOT OF ALL EVIL, BUT... >>>

It can buy you a house — but not a home.
It can buy you a bed — but not sleep.
It can buy you a clock — but not time.
It can buy you a book — but not knowledge.
It can buy you a position — but not respect.
It can buy you medicine — but not health.
It can buy you blood — but not life.
It can buy you sex — but not love.

So you see money isn't everything. And it often causes pain and suffering. I tell you all this because as your friend, I want to take away your pain and suffering. So send me all your money — and I will suffer for you.

QUIZ TIME >>>

The following short quiz consists of four questions and will tell you whether you are qualified to be a ' professional'.

1. *How do you put a giraffe into a refrigerator?*
   The correct answer: Open the refrigerator, put in the giraffe, and close the door. This question tests whether you tend to do simple things in an overly complicated way.
2. *How do you put an elephant into a refrigerator?*
   Did you say, 'Open the refrigerator, put in the elephant, and close the refrigerator'? Wrong answer. Correct answer: Open the refrigerator, take out the giraffe, put in the elephant and close the door. This tests your ability to think through the repercussions of your previous actions.
3. *The Lion King is hosting an animal conference. All the animals attend except one. Which animal does not attend?*
   Correct answer: The elephant. The elephant is in the refrigerator. You just put him in there. This tests your memory. OK, even if you did not answer the first three questions correctly, you still have one more chance to show your true abilities.
4. *There is a river you must cross but it is inhabited by crocodiles. How do you manage it?*
   Correct answer: You swim across. All the crocodiles are attending the animal meeting.

This tests whether you learn quickly from your mistakes. According to Anderson Consulting Worldwide, around 90 percent of the professionals they tested got all questions wrong. But many pre-schoolers got several correct answers. Anderson Consulting says this conclusively disproves the theory that most professionals have the brains of a four-year-old.

✉ ANOTHER LUDICROUS AMERICAN LAWSUIT

A North Carolina lawyer purchased a box of very rare and expensive cigars, then insured them against fire among other things. Within a month, having smoked his entire stockpile of these great cigars and without yet having made even his first premium payment on the policy, the lawyer filed a claim against the insurance company.

In his claim, the lawyer stated the cigars were lost 'in a series of small fires'. The insurance company refused to pay, citing the obvious reason: that the man had consumed the cigars in the normal fashion.

The lawyer sued … and won!

In delivering the ruling the judge agreed with the insurance company that the claim was frivolous. The judge stated, nevertheless, that the lawyer held a policy from the company in which it had warranted that the cigars were insurable and also guaranteed that it would insure them against fire, without defining what is considered to be unacceptable fire, and was obligated to pay the claim.

Rather than endure a lengthy and costly appeal process, the insurance company accepted the ruling and paid $15,000 to the lawyer for his loss of the rare cigars in the 'fires'.

But after the lawyer cashed the cheque, the insurance company had him arrested on 24 counts of arson. With his own insurance claim and testimony from the previous case being used against him, the lawyer was convicted of intentionally burning his insured property and was sentenced to 24 months in jail and a $24,000 fine.

This is a true story and was the first-place winner in the recent Criminal Lawyers Award Contest.

 IT, YOU SEE! >>>

Comprehending the IT guy — Take One

Two IT guys were walking across the park when one said, 'Where did you get such a great bike?' The second IT guy replied, 'Well, I was walking along yesterday minding my own business when a beautiful woman rode up on this bike. She threw the bike to the ground, took off all her clothes and said, "Take what you want".' The second IT guy nodded approvingly, 'Good choice. The clothes probably wouldn't have fit.'

Comprehending the IT guy — Take Two

An architect, an artist and an IT guy were discussing whether it was better to have a wife or a mistress. The architect said he enjoyed time with his wife, building a solid foundation for an enduring relationship. The artist said he enjoyed time with his mistress, because of the passion and mystery he found there. The IT guy said, 'I like both.' The artist said 'BOTH?' The IT guy replied, 'Yeah. If you have a wife and a mistress, they will each assume you are spending time with the other woman, and you can go to the office and get some work done.'

Comprehending the IT guy — Take Three
To the optimist, the glass is half full. To the pessimist, the glass is half empty. To the IT guy, the glass is twice as big as it needs to be.

Comprehending the IT guy — Take Four
An IT guy was crossing a road one day when a frog called out to him and said, 'If you kiss me, I'll turn into a beautiful princess.' He bent over, picked up the frog and put it in his pocket. The frog spoke up again and said, 'If you kiss me and turn me back into a beautiful princess, I will stay with you for one week.' The IT guy took the frog out of his pocket, smiled at it and returned it to his pocket. The frog then cried out, 'If you kiss me and turn me back into a princess, I'll stay with you for a week and do ANYTHING you want.'

Again the IT guy took the frog out, smiled at it and put it back into his pocket. Finally, the frog asked, 'What is the matter? I've told you I'm a beautiful princess, that I'll stay with you for a week and do anything you want. Why won't you kiss me?' The IT guy said, 'Look, I work in IT. I don't have time for a girlfriend, but a talking frog — now that's cool.'

 BIG BUSINESS BLUES >>>

Corporate Lesson 1
A man is preparing to get into the shower just as his wife is finishing hers. The doorbell rings and after a few seconds of arguing over which one should go and answer the door, the wife gives up, quickly wraps herself in a towel and runs downstairs.

When she opens the door, there stands Bob, the next-door neighbour. Before she says a word, Bob says, 'I'll give you $800 to drop that towel you have on.'

After thinking for a moment, the woman drops her towel and stands naked in front of Bob. After a few seconds, Bob hands her $800 and leaves.

Confused, but excited about her good fortune, the woman wraps back up in the towel and goes back upstairs. When she gets back to the bathroom, her husband asks from the shower, 'Who was that?'

'It was Bob the next-door neighbour,' she replies.

'Great,' the husband says, 'did he say anything about the $800 he owes me?'

Moral of the story: If you share critical information pertaining to credit and risk in time with your stakeholders, you may be in a position to prevent avoidable exposure.

Corporate lesson 2

A priest was driving along and saw a nun on the side of the road. He stopped and offered her a lift, which she accepted. She got in and crossed her legs, forcing her gown to open and reveal a lovely leg.

The priest had a look and nearly had an accident. After controlling the car, he stealthily slid his hand up her leg. The nun looked at him and immediately said, 'Father, remember Psalm 129?' The priest was flustered and apologised profusely.

He forced himself to remove his hand. However, he was unable to remove his eyes from her leg. Further on, while changing gear, he let his hand slide up her leg again. The nun once again said, 'Father, remember Psalm 129?'

Once again the priest apologised. 'Sorry sister, but the flesh is weak.' Arriving at the convent, the nun got out, gave him a meaningful glance and went on her way.

On his arrival at the church, the priest rushed to retrieve a Bible and looked up Psalm 129. It said, 'Go forth and seek, further up, you will find glory.'

Moral of the story: Always be well informed in your job, or you might miss a great opportunity!

Corporate Lesson 3

A sales rep, an administration clerk and the manager are walking to lunch when they find an antique oil lamp. They rub it and a genie comes out in a puff of smoke. The genie says, 'I usually only grant three wishes, so I'll give each of you just one.'

'Me first! Me first!' says the admin clerk. 'I want to be in the Bahamas, driving a speedboat, without a care in the world.' Poof! She's gone.

'Me next! Me next!' says the sales rep. 'I want to be in Hawaii, relaxing on the beach with my personal masseuse, an endless supply of pina coladas and the love of my life.' Poof! He's gone.

'OK, you're up,' the genie says to the manager. The manager says, 'I want those two back in the office after lunch.'

Moral of story: Always let your boss have the first say.

✉ MANAGEMENT LEARNING >>>

Lesson 1

A little bird was flying south for the winter. It was so cold, the bird froze and fell to the ground in a large field. While it was lying there, a cow came by and dropped some dung on it. As the frozen bird lay there in the pile of cow dung, it began to realise how warm it was. The dung was actually thawing him out! He lay there all warm and happy, and soon began to sing for joy.

A passing cat heard the bird singing and discovered it under the pile of cow dung, promptly dug him out and ate him!

The moral: Not everyone who drops shit on you is your enemy; not everyone who gets you out of shit is your friend; and when you're in deep shit, keep your mouth shut!

Lesson 2

The boy rode on the donkey and the old man walked. As they went along, they passed some people who remarked it was a shame the old man was walking and the boy was riding.

The man and boy thought maybe the critics were right, so they changed positions. Later, they passed some people who remarked, 'What a shame, he makes that little boy walk.'

They decided they both would walk! Soon they passed some more people who thought they were stupid to walk when they had a decent donkey to ride. So they both rode the donkey!

Now they passed some people who shamed them by saying how awful to put such a load on a poor donkey. The boy and man said they were probably right, so they decided to carry the donkey. As they crossed a bridge, they lost their grip on the animal and he fell into the river and drowned.

The moral: If you try to please everyone, you will eventually lose your ass.

2003 Corporation-style dating

Dearest [Girl]

I am very happy to inform you that I have fallen in love with you since Wednesday, 24 April 2002. With reference to the meeting held between us on 31 March 2001 at 1500 hours, I would like to present myself as a prospective lover.

Our love affair would be on probation for a period of three months, and depending on compatibility would be made permanent. Of course, upon completion of probation, there will be continuous on-the-relationship training and relationship appraisal schemes leading up to promotion from lover to spouse.

The expenses incurred for coffee and entertainment would initially be shared equally between us. Later, based on your performance, I might take up a larger share of the expenses. However, I am broad-minded enough to be taken care of on your expense account.

I request you to kindly respond within 30 days of receiving this letter, failing which, this offer would be cancelled without further notice and I shall be considering someone else. I would be happy if you could forward this letter to your sister, if you do not wish to take up this offer.

Thanking you in anticipation.

Yours sincerely,
[Boy]

Modern reply

Dear [Boy]

Please refer to your letter dated today. I am pleased to inform you that I hope to accept your proposal for romance.

I view the promotional prospects as satisfactory. However, you should be informed that there are certain conditions of acceptance. Please enlighten me as to your retirement benefits. Gratuity should be generous.

I also need to be assured that there is sufficient security with regards to this commitment. If there is any chance at all of retrenchment or consequent disinterest on your part, then I should receive monetary compensation according to union standards.

Due to the nature of my position, I am sure you will agree that an expense account should be arranged for my access in light of the 'VIP' we shall be entertaining.

In addition, housing and transport allowances should be in order and nothing less than a luxury flat and a Jaguar will be considered. Please also note that there should be no moonlighting restrictions placed on myself. If you are still interested in the relationship, please reply on an urgent basis as other prospective lovers have sent indications of interest.

Please also note that my sister is happily employed.

Yours perhaps,
[Girl]

 THAT'S HEAVY, MAN! >>>

A man takes his Rottweiler to the vet. 'My dog's cross-eyed. Is there anything you can do for him?'

'Well,' says the vet, 'let's have a look at him.' So he picks the dog up and examines his eyes, then checks his teeth. Finally, he says, 'I'm going to have to put him down.'

'What? Because he's cross-eyed?'

'No, because he's really heavy!'

 ANSETT — RIP >>>

A difficult customer

A crowded Ansett flight was cancelled after Ansett's 767s had been withdrawn from service. A single attendant was rebooking a long line of inconvenienced travellers. Suddenly, an angry passenger pushed his way to the desk. He slapped his ticket down on the counter and said, 'I HAVE to be on this flight and it HAS to be FIRST CLASS. The attendant replied, 'I'm sorry sir. I'll be happy to try to help you, but I've got to help these people first, then I'm sure we'll be able to work something out.'

The passenger was unimpressed. He asked loudly, so that the passengers behind him could hear, 'DO YOU HAVE ANY IDEA WHO I AM?'

Without hesitating, the attendant smiled and grabbed her public address microphone: 'May I have your attention please, may I have your attention please,' she began, her voice heard clearly throughout the terminal. 'We have a passenger here at Gate 14 WHO DOES NOT KNOW WHO HE IS. If anyone can help him find his identity, please come to Gate 14.'

With the folks behind him in line laughing hysterically, the man glared at the Ansett attendant, gritted his teeth and said, 'F*** you!'

Without flinching, she smiled and said, 'I'm sorry, sir, but you'll have to get in line for that too.'

 FLYING HIGH! >>>

Tower: 'Delta 351, you have traffic at 10 o'clock, 10 kilometres!'
Delta 351: 'Give us another hint! We have digital watches!'

One day, the pilot of a Cherokee 180 was told by the tower to hold short of the runway while a DC-8 landed. The DC-8 landed, rolled out, turned around, and taxied back past the Cherokee. Some quick-witted comedian in the DC-8 crew got on the radio and said, 'What a cute little plane. Did you make it all by yourself?'

Our hero, the Cherokee pilot, not about to let the insult go by, came back with a real zinger: 'I made it out of DC-8 parts. Another landing like that and I'll have enough parts for another one.'

There's a story about the military pilot calling for a priority landing because his single-engine jet fighter was running 'a bit peaked'. Air Traffic Control told the fighter jock that he was number two behind a B-52 that had one engine shut down.

'Ah,' the pilot remarked, 'the dreaded seven-engine approach'.

A student became lost during a solo cross-country flight. While attempting to locate the aircraft on radar, ATC asked, 'What was your last known position?'
Student: 'When I was number one for takeoff.'

Taxiing down the tarmac, the DC-10 abruptly stopped, turned around and returned to the gate. After an hour-long wait, it finally took off. A concerned passenger asked the flight attendant, 'What was the problem?'

'The pilot was bothered by a noise he heard in the engine,' explained the flight attendant, 'and it took us a while to find a new pilot.'

'Flight 2341, for noise abatement turn right 45 degrees.'

'But Centre, we are at 35,000 feet. How much noise can we make up here?'

'Sir, have you ever heard the noise a 747 makes when it hits a 727?'

✉ AND MORE OF FLYING THE FRIENDLY SKIES >>>

All too rarely, airline attendants make an effort to make the in-flight 'safety lecture' and their other announcements a bit more entertaining.

- On a Continental Flight with a very 'senior' flight attendant crew, the pilot said, 'Ladies and gentlemen, we've reached cruising altitude and will be turning down the cabin lights. This is for your comfort and to enhance the appearance of your flight attendants.'
- On landing, the stewardess said, 'Please be sure to take all your belongings. If you're going to leave anything, please make sure it's something we'd like to have.'
- 'There may be 50 ways to leave your lover, but there are only four ways out of this aeroplane.'
- 'Thank you for flying Delta Business Express. We hope you enjoyed giving us the business as much as we enjoyed taking you for a ride.'
- After a particularly rough landing during thunderstorms in Memphis, a flight attendant on a Northwest flight announced, 'Please take care when opening the overhead compartments because, after a landing like that, sure as hell everything has shifted.'

- From a Southwest Airlines employee: 'Welcome aboard Southwest flight XXX to YYY. To operate your seat-belt, insert the metal tab into the buckle, and pull tight. It works just like every other seat-belt; and, if you don't know how to operate one, you probably shouldn't be out in public unsupervised.'
- 'In the event of a sudden loss of cabin pressure, masks will descend from the ceiling. Stop screaming, grab the mask, and pull it over your face. If you have a small child travelling with you, secure your mask before assisting with theirs. If you are travelling with more than one small child, pick your favourite.'
- 'Weather at our destination is 50 degrees with some broken clouds, but we'll try to have them fixed before we arrive. Thank you, and remember, nobody loves you, or your money, more than Southwest Airlines.'
- 'Your seat cushions can be used for flotation; and in the event of an emergency water landing, please paddle to shore and take them with our compliments.'
- 'Should the cabin lose pressure, oxygen masks will drop from the overhead area. Please place the bag over your own mouth and nose before assisting children … or other adults acting like children.'
- 'As you exit the plane, make sure to gather all of your belongings. Anything left behind will be distributed evenly among the flight attendants. Please do not leave children or spouses.'
- And from the pilot during his welcome message: 'Delta Airlines is pleased to have some of the best flight attendants in the industry. Unfortunately, none of them are on this flight.'
- Heard on Southwest Airlines just after a very hard landing in Salt Lake City: The flight attendant came on the intercom and said, 'That was quite a bump, and I know what y'all are thinking, I'm here to tell you it wasn't the airline's fault, it wasn't the pilot's fault, it wasn't the flight attendant's fault — it was the asphalt.'
- Overheard on an American Airlines flight into Amarillo, Texas, on a particularly windy and bumpy day: During the final approach, the captain was really having to fight it. After an extremely hard landing, the flight attendant said, 'Ladies and gentlemen, welcome to Amarillo. Please remain in your seats with your seat-belts fastened while the captain taxis what's left of our aeroplane to the gate.'

- Part of a flight attendant's arrival announcement: 'We'd like to thank you folks for flying with us today. And, the next time you get the insane urge to go blasting through the skies in a pressurised metal tube, we hope you'll think of US Airways.'

 PILOT CAUSES ACCIDENT >>>

A plane was taking off from Kennedy Airport. After it reached a comfortable cruising altitude, the captain made an announcement over the intercom: 'Ladies and gentlemen, this is your captain speaking. Welcome to flight number 293, non-stop from New York to Los Angeles. The weather ahead is good and, therefore, we should have a smooth and uneventful flight. Now sit back and relax — OH, MY GOD!'

Silence followed and after a few minutes, the captain came back on the intercom and said, 'Ladies and gentlemen, I am so sorry if I scared you earlier; but, while I was talking, the flight attendant brought me a cup of coffee and spilled the hot coffee in my lap. You should see the front of my pants!'

A passenger was heard saying, 'That's nothing. He should see the back of mine!'

 THE BEST JOB IN THE WORLD? >>>

POSITION: Mother, Mum, Mama

JOB DESCRIPTION: Long term, team players needed, for challenging permanent work in an often chaotic environment. Candidates must possess excellent communication and organisational skills and be willing to work variable hours, which will include evenings and weekends and frequent 24-hour shifts, on call. Some overnight travel required, including trips to primitive camping sites on rainy weekends and endless sports tournaments in faraway cities. Travel expenses not reimbursed. Extensive courier duties also required.

RESPONSIBILITIES: The rest of your life. Must be willing to be hated, at least temporarily, until someone needs $5. Must be willing to bite tongue repeatedly. Also, must possess the physical stamina of a pack mule and be able to go from zero to 100kph in three seconds flat in case, this time, the screams from the backyard are not someone just crying wolf. Must be willing to face stimulating technical challenges, such as small gadget repair, mysteriously sluggish toilets and stuck zippers. Must screen phone calls, maintain calendars and co-ordinate production of multiple homework projects. Must have ability to plan and organise social gatherings for clients of all ages and mental outlooks. Must be willing to be indispensable one minute and embarrassing the next. Must handle assembly and product safety testing of a half million cheap plastic toys, and battery-operated devices. Must always hope for the best but be prepared for the worst. Must assume final, complete accountability for the quality of the end product. Responsibilities also include floor maintenance and general cleaning work throughout the facility.

POSSIBILITY FOR ADVANCEMENT AND PROMOTION: Virtually none. Your job is to remain in the same position for years, without complaining, constantly retraining and updating your skills, so that those in your charge can ultimately surpass you.

PREVIOUS EXPERIENCE: None required unfortunately. On-the-job training offered on a continually exhausting basis.

WAGES AND COMPENSATION: You pay them. Offering frequent rises and bonuses. A balloon payment is due when they turn 18 because of the assumption that tertiary education will help them become financially independent. When you die, you give them whatever is left. The oddest thing about this reverse-salary scheme is that you actually enjoy it and only wish you could do more.

 GOOD GRIEF >>>

A guy walks into the psychiatrist wearing only plastic wrap for shorts. The shrink says, 'Well, I can clearly see you're nuts.'

Doctor Dave had slept with one of his patients and felt guilty all day long. No matter how much he tried to forget about it, he couldn't. The guilt and sense of betrayal was overwhelming. But every once in a while he'd hear an internal, reassuring voice that said, 'Dave, don't worry about it. You aren't the first doctor to sleep with one of their patients and you won't be the last. And you're single. Just let it go.'

But invariably the other voice would bring him back to reality, whispering, 'Dave, you're a vet!'

 FIERY FERRARI >>>

Modena, Italy: The Ferrari F1 Team fired their entire pit-crew yesterday. The announcement was followed by Ferrari's decision to take advantage of the New Zealand Government's 'Work For the Dole' scheme and hire unemployed youths from Auckland.

The decision to hire them was brought on by a recent documentary on how unemployed youths in South Auckland were able to remove a set of car wheels in less than six seconds without proper equipment, whereas Ferrari's existing crew can only do it in eight seconds.

This was thought to be an excellent yet bold move by Ferrari management and, as most races are won and lost in the pits, Ferrari would have an advantage over every team.

However Ferrari expectations were easily exceeded, as during the crew's first practice session not only were 'da boyz' able to change the tyres in under six seconds, but within 12 seconds they had resprayed, rebadged and sold the vehicle over to the McLaren Team for four dozen Lion Red stubbies and a tinnie.

 SHRED OF EVIDENCE >>>

A young executive was leaving the office at 6pm when he found the CEO standing in front of a shredder with a piece of paper in his hand.

'Listen,' said the CEO, 'this is a very sensitive and important document, and my secretary has left. Can you make this thing work?'

'Certainly,' said the young executive. He turned the machine on, inserted the paper and pressed the start button.

'Excellent, excellent!' said the CEO as his paper disappeared inside the machine. 'I just need one copy.'

Lesson learnt: Never, never assume that your boss knows everything.

earning a crust

A crusty old man walks into a bank and says to the teller at the window: 'I want to open a damn cheque account.'

The astonished woman replies: 'I beg your pardon, sir; I must have misunderstood you. What did you say?'

'Listen up bitch! I said, I want to open a damn cheque account right now!'

'I'm very sorry sir, but we do not tolerate that kind of language in this bank.' Having said this, the teller leaves the window and goes over to the bank manager to tell him about her problem customer.

They both return and the manager asks the old geezer: 'What seems to be the problem here?'

'There's no damn problem, sonny,' the elderly man says. 'I just won 50 million bucks in the damn lottery and I want to open a damn cheque account in this damn bank!'

'I see,' says the manager thoughtfully. 'And you're saying that this bitch here is giving you a hard time?'

Lesson learnt: If you are rich, you can get away with almost anything.

COMPANY CAR CHARACTERISTICS >>>

- Accelerates at a phenomenal rate.
- Has a much shorter braking distance than the private car.
- Can take speed humps at twice the speed of private cars.
- The battery, radiator water, oil and tyres never have to be checked.
- It can be driven up to 100kms with the oil warning-light flashing.
- It needs cleaning less often than private cars.
- The suspension is reinforced to allow for weekend loads of bricks, concrete slabs and other building materials.
- Unusual and alarming engine noises are easily eliminated by turning up the radio.
- It needs no security system and may be left anywhere, unlocked and with the keys in the ignition.
- It is especially sand and waterproof for barbecues and fishing expeditions on remote beaches.

HEARTFELT CONDOLENCES >>>

A well-known cardiologist died, and an elaborate funeral was planned. A huge heart covered in flowers stood behind the casket during the service. Following the eulogy, the heart opened, and the casket rolled inside. The heart then closed, sealing the doctor in the beautiful heart forever.

At that point, one of the mourners burst into laughter. When confronted, he said, 'I'm sorry, I was just thinking of my own funeral ... I'm a gynaecologist.'

 SIGNS OF THE TIMES >>>

- Sign over a gynaecologist's office: 'Dr Jones, at your cervix.'
- On a plumber's truck: 'We repair what your husband fixed.'
- On the trucks of a local plumbing company in Pennsylvania: 'Don't sleep with a drip. Call your plumber.'
- On an electrician's truck: 'Let us remove your shorts.'
- In a non-smoking area: 'If we see smoke, we will assume you are on fire and take appropriate action.'
- On a maternity room door: 'Push. Push. Push.'
- At an optometrist's office: 'If you don't see what you're looking for, you've come to the right place.'
- In a podiatrist's office: 'Time wounds all heels.'
- On a fence: 'Salesmen welcome! Dog food is expensive.'
- Outside a muffler shop: 'No appointment necessary. We hear you coming.'
- In a veterinarian's waiting room: 'Be back in five minutes. Sit! Stay!'
- In the front garden of a funeral home: 'Drive carefully. We'll wait.'
- At the entrance to a sperm bank: 'The customer always comes first.'

 SKETCHY STUFF >>>

This is our new IT strategy; all laptop computers will be disposed of by May 2003 and all desktop computers by April 2003 as a part of the ongoing cost-cutting around the company. Instead, everyone will be provided with an Etch-A-Sketch. There are many sound reasons for doing this:

1. No boot-up problems.
2. No technical glitches keeping work from being done.
3. No more wasted time reading and writing e-mails.
4. No more worries about power cuts.
5. Budget savings on Upgrades unparalleled.

Frequently Asked Questions from the Etch-A-Sketch Help Desk

Q: My Etch-A-Sketch has all of these funny little lines all over the screen.
A: Pick it up and shake it.

Q: How do I turn my Etch-A-Sketch off?
A: Pick it up and shake it.

Q: What's the shortcut for Undo?
A: Pick it up and shake it.

Q: How do I create a New Document window?
A: Pick it up and shake it.

Q: How do I set the background and foreground to the same colour?
A: Pick it up and shake it.

Q: What is the proper procedure for rebooting my Etch-A-Sketch?
A: Pick it up and shake it.

Q: How do I delete a document on my Etch-A Sketch?
A: Pick it up and shake it.

Q: How do I save my Etch-A-Sketch document?
A: Don't shake it.

If you have any further queries, please feel free to contact the IT department.

✉ I HEREBY STATE... >>>

These are taken from résumés and cover letters that were printed in the 21 July 1997 issue of *Fortune Magazine*. The spelling is exactly the way it appeared in the magazine.

1. 'I demand a salary commiserate with my extensive experience.'
2. 'You will want me to be Head Honcho in no time.'
3. 'Am a perfectionist and rarely, if ever, forget details.'
4. 'I have become completely paranoid, trusting completely no one and absolutely nothing.'
5. 'My goal is to be a meteorologist. But since I possess no training in meteorology, I suppose I should try stock brokerage.'
6. 'As indicted, I have over five years of analysing investments.'
7. 'Personal interests: donating blood. Fifty-three litres so far.'
8. 'Instrumental in ruining entire operation for a Midwest chain store.'
9. 'Marital status: often. Children: various.'
10. 'Reason for leaving last job: They insisted that all employees get to work by 8.45am every morning. Could not work under those conditions.'
11. 'The company made me a scapegoat, just like my three previous employers.'
12. 'Finished eighth in my class of 10.'
13. 'References: None. I've left a path of destruction behind me.'

✉ NIGEL NO-MATES OBVIOUSLY >>>

Sunday Mercury, Birmingham

Bosses of a publishing firm are trying to work out why no one noticed that one of their employees had been sitting dead at his desk for five days before anyone asked if he was feeling OK.

George Turklebaum, 51, who had been employed as a proofreader at a New York firm for 30 years, had a heart attack in the open-plan office he shared with 23 other workers.

He quietly passed away on Monday, but nobody noticed until

earning a crust

Saturday morning when an office cleaner asked why he was still working during the weekend.

His boss Elliot Wachiaski said: 'George was always the first guy in each morning and the last to leave at night, so no one found it unusual that he was in the same position all that time and didn't say anything. He was always absorbed in his work and kept much to himself.'

A post-mortem examination revealed that he had been dead for five days after suffering a coronary. Ironically, George was proofreading manuscripts of medical textbooks when he died.

You may want to give your co-workers a nudge occasionally.

And the moral of the story: Don't work too hard — nobody notices anyway.

PANIC AND SCREAM >>>

Passengers on a small commuter plane are waiting for the flight to leave. They're getting a little impatient, but the airport staff has assured them that the pilots will be there soon, and the flight can take off immediately after that.

The entrance opens, and two men walk up the aisle, dressed in pilots' uniforms — both are wearing dark glasses, one is using a seeing-eye dog, and the other is tapping his way up the aisle with a cane. Nervous laughter spreads through the cabin; but the men enter the cockpit and the plane starts up. The passengers begin glancing nervously around, searching for some sign that this is just a little practical joke. None is forthcoming.

The plane moves faster and faster down the runway, and people at the windows realise that they're headed straight for the water at the edge of the airport territory. As it begins to look as though the plane will never take off, that it will plough into the water, panicked screams fill the cabin — but at that moment, the plane lifts smoothly into the air.

The passengers relax and laugh a little sheepishly, and soon they have all retreated into their magazines, secure in the knowledge that the plane is in good hands.

Up in the cockpit, the co-pilot turns to the pilot and says, 'You know, Bob, one of these days they're going to scream too late, and we're all gonna die.'

A timeless lesson on how consultants can make a difference for an organisation …

Last week, we took some friends out to a new restaurant and noticed that the waiter who took our order carried a spoon in his shirt pocket. It seemed a little strange, but I ignored it. However, when they brought out water and utensils, I noticed that worker also had a spoon in his shirt pocket, then I looked around the room and saw that all the staff had spoons in their pockets.

When the waiter came back to serve our soup I asked, 'Why the spoon?'

'Well,' he explained, 'the restaurant's owners hired Andersen Consulting, experts in efficiency, in order to revamp all our processes. After several months of statistical analysis, they concluded that the spoon was the most frequently dropped utensil. This represents a drop frequency of approximately three spoons per table per hour. If our personnel are prepared to deal with that contingency, we can reduce the number of trips back to the kitchen and save 15 man-hours per shift.'

As luck would have it I dropped my spoon and he was able to replace it with his spare spoon. 'I'll get another spoon next time I go to the kitchen instead of making an extra trip to get it right now.' I was rather impressed.

I noticed that there was a very thin string hanging out of the waiter's fly. Looking around, I noticed that all the waiters had the same string hanging from their flies. My curiosity got the better of me and before he walked off, I asked the waiter, 'Excuse me, but can you tell me why you have that string right there?'

'Oh, certainly!' he answered, lowering his voice. 'Not everyone is as observant as you are. That consulting firm I mentioned also found out that we can save time in the toilet.'

'How so?'

'See,' he continued, 'by tying this string to the tip of you-know-what, we can pull it out over the urinal without touching it and that way eliminate the need to wash the hands, shortening the time spent in the toilet by 76.39 percent.'

'After you get it out, how do you put it back?'

'Well,' he whispered, lowering his voice even further, 'I don't know about the others, but I use the spoon.'

✉ YOU HAVE BEEN WARNED >>>

IMPORTANT: This e-mail is intended for the use of the individual addressee(s) named above and may contain information that is confidential, privileged or unsuitable for overly sensitive persons with low self-esteem, no sense of humour or irrational religious beliefs. If you are not the intended recipient, any dissemination, distribution or copying of this e-mail is not authorised (either explicitly or implicitly) and constitutes an irritating social faux pas.

Unless the word absquatulation has been used in its correct context somewhere other than in this warning, it does not have any legal or grammatical use and may be ignored. No animals were harmed in the transmission of this e-mail, although the kelpie next door is living on borrowed time, let me tell you.

Those of you with an overwhelming fear of the unknown will be gratified to learn that there is no hidden message revealed by reading this backwards, so just ignore that Alert Notice from Microsoft.

However, by pouring a complete circle of salt around yourself and your computer you can ensure that no harm befalls you and your pets. If you have received this e-mail in error, please add some nutmeg and egg whites, whisk, and place in a warm oven for 40 minutes.

✉ OFFICE HI-JINKS >>>

1. Run one lap around the office at top speed.
2. Groan out loud in the toilet cubicle (at least one other 'non-player' must be in the toilet at the time).
3. Ignore the first five people who say 'Good morning' to you.
4. Phone someone in the office you barely know, leave your name and say, 'Just called to say I can't talk right now. Bye.'
5. To signal the end of a conversation, clamp your hands over your ears and grimace.

6. When someone hands you a piece of paper, finger it, and whisper huskily, 'Mmmmmmm, that feels soooooo good!'
8. Walk sideways to the photocopier.
9. While riding a lift, gasp dramatically every time the doors open.

Three-point dares

1. Say to your boss, 'I like your style,' and shoot him with double-barrelled fingers.
2. Babble incoherently at a fellow employee then ask, 'Did you get all that, I don't want to have to repeat it.'
3. Page yourself over the intercom (do not disguise your voice).
4. Kneel in front of the water cooler and drink directly from the nozzle (there must be a 'non-player' within sight).
5. Shout random numbers while someone is counting.

Five-point dares

1. At the end of a meeting, suggest that, for once, it would be nice to conclude with the singing of the national anthem (extra points if you actually launch into it yourself).
2. Walk into a very busy person's office and while they watch you with growing irritation, turn the light switch on/off 10 times.
3. For an hour, refer to everyone you speak to as 'Bob'.
4. Announce to everyone in a meeting that you 'really have to go do a number two'.
5. After every sentence, say 'mon' in a really bad Jamaican accent. As in 'The report's on your desk, mon'. Keep this up for one hour.
6. While an officemate is out, move their chair into the lift.
7. In a meeting or crowded situation, slap your forehead repeatedly and mutter, 'Shut up, damn it, all of you just shut up!'
8. At lunchtime, get down on your knees and announce, 'As God is my witness, I'll never go hungry again.'
9. In a colleague's diary, write in '10am — see how I look in tights'.
10. Carry your keyboard over to your colleague and ask, 'You wanna trade?'
11. Repeat the following conversation 10 times to the same person: 'Do you hear that?' 'What?' 'Never mind, it's gone now.'

12. Come to work in army fatigues and when asked why, say, 'I can't talk about it.'
13. Posing as a maître d', call a colleague and tell him he's won a lunch for four at a local restaurant. Let him go.
14. Speak with an accent (French, German, Porky Pig etc.) during a very important conference call.
15. Find the vacuum and start vacuuming around your desk.
16. Hang a two-foot long piece of toilet roll from the back of your pants and act genuinely surprised when someone points it out.
17. Present meeting attendees with a cup of coffee and biscuit — smash each biscuit with your fist.
18. During the course of a meeting, slowly edge your chair towards the door.
19. Arrange toy figures on the table to represent each meeting attendee, then move them according to the movements of their real-life counterparts.

✉ THE RULES OF THE GAME >>>

- Rome did not create a great empire by having meetings; they did it by killing all those who opposed them.
- If you can stay calm, while all around you is chaos ... then you probably haven't completely understood the seriousness of the situation.
- Doing a job RIGHT the first time gets the job done. Doing the job WRONG 14 times gives you job security.
- Eagles may soar, but weasels don't get sucked into jet engines.
- Artificial Intelligence is no match for Natural Stupidity.
- A person who smiles in the face of adversity ... probably has a scapegoat.
- Plagiarism saves time.
- If at first you don't succeed, try management.
- Never put off until tomorrow what you can avoid altogether.
- Teamwork means never having to take all the blame yourself.
- The beatings will continue until morale improves.
- Never underestimate the power of very stupid people in large groups.
- We waste time, so you don't have to.
- Hang in there, retirement is only 30 years away!

- Go the extra mile. It makes your boss look like an incompetent slacker.
- A snooze button is a poor substitute for no alarm clock at all.
- When the going gets tough, the tough take a coffee break.
- INDECISION is the key to FLEXIBILITY.
- Succeed in spite of management.
- Aim low, reach your goals, avoid disappointment.

 SURGEON CUTS TO THE BONE! >>>

A mechanic was removing a cylinder head from the motor of a Harley when he spotted a world-famous heart surgeon in his shop. The heart surgeon was waiting for the service manager to come and have a look at his bike.

The mechanic shouted across the garage, 'Hey doctor, can I ask you a question?' The famous surgeon, a bit surprised, walked over to the mechanic working on the motorbike.

The mechanic straightened up, wiped his hands on a rag and asked, 'Have a look at this engine. I can also open hearts, take valves out, fix 'em, put in new parts, and when I finish this will work just like a new one. So how come I get a pittance and you get the really big money, when you and I are doing basically the same work?'

The surgeon paused, smiled, leaned over and whispered to the mechanic, 'Try doing it with the engine running!'

 SMELLY DIGITS >>>

First-year students at Med School were receiving their first anatomy class with a real dead human body. They all gathered around the surgery table with the body covered with a white sheet. The professor started the class by telling them, 'In medicine, it is necessary to have two important qualities as a doctor: the first is that you must not be disgusted by anything involving the human body.'

As an example, the professor pulled back the sheet, stuck his finger up the rectum of the corpse, withdrew it and stuck it in his mouth.

earning a crust

'Go ahead and do the same thing,' he told his students. The students freaked out, hesitated for several minutes, but eventually took turns sticking a finger in the arse of the dead body and sucking on it.

When everyone finished, the professor looked at them and told them, 'The second most important quality is observation. I stuck in my middle finger and sucked on my index finger. Now learn to pay attention.'

✉ GETTING STRUNG ALONG >>>

A man has spent many days crossing the desert without water. His camel dies of thirst. He's crawling through the sands, certain that he has breathed his last, when all of a sudden he sees an object sticking out of the sand several metres ahead of him.

He crawls to the object, pulls it out of the sand, and discovers what looks to be an old briefcase. He opens it and out pops a genie. But this is no ordinary genie. He is wearing an Inland Revenue tax inspector ID badge and a dull grey suit. There's a calculator in his pocket. He has a pencil tucked behind one ear.

'Well, kid,' says the genie, 'you know how it works. You have three wishes.'

'I'm not falling for this,' says the man. 'I'm not going to trust an Inland Revenue tax inspector.'

'What do you have to lose? You've got no transportation, and it looks like you're a goner anyway!'

The man thinks about this for a minute, and decides that the genie is right. 'OK, I wish I were in a lush oasis with plentiful food and drink.' POOF! The man finds himself in the most beautiful oasis he has ever seen. And he is surrounded with jugs of wine and platters of delicacies.

'OK, kid, what's your second wish?'

'My second wish is that I were rich beyond my wildest dreams.' POOF! The man finds himself surrounded by treasure chests filled with rare gold coins and precious gems.

'OK, kid, you have just one more wish. Better make it a good one!'

After thinking for a few minutes, the man says, 'I wish that no matter where I go, beautiful women will want and need me.'

POOF! He is turned into a tampon.

The moral of the story? If the Inland Revenue offers you anything, there's going to be a string attached.

✉ TOO MUCH PISSING ABOUT, MR SCHUBERT >>>

A company chairman was given a ticket for a performance of Schubert's Unfinished Symphony. Since he was unable to go, he passed the invitation to the company's Quality Assurance Manager. The next morning, the chairman asked him how he enjoyed it, and, instead of a few plausible observations, he was handed a memorandum which read as follows:

For a considerable period, the oboe players had nothing to do. Their number should be reduced, and their work spread over the whole orchestra, thus avoiding peaks of inactivity.

All 12 violins were playing identical notes. This seems unnecessary duplication, and the staff of this section should be drastically cut. If a large volume of sound is really required, this could be obtained through the use of an amplifier.

Much effort was involved in playing the demisemiquavers. This seems an excessive refinement, and it is recommended that all notes should be rounded up to the nearest semiquaver. If this were done, it would be possible to use trainees instead of craftsmen.

No useful purpose is served by repeating with horns the passage that has already been handled by the strings. If all such redundant passages were eliminated, the concert could be reduced from two hours to 20 minutes.

In light of the above, one can only conclude that had Schubert given attention to these matters, he probably would have had the time to finish his symphony.

✉ WORKPLACE HOROSCOPE >>>

MARKETING: You are ambitious yet stupid. You chose a marketing degree to avoid having to study, concentrating instead on drinking and socialising, which is pretty much what your job responsibilities are now. Least compatible with Sales.

SALES: Laziest of all signs, often referred to as 'marketing without a degree', you are also self-centred and paranoid. Unless someone calls you and begs you to take their money, you like to avoid contact with 'customers' so you can 'concentrate on the big picture'. You seek admiration for your golf game throughout your life.

TECHNOLOGY: Unable to control anything in your personal life, you are instead content to completely control everything that happens at your workplace. Often even YOU don't understand what you are saying, but who the hell can tell? It's written that the geeks shall inherit the Earth.

ENGINEERING: One of only two signs that actually studied in school, it is said that 90 percent of all personal ads are placed by engineers. You can be happy with yourself: your office is typically full of all the latest 'ergodynamic' gadgets. However, we all know what is really causing your 'carpal tunnel' ...

ACCOUNTING: The only other sign that studied in school, you are mostly immune from office politics. You are the most feared person in the organisation, combined with your extreme organisational traits. The majority of rumours concerning you say that you are completely insane.

HUMAN RESOURCES: Ironically, given your access to confidential information, you tend to be the biggest gossip within the organisation. Possibly the only other person that does less work than marketing, you are unable to return any calls today because you have to get a haircut, have lunch and mail a letter.

MIDDLE MANAGEMENT/DEPARTMENT OF MANAGEMENT/'TEAM LEADERS': Catty, cut-throat, yet completely spineless, you are destined to remain at your current job for the rest of your life. Unable to make a single decision, you tend to measure your worth by the number of meetings you can schedule for yourself. Best suited to marry other 'middle managers' as everyone in your social circle is a 'middle manager'.

SENIOR MANAGEMENT: Catty, cut-throat, yet completely spineless, you are destined to remain at your current job for the rest of your life. Unable to make a single decision, you tend to measure your worth by the number of meetings you can schedule for yourself. Best suited to marry other 'senior managers' as everyone in your social circle is a 'senior manager'.

CUSTOMER SERVICE: Bright, cheery, positive, you are a 50c taxi ride from taking your own life. As a child very few of you asked your parents for a little cubicle for your room and a headset so you could pretend to play 'customer service'. Continually passed over for promotions, your best bet is to sleep with your boss.

god
forbid

Having a go at religion is probably about as old as the religions themselves, although these days the punishments aren't as drastic. We aren't in danger of being stoned for joking about adulterous couples — although depending on where they live in this world, the couples playing away from home could very well feel the wrath behind a well-aimed boulder.

Although we can joke about the world's religions, it has become the root of many of the world's conflicts, with Osama bin Laden using the book of Islam to beat up on the Americans and the ever-so pious Jews of Israel — who should know a thing or two about religious intolerance — in the occupied lands suffering revenge attacks from self-sacrificing Palestinians, also in the name of Islam.

> And the Christians? Well, they're not blameless either when you think of Northern Ireland and the former Yugoslavia. Hypocrites in the name of religion are all over the place; so they deserve to have some borax poked at them, don't you think?

 PONTIFICATION >>>

After getting all Pope John-Paul II's luggage loaded into the limo (and His Holiness doesn't travel light), the driver notices that the Pope is still standing on the curb.

'Excuse me, Your Holiness,' says the driver. 'Would you please take your seat so we can leave?'

'Well, to tell you the truth,' says the Pope, 'they never let me drive at the Vatican, and I'd really like to drive today.'

'I'm sorry but I cannot let you do that. I'd lose my job. And what if something should happen?' protests the driver, wishing he'd never gone to work that morning.

'There might be something extra in it for you,' says the Pope.

Reluctantly, the driver gets in the back as the Pope climbs in behind the wheel. The driver quickly regrets his decision when, after exiting the airport, the Supreme Pontiff floors it, accelerating the limo to 150kph.

'Please slow down, Your Holiness,' pleads the petrified and worried driver, but the Pope keeps the pedal to the metal until they hear sirens.

'Oh, my God, I'm gonna lose my licence,' moans the driver.

The Pope pulls over and rolls down the window as the patrolman approaches, but the cop takes one look at him, goes back to his motorbike and gets on the radio. 'I need to talk to the chief,' he says to the dispatcher.

The chief gets on the radio and the cop tells him that he had stopped a limo going 150kph. 'So bust him,' says the chief.

'I don't think we want to do that; he's really important.'

'All the more reason!'

'No, I mean really important,' says the cop.

'What've you got there, the mayor?'

'Bigger.'

'Governor?'

'Bigger.'

'Well,' said the chief, 'who is it?'

'I think it's God.'

'What makes you think it's God?'

'He's got the Pope driving for him!'

 SPEAK UP, MAN >>>

A man is lying in bed in a Catholic hospital with an oxygen mask over his mouth. A young auxiliary nurse appears to sponge his face and hands. 'Nurse,' he mumbles from behind the mask, 'are my testicles black?'

Embarrassed, the young nurse replies, 'I don't know, I'm only here to wash your face and hands.'

He struggles again to ask, 'Nurse, are my testicles black?'

Again the nurse replies, 'I can't tell. I'm only here to wash your face and hands.'

The ward sister was passing and saw the man getting a little distraught, so marched over to inquire what was wrong. 'Sister,' he mumbled, 'are my testicles black?'

Being a nurse of long standing, the sister was undaunted. She whipped back the bedclothes, pulled down his pyjama trousers, moved his penis out of the way, had a right good look, pulled up the pyjamas, replaced the bedclothes and announced, 'Nothing wrong with them.'

At this, the man pulled off his oxygen mask and asked again, 'Are my test results back?'

 PEARLY CHRISTMAS >>>

Three men died on Christmas Eve and were met by Saint Peter at the Pearly Gates. 'In honour of the season,' Saint Peter said, 'you

god forbid

must each possess something that symbolises Christmas to get into Heaven on this holy day.'

The first man fumbled through his pockets and pulled out a lighter. He flicked it on. 'It represents a holy candle,' he said.

'You may pass through the pearly gates,' Saint Peter said.

The second man reached into his pocket and pulled out a set of keys. He shook them and said, 'They're bells.'

Saint Peter said, 'You may pass through the pearly gates.'

The third man started searching desperately through his pockets and finally pulled out a pair of women's panties.

'What do these symbolise?' Saint Peter asked.

The man replied, 'They're Carols.'

 DEAR GOD! >>>

Dr Laura Schlessinger is a US radio personality who dispenses advice to people who call in to her radio show. Recently, she said that, as an observant Orthodox Jew, homosexuality was an abomination according to Leviticus 18:22, and cannot be condoned under any circumstance. The following is an open letter to Dr Schlessinger penned by a US resident, Jim, which was posted on the Internet.

Dear Dr Laura

Thank you for doing so much to educate people regarding God's law. I have learned a great deal from your show, and try to share that knowledge with as many people as I can. When someone tries to defend the homosexual lifestyle, for example, I simply remind them that Leviticus 18:22 clearly states it to be an abomination. End of debate. I do need some advice from you, however, regarding some of the other specific laws and how to follow them.

1. When I burn a bull on the altar as a sacrifice, I know it creates a pleasing odour for the Lord (Lev. 1:9). The problem is my neighbours. They claim the odour is not pleasing to them. Should I smite them?

2. I would like to sell my daughter into slavery, as sanctioned in Exodus 21:7. In this day and age, what do you think would be a fair price for her?

3. I know that I am allowed no contact with a woman while she is in her period of menstrual cleanliness (Lev. 15:19–24). The problem is, how do I tell? I have tried asking, but most women take offence.

4. Lev. 25:44 states that I may indeed possess slaves, both male and female, provided they are purchased from neighbouring nations. A friend of mine claims that this applies to Mexicans, but not Canadians. Can you clarify? Why can't I own Canadians?

5. I have a neighbour who insists on working on the Sabbath. Exodus 35:2 clearly states he should be put to death. Am I morally obligated to kill him myself?

6. A friend of mine feels that even though eating shellfish is an abomination (Lev. 11:10), it is a lesser abomination than homosexuality. I don't agree. Can you settle this?

7. Lev. 21:20 states that I may not approach the altar of God if I have a defect in my sight. I have to admit that I wear reading glasses. Does my vision have to be 20/20, or is there some wiggle room here?

8. Most of my male friends get their hair trimmed, including the hair around their temples, even though this is expressly forbidden by Lev. 19:27. How should they die?

9. I know from Lev. 11:6–8 that touching the skin of a dead pig makes me unclean, but may I still play football if I wear gloves?

10. My uncle has a farm. He violates Lev. 19:19 by planting two different crops in the same field, as does his wife by wearing garments made of two different kinds of thread (cotton/polyester blend). He also tends to curse and blaspheme a lot. Is it really necessary that we go to all the trouble of getting the whole town together to stone them? (Lev. 24:10–16). Couldn't we just burn them to death at a private family affair like we do with people who sleep with their in-laws? (Lev. 20:14)

I know you have studied these things extensively, so I am confident you can help. Thank you again for reminding us that God's word is eternal and unchanging.

Your devoted fan,
Jim

A management consultant dies in a car accident on his 40th birthday and finds himself at the Pearly Gates. A brass band is playing, the Angels are singing, there is a huge crowd cheering and shouting his name, and absolutely everyone wants to shake his hand.

Just when he thinks things can't get any better, St Peter himself runs over, apologises for not greeting him personally at the Pearly Gates, shakes his hand and says, 'Congratulations son, we've been waiting a long time for you.'

Totally confused and a little embarrassed, the consultant looks sheepishly at St Peter and says, 'St Peter, I tried to lead a God-fearing life. I love my family. I tried to obey the 10 Commandments, but congratulations for what? I honestly don't remember doing anything really special when I was alive.'

'Congratulations for WHAT?' says St Peter, totally amazed at the consultant's modesty. 'We're celebrating the fact that you lived to be 160 years old. God himself wants to see you!'

The man is awestruck and can only look at St Peter with his mouth agape. When he regains his power of speech, he looks up at St Peter and says, 'St Peter, I lived my life in the eternal hope that when I died I would be judged by God and be found worthy, but I only lived until I was 40.'

'That's impossible,' says St Peter. 'We've added up your timesheets.'

✉ PRIEST AT THE MERCY OF A SMART-ARSE >>>

A little boy got on the bus, sat next to a man reading a book, and noticed he had his collar on backwards. The little boy asked why he wore his collar that way.

The man, who was a priest, said, 'I am a Father.'

The little boy replied, 'My daddy doesn't wear his collar like that.'

The priest looked up from his book and answered, 'I am the Father of many.'

The boy said, 'My dad has four boys, four girls and two grandchildren and he doesn't wear his collar that way.'

The priest, getting impatient said, 'I am the Father of hundreds,' and went back to reading his book.

The little boy sat quietly … but on leaving the bus he leaned over and said … 'Well, maybe you should wear your pants backwards instead.'

 ## TOGETHER AGAIN >>>

Maria is a devout Catholic. She gets married and has 17 children. Soon after the last child is born her husband dies. A few weeks later she remarries and over the following years has another 22 children with her second husband. After the last child is born her second husband also dies.

Within a month Maria is engaged to be married a third time. Unfortunately, she becomes very ill and dies. At her wake, the priest looks tenderly at Maria as she lies in her coffin, looks up to the heavens and says, 'At least they're finally together.'

A man standing next to the priest asks, 'Excuse me, Father, but do you mean Maria and her first husband, or Maria and her second husband?'

The priest says, 'I mean her legs.'

 ## PRIESTS IN DISGUISE >>>

Two priests were going to Hawaii on holiday. To improve their chances of having a real holiday, they decided not to wear anything that would identify them as clergy. As soon as the plane landed, they headed for a mall and bought some really outrageous shorts, shirts, sandals, sunglasses, and anything that would not mark them as priests.

The next morning, they went to the beach, dressed in their 'tourist' garb. They were sitting on deckchairs, enjoying their drinks, the sunshine and the scenery when a drop-dead gorgeous blonde in a tiny bikini came walking straight towards them. They couldn't help but stare.

When she passed them, she smiled and said, 'Good morning, Father,' nodding and addressing each of them individually, then passed on by.

They were both stunned. How in the world did she recognise them as priests? The next day they went back to the shop and bought even more outrageous outfits — outfits so loud you could hear them coming before you even saw them. Once again, they settled down on the beach to enjoy the sunshine. After a while, the same gorgeous blonde came walking toward them.

Again, she approached them and greeted them individually, said 'Good morning Father,' and walked away.

One of the priests couldn't stand it. 'Just a minute young lady,' he said. 'Yes, we are priests, and proud of it, but I have to know how in the world did you know we are priests?'

'Father, it's me, Sister Veronica.'

THE MEANING OF LIFE >>>

On the first day, God created the cow. God said, 'You must go to the field with the farmer all day long and suffer under the sun, have calves and give milk to support the farmer. I will give you a life span of 60 years.'

The cow said, 'That's kind of a tough life you want me to live for 60 years. Let me have 20 years and I'll give back the other 40.' And God agreed.

On the second day, God created the dog. God said, 'Sit all day by the door of your house and bark at anyone who comes in or walks past. I will give you a lifespan of 20 years.'

The dog said, 'That's too long to be barking. Give me 10 years and I'll give back the other 10.' So God agreed.

On the third day, God created the monkey. God said, 'Entertain people, do monkey tricks, make them laugh. I'll give you a 20-year lifespan.'

The monkey said, 'How boring. Monkey tricks for 20 years? I don't think so. Dog gave you back 10, so that's what I'll do too, OK?' And God agreed again.

On the fourth day, God created man. God said, 'Eat, sleep, play, have sex, enjoy doing nothing, just enjoy, enjoy. I'll give you 20 years.'

Man said, 'What? Only 20 years? No way, man. Tell you what, I'll take my 20, and the 40 Cow gave back, and the 10 Dog gave back and the 10 Monkey gave back. That makes 80, OK?'

'OK,' said God. 'You've got a deal.'

So that is why for the first 20 years we eat, sleep, play, have sex, enjoy doing nothing. For the next 40 years we slave in the sun to support our family. For the next 10 years, we do monkey tricks to entertain our grandchildren and for the last 10 years, we sit around the house and bark at everybody.

Life has now been explained.

 MANY–HUED JESUS >>>

There were three equally good arguments that Jesus was BLACK:
1. He called everyone 'brother'.
2. He liked Gospel.
3. He couldn't get a fair trial.

But then there were three equally good arguments that Jesus was INDIAN:
1. He went into His Father's business.
2. He lived at home until he was 33.
3. He was sure his Mother was a virgin and his mother was sure he was God.

But then there were three equally good arguments that Jesus was ITALIAN:
1. He talked with his hands.
2. He had wine with every meal.
3. He used olive oil.

But then there were three equally good arguments that Jesus was a CALIFORNIAN:
1. He never cut his hair.
2. He walked around barefoot all the time.
3. He started a new religion.

But then there were three equally good arguments that Jesus was IRISH:
1. He never got married.
2. He was always telling stories.
3. He loved green pastures.

But the most compelling evidence of all is that Jesus was a WOMAN:

god forbid

1. He had to feed a crowd at a moment's notice when there was no food.
2. He kept trying to get a message across to a bunch of men who just didn't get it.
3. Even when he was dead, he had to get up because there was more work for him to do.

 ## NOAH GETTING THE HUMP >>>

One day God calls down to Noah and says, 'Noah, me old china, I want you to make me a new ark.'

Noah replies, 'No probs God, me old Supreme Being. Anything you want. After all, you're the guv.'

But God says, 'Ah, but there's a catch. This time Noah, I want not just a couple of decks, I want 20 decks — one on top of the other.'

'Twenty DECKS!' screams Noah. 'Well, OK Big Man, whatever you say. Should I fill it up with all the animals just like last time?'

'Yep, that's right, well ... sort of right ... this time I want you to fill it up with fish,' God answers.

'Fish?' queries Noah.

'Yep, fish ... well, to make it more specific Noah, I want carp — wall-to-wall, floor-to-ceiling carp!'

Noah looks to the skies. 'OK God, me old mucker, let me get this right. You want a new ark?'

'Correct.'

'With 20 decks, one on top of the other?'

'Correct.'

'And you want it full of carp?'

'Correct.'

'Why?' asks the perplexed Noah, who was slowly but surely getting to the end of his tether.

'Dunno,' says God, 'I just fancied a multi-storeyed carp ark.'

THE KEY TO HEAVEN >>>

It was time for Father John's Saturday night bath, and the young nun Sister Magdalene had prepared the bath water and towels just the way the old nun had instructed.

Sister Magdalene was also instructed not to look at Father John's nakedness if she could help it. Do whatever he told her to do, and pray.

The next morning the old nun asked Sister Magdalene how the Saturday night bath had gone. 'Oh, Sister,' said the young nun dreamily, 'I've been saved.'

'Saved? And how did that fine thing come about?' asked the old nun.

'Well, when Father John was soaking in the tub, he asked me to wash him, and while I was washing him he guided my hand down between his legs where he said the Lord keeps the Key to Heaven.'

'Did he now?' said the old nun evenly.

Sister Magdalene continued, 'And Father John said that if the Key to Heaven fitted my lock, the portals of Heaven would be opened to me and I would be assured salvation and eternal peace. And then Father John guided his Key to Heaven into my lock.'

'Is that a fact?' said the old nun even more evenly.

'At first it hurt terribly, but Father John said the pathway to salvation was often painful and that the glory of God would soon swell my heart with ecstasy. And it did, it felt so good being saved.'

'That wicked old devil!' said the old nun. 'He told me it was Gabriel's Horn, and I've been blowing it for 40 years!'

✉ THAT OLD FAT, RED-SUITED BASTARD! >>>

'Twas the night before Christmas and all through the flat
The techno was blaring, 'twas too loud to chat
The Rizlas were perched on the table with care
And smoke full of chemicals soon filled the air

We'd just been out clubbing, I truly was trashed
My faithful companions were equally mashed
We'd popped a few pills and we'd had a quick sniff
And just settled down to a nice tasty spliff

When out on the balcony rose such a clatter
We looked slowly up to see what was the matter
I got to my feet and I swayed to the door
And only occasionally fell on the floor

I peered through the glass as I took a long puff
The moon glistened through the pollution and stuff
When what to my wandering eyes should appear
But a fat man in red and a team of reindeer

He yelled and he ranted, gave each one a kick
I knew in a second it must be Saint Nick
He shrieked at each reindeer and cursed them alike
'F*** you!' yelled Rudolph. 'We're going on strike!'

The reindeer did turn and soar into the sky
And Santa growled something that wasn't goodbye
I watched as they went in a puff of pink smoke
And vowed from now on to stay off the coke

As debris did settle St Nick turned around
He swore as he angrily kicked at the ground
He gave me a gesture that clearly implied
He'd be very pleased if I let him inside

I threw the doors open and ushered him in
Invited him through with a welcoming grin
'So where are our presents?' my wasted mates cried
With a look of astonishment, Santa replied ...

'You seriously think you might be on my list?
You've got to be kidding; you're taking the piss!
Have you lot considered your actions this year?
Stop being stupid and get me a beer.'

He opened a Stella, but still looked depressed
We asked him to tell us what made him so stressed
'My reindeer have left me,' he said with a sigh
'Unless I have reindeer, I've no way to fly!'

'Now look here,' I told him, 'we may not know much
We don't help old ladies, kiss babies and such
But Santa, there's no need for you to despair
We know how to get you back up in the air!'

I chopped up a line with precision and skill
And rolled him up neatly a 20-pound bill
His face lit up quickly with real Christmas cheer
'Perhaps you kids WILL get some presents this year!'

He spoke not a word but got straight to his mission
He snorted that line with wholehearted ambition
Then Santa skinned up and he smiled as he puffed
We knew that our stockings this year would be stuffed

He sprang to the balcony, leapt from the railing
Soared to the sky with his present-sack trailing
I heard him exclaim as he flew out of sight
'Happy Christmas to all, and to all a good night!'

 VANITY RULES OK >>>

A middle-aged woman had a heart attack and was taken to the hospital. While on the operating table, she had a near-death experience. Seeing God, she asked, 'Is my time up?'

God said, 'No, you have another 43 years, two months and eight days to live.'

Upon recovery, the woman decided to stay in the hospital and have a face-lift, liposuction and a tummy tuck. She even had someone come in and change her hair colour. Since she had so much more time to live, she figured she might as well make the most of it.

After her last operation, she was released from the hospital. While crossing the street on her way home, she was killed by an ambulance.

Arriving in front of God, she demanded, 'I thought you said I had another 40 years. Why didn't you pull me out from the path of the ambulance?'

God replied, 'I didn't recognise you.'

Answers below, but no cheating

1. Bleached Yule
2. Castaneous-coloured Seed Vesicated in a Conflagration
3. Singular Yearning for the Twin Anterior Incisors
4. Righteous Darkness
5. Arrival Time 2400 hrs, Weather Cloudless
6. Loyal Followers Advance
7. Far Off in a Feeder
8. Array the Corridor
9. Bantam Male Percussionist
10. Monarchial Triad
11. Nocturnal Noiselessness
12. Jehovah Deactivate Blithe Chevaliers
13. Red Man En Route to Borough
14. Frozen Precipitation Commence
15. Proceed and Enlighten on the Pinnacle
16. The Quadruped with the Vermilion Proboscis
17. Query Regarding Identity of Descendant
18. Delight for this Planet
19. Give Attention to the Melodious Celestial Beings
20. The Dozen Festive 24-Hour Intervals

Answers:

1. White Christmas
2. Chestnuts Roasting on an Open Fire
3. All I Want for Christmas is My Two Front Teeth
4. O Holy Night
5. It Came Upon a Midnight Clear
6. O Come, All Ye Faithful
7. Away in a Manger
8. Deck the Hall
9. Little Drummer Boy
10. We Three Kings
11. Silent Night
12. God Rest Ye, Merry Gentlemen
13. Santa Claus is Coming to Town
14. Let It Snow

HEAVEN'S DEARTH OF PRIESTS >>>

On their way to get married, a young couple are involved in a fatal car accident. The couple find themselves sitting outside the Pearly Gates waiting for Saint Peter to process them into Heaven. While waiting, they begin to wonder: could they possibly get married in Heaven?

When Saint Peter showed up, they asked him. St Peter said, 'I don't know. This is the first time anyone has asked. Let me go find out,' and he left. The couple sat and waited for an answer … for a couple of months. While they waited, they discussed that IF they were allowed to get married in Heaven, SHOULD they get married, what with the eternal aspect of it all.

'What if it doesn't work?' they wondered. 'Are we stuck together FOREVER?'

After yet another month, St Peter finally returned looking somewhat bedraggled. 'Yes,' he informed the couple. 'You CAN get married in Heaven.'

'Great!' said the couple. 'But we were just wondering … what if things don't work out? Could we also get a divorce in Heaven?'

St Peter, red-faced with anger, slams his clipboard onto the ground. 'What's wrong?' asked the frightened couple.

'OH, COME ON!!' St Peter shouts. 'It took me three months to find a priest up here! Do you have ANY idea how long it'll take me to find a lawyer?'

 ## MAKING MONEY IN DARK PLACES >>>

A woman takes a lover during the day while her husband is at work. Her nine-year-old son comes home unexpectedly, sees them and hides in the wardrobe to watch. The woman's husband also comes

god forbid

home. She puts her lover in the wardrobe, not realising that the little boy is in there already.

The little boy says, 'Dark in here.'

The man says, 'Yes, it is.'

Boy: 'I have a baseball.'

Man: 'That's nice.'

Boy: 'Want to buy it?'

Man: 'No thanks.'

Boy: 'My dad's outside.'

Man: 'OK, how much?'

Boy: '$250.'

In the next few weeks, it happens again that the boy and the lover are in the wardrobe together.

Boy: 'It's dark in here.'

Man: 'Yes, it is.'

Boy: 'I have a baseball glove.'

The lover, remembering the last time, asks the boy, 'How much?'

Boy: '$750.'

Man: 'Fine.'

A few days later, the father says to the boy, 'Grab your glove, let's go outside and have a game of catch.'

The boy says, 'I can't, I sold my baseball and my glove.'

The father asks, 'How much did you sell them for?'

The boy says, '$1000.'

The father says, 'That's terrible to overcharge your friends like that … that is way more than those two things cost. I'm going to take you to church and make you confess.'

They go to the church and the father makes the boy sit in the confession booth and he closes the door.

The boy says, 'It's dark in here.'

The priest says, 'Don't start that shit again.'

 THE OLD BROTHER-IN-LAW >>>

A few minutes before the church service started, the townspeople were sitting in their pews and talking. Suddenly, Satan appeared at the front of the church.

Everyone started screaming and running for the front entrance, trampling each other in a frantic effort to get away from evil incarnate. Soon, everyone had exited the church except for one elderly gentleman who sat calmly in his pew without moving, seeming oblivious to the fact that God's ultimate enemy was in his presence.

So Satan walked up to the old man and said, 'Don't you know who I am?'

The man replied, 'Yep, sure do.'

'Aren't you afraid of me?' Satan asked.

'Nope, sure ain't,' said the man.

'Don't you realise I can kill you with a word?' asked Satan.

'Don't doubt it for a minute,' returned the old man, in an even tone.

'Did you know that I could cause you profound, horrifying, physical AGONY for all eternity?' persisted Satan.

'Yep,' was the calm reply.

'And you're still not afraid?' asked Satan.

'Nope.'

More than a little perturbed, Satan asked, 'Well, why aren't you afraid of me?'

The man calmly replied, 'Been married to your sister for over 48 years.'

 HE'S A SPOOK >>>

I was coming out of church the other day, and the priest was standing at the door as he always does to shake hands. As I was trying to shuffle past, he grabbed my hand and pulled me aside.

The priest said to me, with that same smile he always has, 'You need to join the Army of the Lord!'

I replied, 'I'm already in the Army of the Lord, Father.'

Father questioned, 'How come I don't see you except at Christmas and Easter?'

I whispered, 'I'm in the secret service.'

(**god forbid**)

across
the seas

> This chapter is the one that has a poke at the foreigners.
> No one is spared, although the Irish are given the job of giving us a laugh, as they generally do.
> And we promise that the Kiwi taunts have not been changed to make some other country bear the brunt — like the Australians. We are not that devious!

General

1. Never take a beer to a job interview.
2. Always identify people in your backyard before shooting them.
3. It's tacky to take an esky to church.
4. If you have to vacuum the bed, it's time to change the sheets.
5. Even if you're certain you're included in the will, it's rude to take the trailer to the funeral home.

Dining out

1. When decanting wine from the box, tilt the paper cup and pour slowly so as not to 'bruise' the wine.
2. If drinking directly from the bottle, hold it with both hands.

Entertaining in your home

1. A centrepiece for the table should never be anything prepared by a taxidermist.
2. Don't allow the dog to eat at the table, no matter how good his manners are.

Personal hygiene

1. While ears need to be cleaned regularly, this should be done in private, using one's own ute keys.
2. Even if you live alone, deodorant isn't a waste of money.
3. Use of toiletries can only delay bathing a few days.
4. Dirt and grease under the fingernails is a no-no, as they detract from a woman's jewellery and alter the taste of finger-foods.

Dating (outside the family)

1. Always offer to bait your date's hook, especially on the first date.
2. Be assertive. Let him/her know you're interested: 'I've been wanting to go out with you since I read that stuff on the bathroom wall two years ago.'
3. Establish with her parents what time she's expected back. Some will say 10pm and others might say 'Monday'. If the latter is the answer, it's the man's responsibility to get her to school on time.

Theatre etiquette
1. Crying babies should be taken to the lobby and picked up after the movie has ended.
2. Refrain from talking to characters on the screen. Tests have proven they can't hear you.

Weddings
1. Livestock is a poor choice for a wedding gift.
2. Kissing the bride for more than five seconds may get you shot.
3. For the groom, at least, rent a tux. A tracksuit with a cummerbund and a clean football jumper can create a tacky appearance.
4. Though uncomfortable, say 'Yes' to socks and shoes for the occasion.

Driving etiquette
1. Dim your headlights for approaching vehicles, even if the gun's loaded and the pig's in sight.
2. When approaching a roundabout, the vehicle with the largest tyres doesn't always have the right of way.
3. Never tow another car using pantyhose and duct tape.
4. Don't burn rubber while travelling in a funeral procession.
5. When sending your wife down the road with a petrol can, it's impolite to ask her to bring back beer, too.

 YOU HAVE BEEN WARNED >>>

From the Province of Inhambane Ministry of Fish and Wildlife, Mozambique

Warning
Due to the rising frequency of human-lion encounters, the Ministry of Fish and Wildlife, Inhambane Province, Mozambique, is advising hikers, hunters, fishermen and any motorcyclists who use the out-of-doors in a recreational or work-related function to take extra precautions while in the bush.

We advise outdoorsmen to wear little noisy bells on clothing so as to give advanced warning to any lions that might be close by, so you don't take them by surprise.

We also advise anyone using the out-of-doors to carry 'Pepper Spray' with him or her in case of an encounter with the lion.

Outdoorsmen should also be on the watch for fresh lion activity, and be able to tell the difference between lion cub shit and big lion shit. Lion cub shit is smaller and contains lots of berries and dassie fur. Big lion shit has bells in it, and smells like pepper.

 ## SORRY UNCLE SAM >>>

Courtesy Rick Mercer, CBC Television

On behalf of Canadians everywhere I'd like to offer an apology to the United States of America. We haven't been getting along very well recently and for that, I am truly sorry.

I'm sorry we called George Bush a moron. He is a moron, but it wasn't nice of us to point it out. If it's any consolation, the fact that he's a moron shouldn't reflect poorly on the people of America. After all it's not like you actually elected him.

I'm sorry about our softwood lumber. Just because we have more trees than you, doesn't give us the right to sell you lumber that's cheaper and better than your own.

I'm sorry we beat you in Olympic hockey. In our defence, I guess our excuse would be that our team was much, much, much, much better than yours was.

I'm sorry we burnt down your White House during the war of 1812. I notice that you've rebuilt it! It's very nice.

I'm sorry about your beer. I know we had nothing to do with your beer but we feel your pain.

I'm sorry about our waffling on Iraq. I mean, when you're going up against a crazed dictator, you want to have your friends by your side. I realise it took more than two years before you guys pitched in against Hitler, but that was different. Everyone knew he had weapons.

And finally on behalf of all Canadians, I'm sorry that we're constantly apologising for things in a passive-aggressive way, which is really a thinly veiled criticism. I sincerely hope that you're not upset over this. We've seen what you do to countries you get upset with.

SUICIDE BUMMER >>>

Everyone seems to be wondering why the Muslim terrorists are so quick to commit suicide.

Hmmm ... let's see now:

No beer.	No spirits.
No bars.	No television.
No Internet.	No sport but soccer and only on dirt fields.
No tailgate parties.	No tailgates on camels.
No hooters.	No BBQ.
No hot dogs.	No burgers.

No lobster, shellfish, or even frozen fish sticks. Ever try to fish at an oasis?

Rags for clothes and hats.

Eating only with your right hand cause you wipe only with your left. (Like life isn't complicated enough already.)

Constant wailing from the guy in the prayer tower.

No music.	No radio.
You can't shave.	Your wife can't shave.

You can't shower to wash off the smell of donkey cooked over burning camel dung.

The women have to wear baggy dresses and veils at all times.

Your bride is picked by someone else.

She smells just like your donkey.

But your donkey has a better disposition.

Then they tell you that when you die it all gets better!

No mystery here.

 WINTER WONDERLAND >>>

20 December

It's starting to snow. The first of the season and the first we've seen for years. The wife and I took our hot toddies and sat on the porch watching the fluffy soft flakes drift gently down clinging to the trees and covering the ground. It's so beautiful and peaceful.

24 December

We awoke to a blanket of crystal-white glistening snow covering as far as the eye could see. What a fantastic sight, every tree and bush covered with a beautiful white mantle. I shovelled snow for the first time ever and loved it. I did both our driveway and the pavement. Later that day a snowplough came along and accidentally covered up our driveway with compacted snow from the street.

The driver smiled and waved. I waved back and shovelled it away again. The children next door built a snowman with coal for eyes and a carrot for a nose, and had a snowball fight. A couple just missed me and hit the car, so I threw a couple back and joined in their fun.

26 December
It snowed an additional 10cm last night and the temperature dropped to around minus 20 degrees. Several branches on our trees and bushes snapped due to the weight of the snow. I shovelled our driveway again. Shortly afterwards the snowplough came by and did his trick again. Much of the snow is now a brownish-grey.

1 January
Warmed up enough during the day to create some slush which soon became ice when the temperature dropped again. Bought snow tyres for both our cars. Fell on my arse in the driveway. Went to a physio but nothing was broken.

5 January
Still cold. Sold the wife's car and bought her a 4x4 to get her to work. She slid into a wall and did considerable damage to the right wing. Had another 12cm of white shite last night. Both vehicles are covered in salt and iced-up slush. That bastard snowplough came by twice today. Where's that bloody shovel?

9 January
More damn snow. Not a tree or a bush on our property that hasn't been damaged. Power was off most of the night. Tried to keep from freezing to death with candles and a paraffin heater which tipped over and nearly torched the house. I managed to put the flames out but suffered second-degree burns on my hands. Lost all my eyebrows and eyelashes. Car hit a f***ing deer on the way to casualty and was written off.

13 January

F***ing bastard white shite just keeps coming down. Have to put on every item of clothing just to go to the post-box. Little shits next door ambushed me with snowballs on the way back — I'll shove that carrot so far up the little pricks' arses it'll take a good surgeon hours to find it. If I ever catch the arsehole that drives the snowplough I'll chew open his chest and rip out his heart with my teeth. I think the bastard hides round the corner and waits for me to finish shovelling and then he accelerates down the street like Michael Schumacher and buries the f***ing driveway again.

17 January

Twenty more f***ing centimetres of snow and f***ing ice and f***ing sleet and God knows what other white shite fell last night. I am in court in three months' time for assaulting the snowplough driver with an ice-pick. Can't move my f***ing toes. Haven't seen the sun for five weeks. Minus 20 and more f***ing snow forecast.

F*** this, I'm moving back to Australia.

✉ IN THE DEAD OF NIGHT >>>

Ireland's worst air disaster occurred early this morning when a small two-seater Cessna plane crashed into a cemetery just outside Dublin. Irish search and rescue workers have so far recovered 1826 bodies and expect that number to climb as digging continues into the night.

✉ TO WHOM IT MAY CONCERN >>>

Genuine written complaints received by local councils in the UK during 2002:

- My bush is really overgrown round the front and my back passage has fungus growing in it.
- … and he's got this huge tool that vibrates the whole house and I just can't take it any more.
- … it's the dog's mess that I find hard to swallow.
- I want some repairs done to my cooker as it has backfired and burnt my knob off.

- I wish to complain that my father hurt his ankle very badly when he put his foot in the hole in his back passage.
- ... and their 18-year-old son is continually banging his balls against my fence.
- I wish to report that tiles are missing from the outside toilet roof. I think it was bad wind the other night that blew them off.
- My lavatory seat is cracked. Where do I stand?
- I am writing on behalf of my sink, which is coming away from the wall.
- Will you please send someone to mend the garden path. My wife and I fell on it yesterday and now she is pregnant.
- We are getting married in September and we would like it in the garden before we move into the house.
- I request permission to remove my drawers in the kitchen ...
- Fifty percent of the walls are damp, 50 percent have crumbling plaster and the rest are plain filthy.
- I am still having problems with smoke in my new drawers.
- The toilet is blocked and we cannot bathe the children until it is cleared.
- Will you please send a man to look at my water, it is a funny colour and not fit to drink.
- Our lavatory seat is broken in half and is now in three pieces.
- Would you please send a man to repair my spout. I am an old-age pensioner and need it badly.
- I want to complain about the farmer across the road; every morning at 6am his cock wakes me up and it's now getting too much for me.
- The man next door has a large erection in the back garden, which is unsightly and dangerous.
- Our kitchen floor is damp. We have two children and would like a third so please send someone round to do something about it.
- I am a single woman living in a downstairs flat and would you please do something about the noise made by the man I have on top of me every night.
- Please send a man with the right tool to finish the job and satisfy my wife.
- I have had the clerk of the works down on the floor six times but I still have no satisfaction.
- This is to let you know that our lavatory seat is broke and we can't get BBC2.

GETTING ABREAST OF THE SITUATION >>>

Into a Belfast pub comes Paddy Murphy, looking like he'd just been run over by a train. His arm is in a sling, his nose is broken, his face is cut and bruised and he's walking with a limp.

'What happened to you?' asks Sean, the barman.

'Jamie O'Conner and me had a fight,' says Paddy.

'That little shit O'Conner,' says Sean. 'He couldn't do that to you, he must have had something in his hand.'

'That he did,' says Paddy. 'A shovel is what he had, and a terrible lickin' he gave me with it.'

'Well,' says Sean, 'you should have defended yourself. Didn't you have something in your hand?'

'That I did,' said Paddy. 'Mrs O'Conner's breast, and a thing of beauty it was, but useless in a fight.'

LAST REQUESTS >>>

Mary Clancy goes up to Father O'Grady after his Sunday morning service, and she's in tears.

He says, 'So what's bothering you, Mary, my dear?'

She says, 'Oh, Father, I've got terrible news. My husband passed away last night.'

The priest says, 'Oh, Mary, that's terrible. Tell me, Mary, did he have any last requests?'

She says, 'That he did, Father.'

The priest says, 'What did he ask, Mary?'

She says, 'He said, "Please Mary, put down that damn gun."'

ACCENT ON CONSTRUCTION >>>

An Italian, a Scotsman and a Chinese fellow are hired at a construction site. The foreman points out a huge pile of sand and says to the Italian guy, 'You're in charge of sweeping.' To the Scotsman he says, 'You're in charge of shovelling.' And to the Chinese guy he says, 'You're in charge of supplies.' He then says, 'Now, I have to leave for a little while. I expect you guys to make a

across the seas

dent in that there pile.'

So the foreman goes away for a couple hours and when he returns, the pile of sand is untouched. He asks the Italian, 'Why didn't you sweep any of it?' The Italian replies, 'I no hava no broom. You saida to the Chinese a fella that he a wasa in a charge of supplies, but he hasa disappeared and I no coulda finda him nowhere.'

Then the foreman turns to the Scotsman and says, 'And you, I thought I told you to shovel this pile.' The Scotsman replies, 'Aye, ye did lad, boot ah couldnay get meself a shoovel! Ye left th' Chinese gadgie in chairge of supplies, boot ah couldnayfin' him either.'

The foreman is really angry now and storms off toward the pile of sand to look for the Chinese guy. Just then, the Chinese guy leaps out from behind the pile of sand and yells, 'SUPPLIES!'

✉ HARVARD MBA BORE WITH ALL THE ANSWERS >>>

A boat docked in a tiny Mexican village. An American tourist complimented the Mexican fisherman on the quality of his fish and asked how long it took him to catch them.

'Not very long,' answered the Mexican.

'Well, then, why didn't you stay out longer and catch more?' asked the American. The Mexican explained that his small catch was sufficient to meet his needs and those of his family.

The American asked, 'But what do you do with the rest of your time?'

'I sleep late, fish a little, play with my children, and take a siesta with my wife. In the evenings, I go into the village to see my friends, have a few drinks, play the guitar, and sing a few songs … I have a full life.'

The American interrupted, 'I have an MBA from Harvard and I can help you! You should start by fishing longer every day. You can then sell the extra fish you catch. With the extra revenue, you can buy a bigger boat. With the extra money the larger boat will bring, you can buy a second one and a third one and so on until you have an entire fleet of trawlers. Instead of selling your fish to a middleman, you can negotiate directly with the processing plants and maybe even open your own plant. You can then leave this little village and move to Mexico City, Los Angeles, or even New York City! From there you can direct your huge enterprise.'

'How long would that take?' asked the Mexican.

'Twenty, perhaps 25 years,' replied the American.

'And after that?'

'Afterwards? That's when it gets really interesting,' answered the American, laughing. 'When your business gets really big, you can start selling stocks and make millions!'

'Millions? Really? And after that?'

'After that you'll be able to retire, live in a tiny village near the coast, sleep late, play with your children, catch a few fish, take siestas with your wife, and spend your evenings drinking and enjoying your friends.'

DRIVER IDENTIFICATION >>>

1. One hand on wheel, one hand on horn: Chicago.
2. One hand on wheel, one finger out window: New York.
3. One hand on wheel, one finger out window, cutting across all lanes of traffic: New Jersey.
4. One hand on wheel, one hand on newspaper, foot solidly on accelerator: Boston.
5. One hand on wheel, one hand on non-fat double-decaf cappuccino, cradling cellphone, brick on accelerator, gun in lap: Los Angeles.
6. Both hands on wheel, eyes shut, both feet on brake, quivering in terror: Ohio, but driving in California.
7. Both hands in air, gesturing, both feet on accelerator, head turned to talk to someone in back seat: Italy.
8. One hand on 12oz. double-shot latte, one knee on wheel, cradling cellphone, foot on brake, mind on radio game, banging head on steering wheel while stuck in traffic: Seattle.
9. One hand on wheel, one hand on hunting rifle, alternating between both feet being on the accelerator and both feet on brake, throwing McDonald's bag out the window: Texas.
10. Four-wheel drive pick-up truck, shotgun mounted in rear window, beer cans on floor, squirrel tails attached to antenna: Alabama.
11. Two hands gripping wheel, blue hair barely visible above

windscreen, driving 35 on the Interstate in the left lane with
the left blinker on: Florida.

12.   Republican sticker on bumper, turning left on a no-left-turn
intersection, kids in back seat screaming and giving the finger
to other drivers: Indiana.

✉ MADAME DE GAULLE'S WAY WITH WORDS >>>

When Charles de Gaulle decided to retire from public life, the British
Ambassador and his wife threw a Gala dinner party in his honour.

At the dinner table the Ambassador's wife was talking with
Madame de Gaulle. 'Your husband has been such a prominent
public figure, such a presence on the French and international
scene for so many years! How quiet retirement will seem in
comparison. What are you most looking forward to in these
retirement years Madame?'

'A penis,' replied Madame de Gaulle.

A huge hush fell over the table. Everyone heard her answer and
no one knew quite what to say next.

Le grand Charles leaned over to his wife and said, 'Ma cherie, I
believe ze English pronounce zat word, "appiness!"'

✉ GENEROUS MOISHE >>>

Moishe took his Passover lunch to eat outside in the park. He sat
down on a bench and began eating. A little while later a blind man
came and sat down next to him. Feeling neighbourly, Moishe
passed a sheet of matzo to the blind man.

The blind man handled the matzo for a few minutes, looked
puzzled, and finally exclaimed, 'Who wrote this shit?'

✉ MARVELS OF LANGUAGE

English: I love you
French: Je t'aime
Japanese: Ai shite imasu

Spanish: Te amo
German: Ich liebe dich
Italian: Ti amo

Chinese: Wo ai ni   Swedish: Jag alskar
Alabama, Arkansas, Oklahoma, Louisiana, North Carolina, South
Carolina, Georgia, Tennessee, Missouri, Mississippi, West Virginia,
Kentucky: Nice ass

 HELPFUL BANK >>>

The Bank of Ireland is very pleased to inform you that we are
installing new drive-thru Cash Point machines where our customers
will be able to withdraw cash without leaving their vehicles. To
enable our customers to make full use of these new facilities, we
have conducted intensive behavioural studies to come up with
appropriate procedures for their use. Please read the procedures that
apply to you and remember them!

Procedures for our male customers:
1. Drive up to the cash machine.
2. Wind down your car window.
3. Insert card into machine and enter PIN.
4. Enter amount of cash required and withdraw.
5. Retrieve card, cash and receipt.
6. Wind up window.
7. Drive off.

Procedures for our female customers:
1. Drive up to cash machine.
2. Reverse back the required amount to align car window with
   cash machine.
3. Re-start the stalled engine.
4. Wind down the window.
5. Find handbag, remove all contents onto passenger seat to
   locate card.
6. Turn the radio down.
7. Attempt to insert card into machine.
8. Open car door to allow easier access to cash machine due to
   its excessive distance from the car.
9. Replace contents of handbag.
10. Insert card.
11. After 'Invalid Card' is displayed, remove the aforementioned

'Tesco' Charge card and insert correct Cash Point card.

12. Remove Cash Point Card.
13. Re-insert Cash Point card the right way up.
14. Re-enter handbag to find diary with your PIN written on the inside back page.
15. Enter PIN.
16. Press 'Cancel' and re-enter correct PIN.
17. Enter amount of cash required.
18. Check make-up in rear-view mirror.
19. Retrieve cash and receipt.
20. Empty handbag again to locate purse and place cash inside.
21. Place receipt in back of chequebook.
22. Re-check make-up.
23. Drive forward two metres.
24. Reverse back to cash machine.
25. Retrieve card.
26. Re-empty handbag, locate card holder, and place card into the slot provided.
27. Re-start stalled engine and pull off.
28. Drive for three or four kilometres.
29. Release handbrake.

✉ SODDING KIWIS >>>

Bob the builder was going through a house he had just built with the woman who owned it. She was telling him what colour to paint each room. They went into the first room and she said, 'I want this room to be painted light blue.'

Bob the builder went to the front door and yelled, 'GREEN SIDE UP!'

When he went back into the house, she told him that the next room was to be bright red. Bob the builder went to the front door and yelled, 'GREEN SIDE UP!'

When he went back into the house, she told him that the next room was to be tan. Bob the builder went to the front door and yelled, 'GREEN SIDE UP!'

When he came back, the lady was pretty curious, so she asked him, 'I keep telling you colours, but you go out the front and yell "Green side up". What is that for?'

Bob the builder said, 'Oh, don't worry about that, I've just got a couple of Kiwis laying the turf out the front.'

 THE TRAIN GANG >>>

Three New Zealanders and three Aussies are travelling by train to a yachting conference in England. At the station, the three Aussies each buy a ticket and watch as the three Kiwis buy just one ticket between them.

'How are the three of you going to travel on only one ticket?' asks one of the Aussies.

'Watch and learn,' answers one of the Kiwis. They all board the train. The Aussies take their respective seats but the three Kiwis cram into a toilet and close the door behind them.

Shortly after the train has departed, the conductor comes around collecting tickets. He knocks on the toilet door and says, 'Ticket please.' The door opens just a crack and a single arm emerges with a ticket in hand. The conductor takes it and moves on.

The Aussies see this and agree it was quite a clever idea. So after the conference, they decide to copy the Kiwis on the return trip and save some money. When they get to the station, they buy a single ticket for the return trip. To their astonishment, the Kiwis don't buy a ticket at all. 'How are you going to travel without a ticket?' asks one perplexed Aussie.

'Watch and learn,' answers one of the Kiwis. When they board the train the three Aussies cram into a toilet and soon after the three Kiwis cram into another nearby.

The train departs. Shortly afterwards, one of the Kiwis leaves the toilet and walks over to the toilet where the Aussies are hiding. He knocks on the door and says, 'Ticket please.'

 INTELLIGENT POM >>>

An Englishman, an Aussie and a South African are in a bar one night, having a beer. All of a sudden the South African downs his beer, throws his glass in the air, pulls out a gun and shoots the glass to pieces and says, 'In Sath Efrika our glasses are so cheap that we don't need to drink from the same one twice.'

The Aussie, obviously impressed by this, drinks his beer, throws his glass into the air, pulls out his gun and shoots the glass to pieces and says, 'Well mate, in 'Straaaaailia we have so much sand to make the glasses that we don't need to drink out of the same glass twice either.'

The Englishman, cool as a cucumber, picks up his beer and drinks it, throws his glass into the air, pulls out his gun, shoots the South African and the Australian and then says, 'In London we have so many South Africans and Australians that we don't need to drink with the same ones twice.'

 ## BAGS MINE >>>

An Englishman, a German, an Irishman and a Scotsman were sitting in a bar drinking, and discussing how stupid their wives were.

The Englishman says, 'I tell you, my wife is so stupid. Last week she went to the supermarket and bought $300 worth of meat because it was on sale, and we don't even have a fridge to keep it in.'

The German says, 'That's nothing! My wife just spent $1000 on ski equipment, and she can't even ski!'

The Scotsman agrees that she sounds pretty thick, but says his wife is thicker. 'Just last week, she went out and spent $17,000 on a new car,' he laments, 'and she doesn't even know how to drive!'

The Irishman nods sagely, and agrees that these three women sound like they all walked through the stupid forest and got hit by every branch. However, he still thinks his wife is dumber.

'Ah, it kills me every time I think of it,' he chuckles. 'My wife left to go on a trip to France. I watched her packing her bag, and she must have put about 100 condoms in there, and she doesn't even have a penis!'

 ## DEFINITION OF AN OCKER >>>

1. The bigger the hat, the smaller the farm.
2. The shorter the nickname, the more they like you.
3. Whether it's the opening of Parliament, or the launch of a

new art gallery, there is no Australian event that cannot be improved by a sausage sizzle.

4. If the guy next to you is swearing like a wharfie he's probably a media billionaire. Or on the other hand, he may be a wharfie.

5. There is no food that cannot be improved by the application of tomato sauce.

6. On the beach, all Australians hide their keys and wallets by placing them inside their sandshoes. No thief has ever worked this out.

7. Industrial design knows of no article more useful than the plastic milk crate.

8. All our best heroes are losers.

9. The alpha male in any group is he who takes the barbecue tongs from the hands of the host and blithely begins turning the snags.

10. It's not summer until the steering wheel is too hot to hold.

11. It is proper to refer to your best friend as 'a total bastard'. By contrast, your worst enemy is 'a bit of a bastard'.

12. If it can't be fixed with pantyhose and fencing wire, it's not worth fixing.

13. The most popular and widely praised family in any street is the one that has the swimming pool.

14. It's considered better to be down on your luck than up yourself.

15. The phrase 'We've got a great lifestyle' means everyone in the family drinks too much.

16. If invited to a party, you should take cheap red wine and then spend all night drinking the host's beer. (Don't worry, he'll have catered for it.)

17. The phrase 'A simple picnic' is not known. You should take everything you own. If you don't need to make three trips back to the car, you're not trying.

18. Unless ethnic or a Pom, you are not permitted to sit down in your front garden, or on your front porch. Pottering about, gardening or leaning on the fence is acceptable. Just don't sit. That's what backyards are for.

19. At picnics, the Esky is always too small, creating a food versus grog battle that can only ever be resolved by leaving the salad at home.

20. When on a country holiday, the neon sign advertising the

21. There comes a time in every Australian's life when he/she realises that the Aerogard is worse than the mozzies.

22. And, finally, the true test for immigration to Australia … Potential new Aussies must pass the following test. Mowing a sloping lawn (at least 20-degree angle) in a pair of thongs, holding a VB while watching the cricket. If you can't pass that, chances are you will never be able to pass yourself off as a true Aussie.

motel's pool will always be slightly larger than the pool itself.

✉ LET THE FORCE BE WITH YOU >>>

The CIA, the FBI and the Los Angeles Police Department are each asked to prove their capability of apprehending terrorists. President Bush releases a white rabbit into a forest and tells each agency to catch it.

The CIA goes first. It sends animal informants into the forest. They question all plant and material witnesses. After three months of intensive investigations the CIA concludes rabbits do not exist.

The FBI goes in. After two weeks with no leads it bombs the forest, killing everything, including the rabbit. It makes no apologies; the rabbit had it coming, it insists.

The LAPD go in. They come out after just two hours with a badly beaten bear. The bear is sobbing, 'OK, OK, I'm a rabbit, I'm a rabbit.'

John Howard hears about George W's idea and decides to test Australian law enforcement agencies. He releases a white rabbit into Stromlo Forest, near Canberra.

The National Crime Authority can't catch it but promises that if it gets a budget increase it can recover $90 million in unpaid rabbit taxes and the proceeds of crime.

The Victorian police go in. They're gone only 15 minutes, returning with a koala, a kangaroo and a tree fern, all three shot to pieces. 'They looked like dangerous rabbits and we acted in self-defence,' they explain.

The NSW police go in. Surveillance tapes later reveal top-ranking officers and rabbits dancing around a gum tree stoned out of their minds.

The Queensland police go in. They reappear driving a brand-new Mercedes, scantily clad rabbits draped all over them.

The WA police actually catch the white rabbit, but it inexplicably hangs itself when the attending officer 'slipped out momentarily' for a cup of tea.

The NT police beat the crap out of every rabbit in the forest, except the white one. They know it is the black ones who cause all the trouble.

The SA police go into the forest and return with the rabbit, however they charge it with being in possession of more than three marijuana plants, lose the evidence (and the case) but discover the head of the Drug Squad stoned out of his mind …

The Australian Federal Police refuse to go in. They examine the issues, particularly cost, and decide that because of low priority, high overtime and the projected expense to the AFP as a whole, the matter should be returned to the referring authority for further analysis.

ASIO goes into the wrong forest.

 CHINESE CHECK! >>>

Apparently, one in five people in the world are Chinese. There are five people in my family, so it must be one of them. It's either my mum or my dad. Or my older brother Colin. Or my younger brother Ho Cha Chu. But I think it's Colin.

 MOVIES ON THE MARAE >>>

The top Maori movies of all time:

- James Tu Meke Bond is 007 in *Paua Finger*
- *Seven Wahines for Seven Bros*
- *Onehunga Jones and the Tiki of Doom*
- *There's Something about Maui*
- *The Wizard of Otara*
- *Tuatara on a Hot Tin Roof*
- *Pa Wars Part 1: Return of Jake Heke*
- *King Arthur: Prince of the Tui Tekas*
- *Rebel without a Holden*
- *Rangi Hood*
- *Gone (after Robbing the Corner Dairy) in 60 Seconds*

- *Four Hangis and a Tangi*
- James Tu Meke Bond is 007 in *Red-Stoned Eye*
- *Nightmare on Eketahuna St Part 2: the Whanau's Back*
- *Goodbye Kumara Pie*
- *The Ngaruawahia Chainsaw Massacre*
- *Pa Wars Part 2: the Kaumatua Strikes Back*
- *I Know What You Stole Last Summer*
- *Fear and Loathing in RotoVegas*
- *My Favourite Maori* (the Disney Classic) starring Winston Peters
- James Tu Meke Bond is 007 in *The South Island Is Not Enough*
- *Pa Wars Part 3: Returning the Land*
- *Onehunga Jones and the Waka Raiders of the Lost Whanau*
- *Aroha Powers: International Bro of Mystery*

 ESE BROTHER >>>

An American man and a Japanese man were sitting on a plane on the way to LA when the American turned to the Japanese and asked, 'What kind of ese are you?'

The Japanese man, confused, replied, 'Sorry, but I don't understand what you mean.'

The American repeated, 'What kind of ese are you?'

Again, the Japanese man was confused over the question. The American, now irritated, then yells, 'What kind of ese are you … are you Chinese, Japanese, Vietnamese, or what?'

The Japanese man then replied, 'Oh, I am Japanese.'

A while later the Japanese man turned to the American man and asked what kind of 'key' he was. The American, frustrated, yelled, 'What do you mean what kind of key am I?'

The Japanese said, 'Are you a monkey, donkey or a Yankee?'

Lesson learnt: Never insult anyone.

 BURNT TOAST >>>

John O'Riley was a member of an Irish Toastmasters Club and one evening, at the local Irish Toastmasters meeting, a contest was held to see who could deliver the best toast.

Well, John O'Riley won the contest for the best toast of the evening: 'Here's to the best years o' me life, spent between the legs o' me wife.'

When John O'Riley arrived home, his beautiful wife asked him how the Toastmasters meeting went and he said, 'I won the contest for the best toast of the evening.'

His wife then asked him what his toast was, and he said, 'Here's to the best years o' me life, spent in church wi' me wife.'

His wife then said, 'Why John, that's so nice of you to include me in your toast.'

The next morning, Mrs O'Riley was downtown shopping and ran into the local policeman on the beat, who was also at the Toastmasters meeting with John O'Riley.

He said, 'Hello Mrs O'Riley, that was some great toast that your husband John gave at the Toastmasters meeting last evening. He won first prize.'

'Yes, that's right,' said the proud Mrs O'Riley, 'but he wasn't quite honest with the facts. He's only been there twice, the first time he fell asleep and the second time he was so drunk I had to push him out.'

 PADDY'S SAD DEMISE >>>

Paddy died in a fire and was burnt pretty badly, so the morgue needed someone to identify the body. So his two best friends, Seamus and Sean were sent for.

Seamus went in and the mortician pulled back the sheet. Seamus said, 'Yup, he's burnt pretty bad. Roll him over.'

So the mortician rolled him over and Seamus looked and said, 'Nope, it ain't Paddy.'

The mortician thought this was rather strange and then he brought Sean in to identify the body. Sean took a look at him and said, 'Yup, he's burnt real bad, roll him over.'

The mortician rolled him over and Sean looked down and said, 'Thank God, no, it ain't Paddy.'

The mortician asked, 'How can you tell?'

Sean said, 'Well, Paddy had two arseholes.'

'What? He had two arseholes?' said the mortician.

'Yup, everyone knew he had two arseholes. Every time we went into town, folks would say, 'Here comes Paddy with them two arseholes …'

FISHY TALE >>>

Recently, Tama was stopped by a Department of Conservation officer, somewhere near Taupo, with two buckets of fish. He was leaving a stream well known for its fishing. The officer asked him, 'Do you have a licence to catch those fish?'

Tama replied, 'These are my pet fish.'

'Pet fish!?' the officer asked.

'Yes, sir. Every night I take these fish down to the stream and let them swim around for a while. I whistle and they jump back into the buckets, and I take them home.'

'That's a lot of crap! Fish can't do that!'

Tama looked at the officer for a moment, and then said, 'Here I'll show you, it really works.'

'OK, I've got to see this!' The officer was curious now. Tama poured the fish into the stream and stood and waited.

After several minutes, the officer turned to him and said, 'Well?'

'Well, what?' Tama responded.

'When are you going to call them back?' the officer prompted.

'Call who back?' Tama asked.

'The fish,' replied the officer.

'What fish?' asked Tama.

OUTBACK LOGIC >>>

A couple of Australian hunters are in the outback when one of them falls to the ground. He doesn't seem to be breathing and his eyes have rolled back in his head.

The other guy whips out his cellphone and calls the emergency number. He gasps to the operator, 'My friend is dead! What can I do?'

The operator, in a calm soothing voice says, 'Just take it easy, I can help. First, let's make sure he's dead.'

There is a silence, then a shot is heard. The hunter says, 'OK, now what?'

- Only in Britain can a pizza get to your house faster than an ambulance.
- Only in Britain do supermarkets make sick people walk all the way to the back of the shop to get their prescriptions while healthy people can buy cigarettes at the front.
- Only in Britain do people order double cheeseburgers, large fries, and a diet coke.
- Only in Britain do banks leave both doors open and chain the pens to the counters.
- Only in Britain do we leave cars worth thousands of pounds on the drive and put our junk and cheap lawnmower in the garage.
- Only in Britain do we buy hot dogs in packs of 10 and buns in packs of eight.
- Only in Britain are there handicapped parking places in front of a skating rink.
- Three Brits die each year testing if a nine-volt battery works on their tongue.
- 142 Brits were injured in 1999 by not removing all pins from new shirts.
- 58 Brits are injured each year by using sharp knives instead of screwdrivers.
- 31 Brits have died since 1996 by watering their Christmas tree while the fairy lights were plugged in.
- British hospitals reported four broken arms last year after cracker-pulling accidents.
- 101 people since 1999 have had to have broken parts of plastic toys pulled out of the soles of their feet.
- 18 Brits suffered serious burns in 2000 from trying on a new jumper with a lit cigarette in their mouth.
- A massive 543 Brits were admitted to A&E in the last two years after opening bottles of beer with their teeth.
- Five Brits were injured last year in accidents involving out-of-control Scalextric cars.
- In 2000, eight Brits cracked their skulls whilst throwing up into the toilet.

UNO, DIOS, TRES, QUATTRO >>>

Five Englishmen in an Audi Quattro arrived at an Irish border checkpoint. Paddy the officer stops them and tells them, 'It is illegal to put five people in a Quattro. Quattro means four.'

'Quattro is just the name of the car,' the Englishman retorts in disbelief. 'Look at the papers: this car is designed to carry five persons.'

'You can't pull that one on me,' replies Paddy. 'Quattro means four. You have five people in your car and you are therefore breaking the law.'

The Englishman replies angrily, 'You idiot! Call your supervisor over. I want to speak to someone with more intelligence!'

'Sorry,' responds Paddy, 'Murphy is busy with two guys in a Fiat Uno.'

AUSSIE BLEEDER! >>>

A Kiwi was sitting with an Australian and an Indian in Saudi Arabia, sharing a smuggled barrel of beer, when all of a sudden, Saudi police entered and arrested them. They were initially sentenced to death but their respective embassies begged for them to be pardoned and the death sentence was commuted to life imprisonment. But, as it was a national holiday, the Sheikh decided they should be released after receiving 20 lashes of the whip.

As they were preparing for their punishment, the Sheikh suddenly said, 'It's my wife's birthday today and she asked me to allow each of you one wish before your whipping.'

So the Indian guy thought for a while and then said, 'Please be tying a pillow to my back.' This was done but the pillow only lasted 10 lashes before the whip went through it.

The Australian, watching the scene, said, 'Please fix two pillows on my back.' But even two pillows could only take 10 lashes before the whip went through again.

Before the Kiwi could say something, the Sheikh turned to him and said: 'As you are from a popular country and your rugby team is terrific and your women beautiful, you can have two wishes!'

'Thank you, Most Royal and Merciful Highness,' the Kiwi replies. 'My first wish is that I would like to have 40 lashes.'

'If you so desire,' the Sheikh replies with a questioning look on his face, 'and your second wish?'

'Tie the Aussie to my back!'

 ## KOREAN LESSON >>>

1. That's not right: Sum ting wong
2. Are you harbouring a fugitive?: Hu yu hai ding?
3. See me ASAP: Kum hia
4. Stupid man: Dum gai
5. Small horse: Tai ni po ni
6. Did you go to the beach?: Wai yu so tan?
7. I bumped the coffee table: Ai bang mai ni
8. I think you need a face-lift: Chin tu fat
9. It's very dark in here: Wao so dim
10. I thought you were on a diet: Wai yu mun ching?
11. This is a towaway zone: No pah king
12. Our meeting is scheduled for next week: Wai yu kum nao?
13. Staying out of sight: Lei ying lo
14. He's cleaning his automobile: Wa shing ka
15. Your body odour is offensive: Yu stin ki pu
16. Great: Fa kin su pah

AUSTRALIAN LOGIC >>>

A Swiss guy visiting Sydney pulls up at a bus stop where two locals are waiting. 'Entschuldigung, können sie Deutsch sprechen?' he asks.

The two Aussies just stare at him. 'Excussez-moi, parlez vous Francais?' he tries. The two continue to stare.

'Parla Italiano?' No response.

'Hablan ustedes Espanol?' Still nothing.

The Swiss guy drives off, extremely disgusted. The first Aussie turns to the second and says, 'Y'know, maybe we should learn a foreign language.'

'Why?' says the other. 'That guy knew four languages, and it didn't do him any good.'

THE STAYER >>>

A virile young Italian gentleman was relaxing at his favourite bar in Rome, when he managed to attract a spectacular young blonde. Things progressed to the point where he invited her back to his apartment, and after some small talk, they retired to his bedroom and made love.

After a pleasant interlude, he asked with a smile, 'So ... you finish?'

She paused for a second, frowned, and replied, 'No.'

Surprised, the young man reached for her and the lovemaking resumed. This time she thrashes about wildly and there are screams of passion. The lovemaking ends, and again, the Italian lover smiles, and again he asks, 'You finish?'

Again, after a short pause, she returns his smile, cuddles closer to him, and softly says, 'No.'

Stunned, but determined this woman was not going to outlast him, the young man reaches for the woman again. Using the last of his strength, he barely manages it, but they climax simultaneously, screaming, bucking, clawing and ripping the bed sheets. The exhausted man falls onto his back, gasping. Barely able to turn his head, he looks into her eyes, smiles proudly and asks again, 'You finish!?'

Barely able to speak, she whispers in his ear, 'No! I Norwegian!'

CANBERRA ON SPEED >>>

Who said there isn't anything to do in Canberra? Two weeks ago a speed camera van in Canberra was approached by four youths. Whilst the camera operator was talking to three boys about the van's equipment and how it works, the fourth boy proceeded to undo the van's front number plate. They then said goodbye to the operator, went home and fixed the number plate to their car and proceeded to drive considerably over the speed limit 17 times through the speed camera radar.

Needless to say, there was considerable embarrassment by urban services when the computer posted their own speeding fines to the department.

It's a relief to know the truth after all those conflicting medical studies. The Japanese eat very little fat and suffer fewer heart attacks than the British or Americans.

The French eat a lot of fat and also suffer fewer heart attacks than the British or Americans.

The Japanese drink very little red wine and suffer fewer heart attacks than the British or Americans.

The Italians drink excessive amounts of red wine and also suffer fewer heart attacks than the British or Americans.

The Germans drink a lot of beers and eat lots of sausages and fats and suffer fewer heart attacks than the British or Americans.

Conclusion: Eat and drink what you like. Speaking English is apparently what kills you.

naughty but nice

Having a laugh over a bit of harmless smut is one of life's joys. It won't give you cancer or any other terminal disease and, believe it or not, it won't make you go blind. But often, it is advisable to pick the right place in which to pass on a particular dirty ditty that may have tickled your fancy the most. There is nothing worse than that horrible silence at the end of a joke ... be warned to save embarrassment.

The tales in this chapter are simply a bit riper than those in other sections but, like we say, perfectly harmless to those of us who have a healthy tilt on sex and life in general and enjoy a chuckle.

THE EARS HAVE IT >>>

A young man rents an apartment in New York, and goes to the lobby to put his name on the group mailbox. While he is there, an attractive young lady comes out of the apartment right next to the mailboxes wearing just a robe.

The young man politely smiles at her and she strikes up a conversation with him. As they talk, she fiddles with the ties and her robe slips open. It is very obvious that she has nothing on underneath. The flustered young man breaks out in a sweat trying desperately to maintain eye contact.

After a few minutes, she places her hand on his arm. 'Let's go into my apartment,' she says. 'I hear someone coming …' So he goes with her into the apartment and, after she closes the door, she leans against it allowing her robe to fall completely off her shoulders — dropping softly to the plush carpeted floor and revealing everything a red-blooded young man could possibly want. 'What would you say is my best feature?' she purrs at him.

The flustered, embarrassed guy stammers, clears his throat several times, and finally squeaks out a reply.

'Oh, it's got to be your ears!' he says. She is astounded.

'My ears? Why my ears? Just look at these breasts!' she indicates. 'They're full, beautifully rounded, don't sag, and they're 100 percent natural. The cheeks of my bum are firm, my legs are long and shapely and I don't have a trace of cellulite anywhere. And,' she continues, her voice getting louder, 'look at this milky white skin of mine all over, no blemishes or scars. Why in heaven's name would you say the best part of my body is my ears?'

Clearing his throat once again, the young man stammers. 'Well … outside, you remember when you said you heard someone coming? That was me.'

QUESTIONS, QUESTIONS >>>

Little Johnny says, 'Mum, what kind of bird brings white babies?' His mum says, 'Why, a stork, little Johnny.'

Little Johnny says, 'Mum, what kind of bird brings black babies?' His mum says, 'A raven, dear.'

Little Johnny then says, 'Then what kind of bird brings no babies at all?'

His mum says, 'A swallow!'

 OH DEAR >>>

The next time you're having a bad day, imagine this: you're a Siamese twin. Your brother, attached to you, is gay. You're not. He has a date coming over today. But you only have one arse. Feel better?

 CHRISTMAS CRACKERS >>>

Things you can get away with saying only at Christmas:

1. I prefer breasts to legs.
2. Tying the legs together keeps the inside moist.
3. Smother the butter all over the breasts.
4. If I don't undo my trousers, I'll burst.
5. I've never seen a better spread.
6. I'm in the mood for a little dark meat.
7. Are you ready for seconds yet?
8. It's a little dry, do you still want to eat it?
9. Just wait your turn, you'll get some.
10. Don't play with your meat.
11. Stuff it up between the legs as far as it will go.
12. Do you think you'll be able to handle all these people at once?
13. I didn't expect everyone to come at the same time.
14. You still have a little bit on your chin.
15. How long will it take after you put it in?
16. You'll know it's ready when it pops up.
17. Just pull the end and wait for the bang.
18. That's the biggest bird I've ever had.
19. I'm so full; I've been gobbling nuts all morning.
20. Wow, I didn't think I could handle all that and still want more!

(naughty but nice)

THE OLD TENT POLE! >>>

A man fell asleep on the beach under the midday sun and suffered severe sunburn to his legs. He was taken to the hospital where his skin had turned bright red, was painful and had started to blister. Anything that touched his legs caused agony. The doctor prescribed continued intravenous feedings of water and electrolytes, a mild sedative and Viagra.

Rather astounded, the nurse inquired, 'What good will Viagra do him in his condition?'

The doctor replied, 'Medically nothing, but it will keep the sheet off his legs.'

IN THE PINK >>>

A couple are attending an art exhibition and they are looking at a portrait that has them a little taken aback. The picture depicts three very black, very naked men sitting on a park bench; two have black penises and the one in the middle has a pink penis.

As the couple is looking somewhat puzzled at the picture, the Irish artist walks by and says, 'Can I help you with this painting? I'm the artist who painted it.'

The man says 'Well, we like the painting but don't understand why you have three African men on a bench, and the one in the middle has a pink penis, while the other two have a black penis.'

The artist says, 'Oh, you are misinterpreting the painting. They're not African men, they are Irish coal miners and the one in the middle went home for lunch.'

THE POLITITIAN AND THE PAPARAZZI >>>

A famous polititian is having a shower. He occasionally feels the need to empty his political scrotal sacs — and this is one of those occasions.

Just as he shoots his load, he sees a photographer taking a picture.

'Hold on a minute,' says the polititian, 'you can't do that. You'll destroy the reputation of the party.'

'This picture is my lottery win,' says the photographer. 'I'll be financially secure for life.'

So the polititian offers to buy the camera off the photographer, and after plenty of negotiation, they eventually arrive at a figure of $2 million.

The polititian then dries himself off and heads off with his new camera. He meets his housekeeper who spots the new purchase.

'That looks like a really good camera,' she says, 'how much did it cost you?'

'Two million dollars,' replies the polititian.

'Two million dollars!' says the housekeeper. 'He must have seen you coming.'

 ## HOT AND SUNNY >>>

A female news-reader who, on the day after it was supposed to have snowed and didn't, turned to the weatherman and asked, 'So Bob, where's that eight inches you promised me last night?' Not only did the weatherman have to leave the set, but half the crew did too because they were all laughing so hard!

 ## LOOK AND LEARN >>>

Who says pornography is not educational? Watching it, you learn that:
1. Women wear high heels to bed.
2. Men are never impotent.
3. When going down on a woman, 10 seconds is more than satisfactory.
4. If a woman gets busted masturbating by a strange man, she will not scream with embarrassment, but rather insist he have sex with her.
5. Women smile appreciatively when men splat them in the face with sperm.
6. Women enjoy having sex with ugly, middle-aged men.
7. Women moan uncontrollably when giving a blowjob.
8. Women always orgasm when men do.
9. A blowjob will always get a woman off a speeding ticket.

naughty but nice

10. All women are noisy on the job.
11. People in the 70s couldn't have sex unless there was a wild guitar solo in the background.
12. Those tits are real.
13. A common and enjoyable sexual practice for a man is to take his half-erect penis and slap it repeatedly on a woman's bum.
14. Men always groan, 'oh yeah!' when they come.
15. If there are two of them they 'high-five' each other (and the girl isn't disgusted!).
16. Double penetration makes women smile.
17. Asian men don't exist.
18. If you come across a guy and his girlfriend having sex in the bushes, the boyfriend won't bash seven shades of shit out of you if you shove your cock in his girlfriend's mouth.
19. There's a plot.
20. When taking a woman from behind, a man can really excite a woman by giving her a gentle slap on the bum.
21. Nurses give blowjobs to patients.
22. Men always pull out.
23. When your girlfriend busts you getting head from her best friend, she'll only be momentarily pissed off before getting on the job with both of you.
24. Women never have headaches … or periods.
25. When a woman is giving a blowjob, it's important for him to remind her to 'suck it'.
26. Arseholes are clean.
27. A man ejaculating on a woman's bum is a satisfying result for all parties concerned.
28. Women always look pleasantly surprised when they open a man's trousers and find a cock there.
29. Men don't have to beg.
30. When standing during a blowjob, a man will always place one hand firmly on the back of the kneeling woman's head and the other proudly on his hip.

✉ **ALL AT SEA >>>**

A depressed young woman was so desperate that she decided to end her life by throwing herself into the ocean. When she went down to the docks, a handsome young sailor noticed her tears, took pity on her and said, 'Look, you've got a lot to live for. I'm off to Europe in the morning and, if you like, I can stow you away on my ship. I'll take good care of you and bring you food every day.' Moving closer, he slipped his arm around her shoulder and added, 'I'll keep you happy, and you'll keep me happy.'

The girl nodded yes, after all, what did she have to lose? That night, the sailor brought her aboard and hid her in a lifeboat. From then on, every night he brought her three sandwiches and a piece of fruit, and they made passionate love until dawn.

Three weeks later, during a routine search, she was discovered by the captain. 'What are you doing here?' the captain asked.

She got up off the ground and explained, 'I have an arrangement with one of the sailors. He's taking me to Europe, and he's screwing me.'

The captain looked at her, 'He sure is lady, this is the Staten Island Ferry.'

 ## PUSHBIKE BLUES >>>

For Christmas Little Patrick asked for a 10-speed bicycle. His father said, 'Son, we'd give you one, but the mortgage on this house is $120,000 and your mother just lost her job. There's no way we can afford it.'

The next day the father saw Little Patrick heading out the front door with a suitcase. So he said, 'Son, where are you going?'

Little Patrick told him, 'I was walking past your bedroom last night and I heard you tell mum you were pulling out. Then I heard her tell you to wait because she was coming too.

And I thought, I'll be damned if I'm sticking around here by myself with a $120,000 mortgage and no bike.'

 ## SHORT, SHARP AND TO THE POINT >>>

If a woman is uncomfortable watching you wank, do you think:
A.   She shouldn't be such a prude.
B.   You need more time together.
C.   She should have sat somewhere else on the bus.

naughty but nice

What's the definition of a bastard?
A man that shags you all night long with a two-inch dick then kisses you goodbye with a nine-inch tongue.

Three things not to say in a gay bar:
1. F*** me, this beer is good.
2. Bugger me, it's hot in here.
3. Can I push your stool in for you?

What have kebabs and pussy got in common? They both make your breath smell, the meat is always hanging out and you only fancy eating them when you are pissed.

ICE CREAM, YOU SCREAM! >>>

There was a guy sunbathing in the nude on the beach. He saw a little girl coming toward him, so he covered himself with the newspaper he was reading.

The girl came up to him and asked, 'What do you have under the newspaper?' Thinking quickly, the guy replied, 'A bird.'

The girl walked away and the guy fell asleep. When he woke up, he was in a hospital in tremendous pain in the groin area. The police asked him what happened. The guy says, 'I don't know. I was lying on the beach, this little girl asked me a question, I guess I dozed off, and the next thing I know is I'm here.'

The police went to the beach, found the girl, and asked her, 'What did you do to that naked fellow?'

After a pause, the girl replied, 'To him? Nothing. I was playing with his bird and it spat on me, so I broke its neck, cracked its eggs, and set its nest on fire.'

MUSICAL OCTOPUS >>>

A man walks into a bar with an octopus. He sits the octopus down on a stool and tells everyone in the bar that this is a very talented octopus. 'He can play any musical instrument in the world.'

Everyone in the bar laughs at the man, calling him an idiot. So he says that he will wager $50 to anyone who has an instrument that the octopus can't play. A bloke walks up with a guitar and sets it beside the octopus.

Immediately the octopus picks up the guitar and starts playing better than Jimmy Hendrix. The guitar man pays up his $50.

Another bloke walks up with a trumpet. This time the octopus plays the trumpet better than Louis Armstrong. The man pays up his $50.

Then a Scotsman walks up with some bagpipes. He sits them down and the octopus fumbles with it for a minute and then sits down with a confused look.

'Ha ha!' the Scot says. 'Ye cannae plae it, can ye?'

The octopus looks up at him and says, 'Play it? I'm going to f*** it as soon as I figure out how to get its pyjamas off.

 ALL THAT SCRATCHIN'... >>>

Nick the Dragon Slayer had a long-standing obsession to nuzzle the beautiful Queen's voluptuous breasts, but he knew the penalty for this would be death. One day he revealed his secret desire to his colleague, Horatio the Physician, who was the King's chief doctor.

Horatio the Physician exclaimed that he could arrange for Nick the Dragon Slayer to satisfy his desire, but it would cost him 1000 gold coins to arrange it. Without pause, Nick the Dragon Slayer readily agreed to the scheme.

The next day, Horatio the Physician made a batch of itching powder and poured a little bit into the Queen's brassiere while she bathed. Soon after she dressed, the itching commenced and grew intense.

Upon being summoned to the Royal Chambers to address this incident, Horatio the Physician informed the King and Queen that only a special saliva, if applied for four hours, would cure this type of itch, and that tests had shown that only the saliva of Nick the Dragon Slayer would work as the antidote to cure the itch.

The King quickly summoned Nick the Dragon Slayer. Horatio the Physician then slipped Nick the Dragon Slayer the antidote for the itching powder, which he quickly put into his mouth, and for the next four hours, Nick worked passionately on the Queen's voluptuous and magnificent breasts. The Queen's itching was eventually relieved, and Nick the Dragon Slayer left satisfied and touted as a hero.

Upon returning to his chamber, Nick the Dragon Slayer found Horatio the Physician demanding his payment of 1000 gold coins. With his obsession now satisfied, Nick the Dragon Slayer couldn't have cared less, and knowing that Horatio the Physician could never report this matter to the King, shooed him away with no payment made.

The next day, Horatio the Physician slipped a massive dose of the same itching powder into the King's loincloth. The King immediately summoned Nick the Dragon Slayer ...

The moral of the story: Pay your bills.

 VATICAN SMOKERS >>>

Two priests were in a Vatican bathroom using the urinals. One of them looked at the other one's penis and noticed a Nicoderm patch on it.

He turned to the other priest and said, 'I believe you're supposed to put that patch on your arm or shoulder, not your penis.'

The other one replied, 'But it's working just fine. I'm down to two butts a day.'

 TIPPER LIPS >>>

At a press conference, Tipper Gore announced she was going on the campaign trail with her husband, former Vice President Al Gore, for the 2004 presidential election.

'To prepare myself,' she said, 'I have shaved off all my pubic hair. From now until the election, I shall sit on the stage with Al and may occasionally flash my legs apart without wearing any panties. This will send a strong message to America.'

'Just what is that message, Mrs Gore?' gasped an astonished reporter at the news of this rather startling announcement.

To which Tipper replied, 'Read my lips, no more Bush.'

Pinocchio had a human girlfriend who would sometimes complain about splinters when they were having sex. Pinocchio, therefore, went to visit Gepetto to see if he could help. Gepetto suggested he try a little sandpaper wherever indicated and Pinocchio skipped away enlightened.

A couple of weeks later, Gepetto saw Pinocchio bouncing happily through town and asked him, 'How's the girlfriend?'

Pinocchio replied, 'Who needs a girlfriend?'

Little Red Riding Hood was walking through the woods when suddenly the Big Bad Wolf jumped out from behind a tree and, holding a sword to her throat, said, 'Red, I'm going to screw your brains out!'

To that, Little Red Riding Hood calmly reached into her picnic basket and pulled out a 44 magnum and pointed it at him and said, 'No, you're not. You're going to eat me, just like it says in the book!'

Did you know Captain Hook died from jock itch?

One day Jane met Tarzan in the jungle. She was very attracted to him and during her questions about his life she asked him how he managed for sex. 'What's that?' he asked.

She explained to him what sex was and he said, 'Oh, I use a hole in the trunk of a tree.' Horrified, she said, 'Tarzan you have it all wrong but I will show you how to do it properly.' She took off her clothes, lay down on the ground and spread her legs wide. 'Here,' she said, 'you must put it in here.'

Tarzan removed his loincloth, stepped closer and then gave her an almighty kick in the crotch. Jane rolled around in agony. Eventually she managed to gasp, 'What the hell did you do that for?'

'Just checking for bees,' said Tarzan.

✉ ONE STONE TOO MANY

In this out-of-the-way village there was a man called 'Onestone'. This wasn't his real name but everyone called him that because he only had one testicle. After years and years of this torment, Onestone cracked and said, 'If anyone calls me Onestone again I will kill them!'

The word got around and nobody called him Onestone any more. Then one day a girl forgot and said, 'Good morning, Onestone.'

He jumped up, grabbed her and took her deep into the forest, where he shagged her all day, he shagged her all night, he shagged her all the next day, until she died from exhaustion.

The word got around that Onestone meant business. Years went by until a woman returned to the village after many years away. She was overjoyed when she saw Onestone and hugged him and said, 'Good to see you, Onestone.'

Again, Onestone grabbed her and took her deep into the forest where he shagged her all day, shagged her all night, shagged her all the next day, shagged her all the next night, but she wouldn't die!

What is the moral of the story? You can't kill two birds with one stone.

✉ UNIVERSITY CHALLENGE >>>

In 1991 Duke University funded a study to see why the head of a man's penis was larger than the shaft. After one year and $180,000, they concluded that the reason the head was larger than the shaft was to give the man more pleasure during sex.

After Duke published the study, Stanford decided to do their own study. After $250,000 and three years of research, they concluded that the reason was to give the woman more pleasure during sex.

Mississippi State University, unsatisfied with these findings, spent $19.27 on a *Playboy*, a *Penthouse*, and a case of Pabst Blue Ribbon, and in less than two hours concluded that it was to keep a man's hand from flying off and hitting him in the forehead.

A first-grade teacher was having trouble with one of her students. 'Harry, what is your problem?' she asked.

Harry answered, 'I'm too smart for the first grade. My sister is in the third grade and I'm smarter than she is. I think I should be in the third grade too.'

The teacher had had enough. She took Harry to the principal's office. While Harry waited in the outer office, the teacher explained to the principal what the situation was.

The principal told the teacher he would give the boy a test and if he failed to answer any of his questions he was to go back to the first grade and behave.

The teacher agreed. Harry was brought in and the conditions were explained to him and he agreed to take the test.

Principal: 'What is three times three?'

Harry: 'Nine.'

Principal: 'What is six times six?'

Harry: '36.'

And so it went, with every question the principal thought a third-grader should know. Finally the principal looks at the teacher and tells her, 'I think Harry can go to the third grade.'

The teacher says to the principal, 'Let me ask him some questions.' The principal and Harry both agree.

The teacher asks, 'What does a cow have four of that I have only two of?'

Harry, after a moment, 'Legs.'

Teacher: 'What is in your pants that you have but I do not have?'

Harry replied, 'Pockets.'

Teacher: 'What does a dog do that a man steps into?'

Harry: 'Pants.'

Teacher: 'What starts with a C and ends with a T, is hairy, oval, delicious and contains thin whitish liquid?'

Harry: 'Coconut.'

Teacher: 'What goes in hard and pink then comes out soft and sticky?'

Harry: 'Bubblegum.'

Teacher: 'What does a man do standing up, a woman do sitting down and a dog do on three legs?'

The principal's eyes open really wide and before he can stop the answer Harry says, 'Shake hands.'

Teacher: 'Now I will ask some "Who am I" sort of questions, OK?'

Harry: 'Yep.'

Teacher: 'You stick your poles inside me. You tie me down to get me up. I get wet before you do.'

Harry: 'Tent.'

Teacher: 'A finger goes in me. You fiddle with me when you're bored. The best man always has me first.'

Principal is looking restless and a bit tense. Harry: 'Wedding ring.'

Teacher: 'I come in many sizes. When I'm not well, I drip. When you blow me, you feel good.'

Harry: 'Nose.'

Teacher: 'I have a stiff shaft. My tip penetrates. I come with a quiver.'

Harry: 'Arrow.'

Teacher: 'What word starts with an 'F' and ends in 'K' that brings a lot of excitement?'

Harry: 'Firetruck.'

The principal breathed a sigh of relief and told the teacher: 'Put Harry in the fifth grade, I missed the last 10 questions myself.'

✉ GIVE ME A RISE! >>>

I, the Penis, do hereby request a raise for the following reasons:

- I do physical labour.
- I work at great depths.
- I plunge headfirst into everything I do.
- I do not get weekends or holidays off.
- I work in a damp environment.
- I do not get paid overtime.
- I work in a dark place that has poor ventilation.
- I work in high temperatures.
- My work exposes me to contagious diseases.

Dear Penis,

After assessing your request, and considering the arguments you have raised, management rejects your request for the following reasons:

- You do not work eight hours straight.
- You fall asleep on the job after brief work periods.
- You do not always follow orders from the management team.
- You do not stay in your allocated position and often visit other areas.
- You do not take initiative — you need to be pressured and stimulated in order to start work.
- You leave the workplace rather messy at the end of your shift.
- You don't always observe necessary safety regulations, such as wearing the correct protective clothing.
- You retire well before 65.
- You're unable to work double shifts.
- You sometimes leave your allocated position before you have completed a day's work.
- And if that were not all, you've been constantly entering and leaving the workplace carrying two suspicious-looking bags.

Sincerely,
Management.

 CLEVER GIRL >>>

One afternoon, a little girl returned from school and announced that her friend had told her where babies come from. Amused, her mother replied, 'Really, sweetie, why don't you tell me all about it?'

The little girl explained, 'Well ... OK ... the mummy and daddy take off all of their clothes, and the daddy's thingee sort of stands up, and then Mummy puts it in her mouth, and then it sort of explodes, and that's how you get babies.'

Her mum shook her head, leaned over to meet her eye to eye and said, 'Oh, darling, that's sweet, but that's not how you get babies. That's how you get jewellery.'

 BECKS BEER >>>

The latest Becks Beer advert in Scotland (displayed in pubs, etc.) is as follows:

'You don't have to be Posh to swallow Becks.'

✉ SEAN AND KYLIE >>>

Sean Connery was interviewed by Michael Parkinson and bragged that despite his 72 years of age, he could still have sex three times a night.

Kylie was intrigued. After the show, Kylie said, 'Sean, if I am not being too forward, I'd love to have sex with an older man. Let's go back to my place.' So they go back to her place and have great sex.

Afterwards, Sean says, 'If you think that was good, let me sleep for half an hour, and we can have even better sex. But while I'm sleeping, hold my balls in your left hand and my dick in your right hand.'

Kylie looks a bit perplexed, but says, 'OK.' He sleeps for half an hour, awakens, and they have even better sex.

Then Sean says, 'Kylie, that was wonderful. But if you let me sleep for an hour, we can have the best sex yet. But again, hold my balls in your left hand, and my dick in your right hand.'

Kylie is now used to the routine and complies. The results are mind-blowing. Once it's all over, and the cigarettes are lit, Kylie asks, 'Sean, tell me, does my holding your balls in my left hand and your dick in my right stimulate you while you're sleeping?'

Sean replies, 'No, but the last time I slept with a slut from Melbourne, she stole my wallet.'

✉ NOT VERY HANDY >>>

There was an elderly man who wanted to make his younger wife pregnant. So, he went to the doctor to have a sperm count done. The doctor told him to take a specimen cup home, fill it, and bring it back the next day.

The elderly man came back the next day and the specimen cup was empty and the lid was on it.

Doctor: What was the problem?

Elderly man: Well, I tried with my right hand ... nothing. So, I tried with my left hand ... nothing. My wife tried with her right hand ... nothing. Her left hand ... nothing. Her mouth ... nothing. Then my wife's friend tried. Right hand, left hand, mouth ... still nothing.

Doctor: Wait a minute. You mean your wife's friend too?!

Elderly man: Yeah, and we still couldn't get the lid off of the specimen cup.

 NUN BETTER >>>

Two nuns are riding their bicycles down the back streets of Rome. One leans over to the other and says, 'I've never come this way before.'

The other nun whispers, 'It's the cobblestones.'

the

sporting

life

In our part of the world sport is king and we tend to agree with that Scotsman Bill Shankly, who managed the great Liverpool sides of the 70s when he said, 'Some people believe football is a matter of life and death. I can assure you it is much more important than that.'

We would lump all sport into that category, especially when you think of all the events that are televised live at ungodly hours because of our exalted status on the date-line, and our living rooms are ablaze with lights as we watch away. Who would watch a Formula One race from Monza beginning at midnight in New Zealand and 10pm in the eastern states of Australia, but petrol-head geeks from either country?

✉ GOLFING BALLS >>>

Two women are playing golf on a sunny afternoon when one of them slices her shot into a group of four men.

To her horror, one of the men collapses in agony with both hands in his crotch. She runs to him apologising profusely, explaining that she is a physical therapist and can help ease his pain.

'No thanks … just give me a few minutes … I'll be fine …' he replies quietly with his hands still between his legs.

Taking it upon herself to help the poor man, she gently undoes the front of his pants and starts massaging his genitals.

'Doesn't that feel better?' she asks.

'Well … yes … that feels pretty good,' he admits. 'But my thumb still hurts like hell.'

✉ THAT'S THE TICKET >>>

I went to the shops the other day, and I was there for only about five minutes. When I came out there was a cop writing a parking ticket. So I went up to him and said, 'Come on, buddy, how about giving a girl a break?'

He ignored me and continued writing the ticket. So I called him a pencil-necked Nazi. He glared at me and started writing another ticket for having worn tyres. So I called him a piece of horse-shit. He finished the second ticket and put it on the windscreen with the first. Then he started writing a third ticket!

This went on for about 20 minutes. The more I abused him, the more tickets he wrote. I didn't care. My car was parked around the corner.

I try to have a little sport each day. It's important …

✉ NAVJOT'S GEMS (OR NONSENSE) >>>

Navjot Siddhu is an Indian cricket commentator.

1. That ball went so high it could have got an airhostess down with it.

2. There is light at the end of the tunnel for India, but it's that of an oncoming train which will run them over.

3. Experience is like a comb that life gives you when you are bald.

4. This quote was made after Ganguly called Dravid for a run and midway sent him back and Dravid was run out in the third test against the West Indies in Barbados. 'Ganguly has thrown a drowning man both ends of the rope.'

5. The Sri Lankan score is running like an Indian taxi meter.

6. Statistics are like miniskirts, they reveal more than what they hide.

7. Wickets are like wives, you never know which way they will turn.

8. He is like an Indian three-wheeler which will suck a lot of diesel but cannot go beyond 30.

9. The Indians are going to beat the Kiwis! Let me tell you, my friend, that the Kiwi is the only bird in the whole world which does not have wings!

10. As uncomfortable as a bum on a porcupine.

11. The ball whizzes past like a bumblebee and the Indians are in the sea.

12. The Indians are finding the gaps like a pin in a haystack.

13. The pitch is as dead as a dodo.

14. Deep Dasgupta is as confused as a child is in a topless bar!

15. … the way Indian wickets fall reminds me of the cycle stand at Rajendra Talkies in Patiala … one falls and everything else falls!

16. An Indian team without Sachin is like giving a kiss without a squeeze.

17. You cannot make omelettes without breaking the eggs.

18. Deep Dasgupta is not a wicket-keeper; he is a goal-keeper. He must be given a free transfer to Manchester United.

19. He will fight a rattlesnake and give it the first two bites, too.

20. One who doesn't throw the dice can never expect to score a six.

21. This quote was made after Eddie Nichols, the third umpire, ruled Shivnarine Chanderpaul not out in the second test at Port of Spain: 'Eddie Nichols is a man who cannot find his own buttocks with his two hands.'

22. Anybody can pilot a ship when the sea is calm.

23. Nobody travels on the road to success without a puncture or two.
24. You've got to choose between tightening your belt or losing your pants.
25. The cat with gloves catches no mice.
26. Age has been a perfect fire extinguisher for flaming youth.
27. You may have a heart of gold, but so does a hard-boiled egg.
28. He is like a one-legged man in a bum-kicking competition.
29. The third umpires should be changed as often as nappies and for the same reason.
30. Rahul Dravid is as dangerous as playing catch with a rattlesnake.

✉ CONCENTRATION INTERRUPTED >>>

It was a sunny Friday morning on the first hole of a busy course and I was beginning my pre-shot routine, visualising my upcoming shot, when a piercing voice came over the clubhouse loudspeaker.

'Would the gentleman on the women's tee back up to the men's tee please?'

I could feel every eye on the course looking at me. I was still deep in my routine, seemingly impervious to the interruption.

Again the announcement, 'Would the MAN on the WOMEN'S tee kindly back up to the MEN'S tee?'

I simply ignored the guy and kept concentrating, when once more, the man yelled, 'Would the man on the women's tee back up to the men's tee, PLEASE?'

I finally stopped, turned, looked through the clubhouse window directly at the person with the microphone, cupped my hands and shouted back, 'Would the bastard in the clubhouse kindly shut the f*** up and let me play my second shot?'

✉ POWER TO THE SLEDGERS >>>

Glenn McGrath (to Otto Brandes, tubby South African No. 11, after a 130kph delivery whistles past OB's chin): 'Why are you so fat?'
OB: 'Because every time I f*** your wife, she gives me a biscuit.'

During Australia's last tour of South Africa it was rumoured that Daryll Cullinan had been consulting a psychologist to exorcise the demons that appeared whenever Shane Warne removed his hat. No sooner had Cullinan arrived at the crease, than Warne snarled: 'I'm going to send you straight back to your shrink.'

Ian Healy once became frustrated with an overweight batsman from a South African provincial side who seemed not the least interested in scoring runs. Eventually Healy called to the bowler: 'Why don't we put a Mars bar on a good length to see if we can lure him out of his crease?'

An English county bowler was having surprising success against the great West Indian Viv Richards, who'd played and missed at several balls. Foolishly, the bowler piped up, 'Hey Viv, it's red and it's round.'
    A steaming Richards cracked the next ball into another postcode and told the bowler, 'You know what it looks like, man, go fetch it.'

Sledging can be plain amusing. It's unlikely Merv Hughes was thinking tactically when he told a struggling English batsman: 'I'll bowl you a f***ing piano, ya pommie poofter. Let's see if you can play that.'

 GET A GRIP >>>

Two old folks got married. As they were lying in their wedding suite, staring at the ceiling, the old man says, 'I haven't been completely honest with you. I think the world of you, but you are only number two to me. Golf is my first love. It's my hobby, my passion, my first love.'
    They both stare at the ceiling for a bit then the woman says, 'While we're baring our souls, I'd guess I better tell you that I've been a hooker all my life.'
    The man jumps out of bed, looks at her a moment then says, 'Have you tried widening your stance and adjusting your grip?'

✉ BROADCASTING BALLS-UPS >>>

- 'Sure, there have been deaths in boxing but none of them serious.' Alan Minter
- 'The lead car is absolutely unique. Except for the one behind it which is identical.' Murray Walker, Formula One racing commentator
- 'And this is Gregoriava from Bulgaria. I saw her snatch this morning and it was truly amazing!' Pat Glenn, weightlifting commentator
- 'Andrew Mehrtens loves it when Darryl Gibson comes inside of him.' Murray Mexted, rugby commentator
- 'I owe a lot to my parents, especially my father and mother.' Greg Norman

✉ CHIP'S A WEE BIT PEEVED >>>

The Australian's sports writer Chip Le Grand sent the following blistering e-mail to everyone in the sports department after two paragraphs were added to his column:

From: Le Grand, Chip
Sent: Monday, 20 January 2003, 2:17
To: Aussport
Subject: chip and charge

To all and sundry and particularly the person responsible for adding two paragraphs to the end of the 'chip and charge' column.

If anyone has suggestions for my column, they would be dearly appreciated. If anyone subbing my column has a query or would like to suggest a change, I'd love to hear it.

Otherwise, it is not the prerogative of anyone working on the sports desk to unilaterally add editorial content — in this case the final two paragraphs — without first raising the matter with me.

This is not some kind of creative writing workshop where anyone in the office who happens to pick up the story (or to have watched some tennis on TV) can add their 20 cents' worth. The column has my name on it, my face on it, and I'll be f***ed if I'm going to sit down here and let some bloody bozo add their own thoughts, moronic or otherwise, to what I have written.

'Lift your game, Seven.' Says who? Not me. Because if I had said it, I would have found a more interesting way to say it than in such a third-rate, chest-thumping manner. I'm surprised it didn't finish with an exclamation mark!

'And while we're having a go at Seven … Who the f*** is we? This is not a co-authorship. I write it, you sub it, and try not to f*** it up. Otherwise you can get on a plane to Melbourne, spend 10 hours a day in the tennis media centre and write the damn thing yourselves.

I don't want to know who did it. I couldn't give a rat's arse. Just don't do it again.

Chip Le Grand

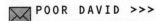 **POOR DAVID >>>**

Why has David Beckham got short hair?
　Coz Victoria was told sex would be 10 times better if she shaved her twat.

FOR SALE >>>

1 x black boat, used only five times, one careful owner (New Zealand) comes with some spares and includes a couple of tacticians and helmsmen. Still has nine months left on Warehouse warranty. Genuine inquiries only, no test pilots please.

DESERT ISLAND RISK >>>

One day, a man who had been stranded on a desert island for over 10 years sees an unusual speck on the horizon.
　'It's certainly not a ship,' he thinks to himself.
　As the speck gets closer and closer he begins to rule out the possibilities of a small boat, then even a raft. Suddenly, emerging from the surf, comes a drop-dead gorgeous blonde woman wearing

a wetsuit and scuba gear. She approaches the stunned guy and says to him, 'Tell me, how long has it been since you've had a cigarette?'

'Ten years,' replies the stunned man. With that she reaches over and unzips a waterproof pocket on her left sleeve and pulls out a pack of cigarettes.

He takes one, lights it, takes a long drag and says, 'Man, oh man! Is that good!!'

'And how long has it been since you've had a sip of whisky?' she asks him.

Trembling, the castaway replies, 'Ten years.' She reaches over, unzips her right sleeve, pulls out a flask and hands it to him. He opens the flask, takes a long swig and says, 'Wow, that's absolutely fantastic!'

At this point she starts slowly unzipping the long zipper that runs down the front of her wetsuit, looks at the man seductively and asks, 'And how long has it been since you've played around?'

With tears in his eyes, the guy falls to his knees and sobs, 'Oh good Lord! Don't tell me you've got golf clubs in there too?'

 AUSSIE JIBES >>>

Who else but the English could invent a game that lasts five days and can still end in a draw? No wonder they had the staying power for two world wars … and an optimist is someone who buys a ticket to the fifth day of an Ashes Test.

 BELOW PAR >>>

A man takes a week off and decides to play a round of golf every day. First thing Monday he sets off on his first round and soon catches up to the person in front.

He sees that this is a woman and as he gets closer to her on the par 3, he notes that she is a stunner.

He's interested and suggests they play the rest of the round together. She agrees and a very close match ensues. She turns out to be a very talented golfer and she wins their little match on the last hole.

He congratulates her in the carpark then offers to give her a lift when he sees she doesn't have a car.

All in all, it's been a highly enjoyable morning. On the way to her place, she thanks him for the morning's company and competition and says she hasn't enjoyed herself so much on the course for a long time.

'In fact,' she says, 'I'd like you to pull over so I can show you how much I appreciated everything.' He pulls over, they kiss and she ends up giving him a blowjob.

The next morning the man spies her at the first tee and suggests they play together again. He's actually quite competitive and slightly peeved that she beat him the previous day. Again they have a magnificent day, enjoying each other's company and playing a tight round of golf.

Again she pips him at the last and again he drives her home and once again she goes down on him in appreciation.

This goes on all week, with her beating him narrowly every day. This is a sore point for his male ego, but nevertheless in the car home on the Friday he tells her that he has had such a fine week that he has a surprise planned. Dinner for two at a candle-lit restaurant followed by a night of passion in the penthouse apartment of a city hotel.

Surprisingly, she bursts into tears and says she can't agree to this. He can't work out what the fuss is about but eventually she admits the truth.

'You see,' she says, 'I'm a transvestite.'

He is aghast. He swerves violently off the road, pulls the car to a screeching halt and curses madly, overcome with emotion.

'I'm sorry,' she says.

'You bastard!' he screams. 'You cheating bastard, you've been playing off the ladies tees all f***ing week!'

ROTT TILL YOU DROP >>>

Two boys are playing with a rugby ball on the street outside Eden Park in Auckland, when one is attacked by a vicious Rottweiler. Thinking quickly, the other boy takes a stick and manages to wedge it down the dog's collar and twist, luckily breaking the dog's neck and stopping its attack.

A reporter who was strolling by sees the incident and rushes over to interview the boy.

'Young Auckland Fan Saves Friend From Vicious Animal,' he starts writing in his notebook.

'But I'm not an Auckland fan,' the little hero replies.

'Sorry, since we are in Auckland, I just assumed you were,' says the reporter and starts again. 'All Black Fan Rescues Friend from Horrific Attack,' he continues writing in his notebook.

'I'm not an All Black fan either!' the boy says.

'I assumed everyone in Auckland was either for Auckland or the All Blacks. So what team DO you support?' the reporter asks.

'I'm a Wallaby fan!' the child beams.

The reporter starts a new sheet in his notebook and writes, 'Little Bastard from Australia Kills Beloved Family Pet.'

 ## SPEECH IMPEDIMENT >>>

A dwarf with a lisp goes into a stud farm. 'I'd like to buy a horth,' he says to the owner of the farm

'What sort of horse?' says the owner.

'A female horth,' the dwarf replies.

So the owner shows him a mare.

'Nithe horth,' says the dwarf, 'can I thee her eyth?'

So the owner picks up the dwarf to show him the horse's eyes.

'Nith eyth,' says the dwarf, 'can I thee her teeth?'

Again the owner picks up the dwarf to show him the horse's teeth. 'Nith teeth, can I see her eerth,' and again the owner picks up the dwarf to show him the horse's ears.

'Nith eerth,' he says 'now can I see her twot?'

With this the owner picks the dwarf up and shoves his head deep inside the horse's private parts, holds him there for a second before pulling him out and putting him down.

The dwarf shakes his head and says, 'Perhaps I should wefwaze that. Can I see her wun wound?'

 ## CRUSADER'S BLUES! >>>

A family of Auckland Blues rugby supporters head out shopping one Saturday before Christmas. While in a sports shop, the son picks up

a Canterbury Crusaders rugby jersey and says to his sister, 'I've decided I'm going to be a Crusaders supporter and I'd like this jersey for Christmas!'

The sister is outraged at this, promptly whacks him round the head and says, 'There is no way I'm going to buy a Crusaders jersey for you. Go talk to your mother.'

Off goes the little lad, with Crusaders jersey in hand, and finds his mother. 'Mum.'

'Yes, son?'

'I've decided I'm going to be a Crusaders supporter and I'd like this jersey for Christmas.'

The mother is outraged at this, promptly whacks him round the head and says, 'Go talk to your father.'

Off he goes, with the Crusaders jersey in hand, and finds his father. 'Dad.'

'Yes, son?'

'I've decided I'm going to be a Crusaders supporter and I would like this jersey for Christmas.'

The father is outraged at this, promptly whacks his son round the head and says, 'No son of mine is ever going to be seen in THAT!'

About half an hour later, they are all back in the car heading home. The father turns to the son and says, 'Son, I hope you've learned an important lesson today?'

The son turns to his father and says, 'Yes, Dad, I have.'

The father says, 'Good son, and what is it?'

The son replies, 'I've only been a Crusaders supporter for an hour and already I hate you Auckland bastards.'

 SWISS MIST >>>

Ernesto Bertarelli, the money-man behind *Alinghi*, the victorious Swiss boat in the America's Cup, has announced the entrance of his new team into the forthcoming Rugby World Cup.

'I have been interested in rugby ever since my childhood,' the Swiss billionaire stated. 'As a child I slept with a rugby ball in my cot, and trained on the greatest rugby fields in Switzerland. I want to follow my interest by entering the Swiss rugby team in the Cup this year.'

Bertarelli's announcement was embraced by the Swiss president, who stated, 'Switzerland has a long and proud rugby history. I think that we can teach the world about tolerance and optimism in rugby instead of the nationalism and backbiting that exists now in the Antipodes.' He added, 'Gaining the Rugby World Cup will be a great achievement for the Swiss nation and show the world our true sporting prowess.'

The Alinghi team has welcomed 27 new immigrants to their rugby team from New Zealand recently. Jonah Lomu, the latest Swiss citizen, was rumoured to be heavily reimbursed for his switch to Alinghi. Lomu evasively answered the question on money saying only 'They gave me MTV.'

Andrew Mehrtens was happy captaining his new team. 'I feel that us Swiss will be able to match any team in the world and bring out the strong Swiss heritage we all possess,' Mehrtens stated. It is rumoured that Mehrtens has been given Liechtenstein as payment for his efforts.

Tana Umaga agreed with his captain. 'As Swiss citizens we are proud of our rugby and we are not just in it for the money,' he added. 'We are honourable professionals just trying to further our sport.'

Ernesto Bertarelli stated that upon winning the World Cup they would be happy to host the next Cup in Switzerland. 'As the new holders we can raise the Cup to new levels of professionalism and integrity, and really make some money out of it.'

A poll of Swiss citizens underscored the enthusiasm of the average Swiss for the team. 'I am looking forward very much to seeing the next World Cup,' Mr Schwartzneger said. 'Ve have been underrated for too long, now we can take our true place in the tennis world.'

Other people interviewed believed rugby to be a new fashion shop or fast food. 'Vatever it is, we are happy to buy it,' stated Mrs Bicknekkle. 'Ve love shiny cups, and have bought a lot of them recently.'

The team members have been released to the media with many familiar players making up their imported side. Players touring include: Christian Von Cullen, Markus Robinssen, Benji Blair, Keith Lowenbrau, Johan Lomustein, Carlos Spencerini, Doug Howlettenbrau, Andrew Von Mehrtenssen, Tana Umatterhorn, Danni Leeberstraum, Regan Skiing, Stephan Devine, Pauli Steinmetz, Taine Randelloosi, Ali Villiams, Sam Broomschtickenhall, Kees

Meeuwsenfarter, Marti Yodel-Holah, Tony Voodcocke, Joe De McDonnelle, Rodni So'oiyodel'ee'oo, Karl Haymanstrasse, Daniel Braidenhorst, Keithe Robinssen, Keven Mealamunchen, Bradley Mika-Hakkinen, Andreu Horemunger.

The team is coached by the former World Cup captain Bukke Schellfforde.

✉ GREAT SICKIE SCORE >>>

Negotiations between union members and their employer were at an impasse. The union denied that their workers were flagrantly abusing their contract's sick-leave provisions.

One morning at the bargaining table, the company's chief negotiator held aloft the morning edition of the newspaper, 'This man,' he announced, 'called in sick yesterday!'

There on the sports page, was a photo of the supposedly ill employee, who had just won a local golf tournament with an excellent score.

The silence in the room was broken by a union negotiator. 'Wow,' he said. 'Just think of what kind of score he could have had if he hadn't been sick!'

✉ HURRICANES' WIND OF CHANGE >>>

Super 12 team the Hurricanes had a meeting, and decided that they desperately needed some new talent in the side. So they set up a big budget and asked their scouts to search every corner of the Earth for fresh and particularly gifted players.

Off they went on a tour of the world, visiting every country possible, finding quite good and quite talented players everywhere they went, but nothing really quite so special that they thought would make any difference to the team.

After some time, and running out of places to look, they started going through the most under-developed and war-torn countries in the world. Whilst walking the streets of Kabul in Afghanistan, and being just about ready to give up, they stopped and watched a group of young lads playing a form of rugby with a ball made of rags, and noticed one youngster who was an absolute demon! He ran rings around the other kids, scored tries galore, side-stepped, kicked goals from anywhere, had ball tricks — the lot. This guy was amazing, and the scouts couldn't believe their eyes.

After watching for some time, they spoke to him, struck a deal, and as soon as they could, had him moving over to play for the Hurricanes. Before long, he had his first match, and sure enough, he was just as good as when they had seen him in Afghanistan.

The Crusaders stood little chance, and hardly touched the ball as he more or less won the game single-handedly.

After the final whistle, the team lifted him in the air, while the crowd at the Cake Tin sang his praises, and he was awarded man-of-the-match. It was the greatest day of his entire life.

While the rest of the team celebrated the highest-scoring game in their history, the only thing he wanted to do was ring his mum and give her the great news. 'Oh Mum, you wouldn't believe it — they absolutely love me! I'm doing so well, Mum — you're going to be so proud of me! I've scored 12 tries in my first match, they're going to pay me loads of money, and I'm so happy! How are things at home?'

Suddenly his mum bursts into tears down the phone. 'What's the matter, Mum?' he asks.

She says, 'I've got some terrible news for you son — your dad was shot dead in the street this morning.'

'Oh, no, that's terrible!' he said.

His mum continued, 'And then I got the news that your sister was gang-raped in the park last night!'

On hearing this, all the excitement of the day was forgotten. 'Oh, Mum, I can't believe it — this is devastating,' he sobbed.

'Then just before you called, I got the news that your brother has been attacked by a bunch of wild dogs roaming the area, and is critically ill.'

'Oh Mum, what can I say — I'm so sorry to hear this!'

'Sorry?' she screamed, 'SORRY? It's your fault we moved to Lower Hutt in the first place!'

✉ CLOSE SHAVE FOR WIREMU >>>

Wiremu, a New Zealander, was in the UK to watch the All Blacks and was not feeling well, so he decided to see a doctor.

'Hey doc, I dun't feel so good, eh,' said Wiremu. The doctor gave him a thorough examination and informed him that he had long-existing and advanced prostate problems and that the only cure was testicular removal.

'No way, Doc,' replied Wiremu. 'I'm gitting a sicond opinion, eh!'

The second pommie doctor gave Wiremu the same diagnosis and also advised him that testicular removal was the only cure.

Not surprisingly, Wiremu refused the treatment. He was devastated, but with only hours to go before the All Blacks' opening game, he found an expat Kiwi doctor and decided to get one last opinion from someone he could trust.

The Kiwi doctor examined him and said, 'Wiremu, you huv prostate suckness, eh.'

'What's the cure thin, Doc, eh?' asked Wiremu, hoping for a different answer.

'Wull, Wiremu,' said the Kiwi doctor. 'We're gonna huv to cut off your balls.'

'Phew, thunk god for thut!' said Wiremu. 'Those pommie bastards wanted to take my test tickets off me!'

✉ LEPRECHAUN DOES THE BUSINESS >>>

One fine day in Ireland, a guy is out golfing and gets up to the sixteenth hole. He tees up and cranks one. Unfortunately, it goes into the woods on the side of the fairway. He goes looking for his ball and comes across this little guy with this huge lump on his head and the golf ball lying right beside him.

'Goodness,' says the golfer, then proceeds to revive the poor little guy.

Upon awakening, the little guy says, 'Well, you caught me fair and square. I am a leprechaun. I will grant you three wishes.'

The man says, 'I can't take anything from you, I'm just glad I didn't hurt you too badly.' And walks away.

Watching the golfer depart, the leprechaun says to himself, 'Well, he was a nice enough guy, and he did catch me, so I have to do something for him. I'll give him the three things that I would want. I'll give him unlimited money, a great golf game, and a great sex life.'

Well, a year goes past and the same golfer is out playing on the same course at the sixteenth hole. He gets up and hits one into the same woods and goes off looking for his ball. When he finds the ball he sees the same little guy and asks how he is doing.

The leprechaun says, 'I'm fine, and might I ask how's your golf game?'

The golfer says, 'It's great! I hit under par every time.'

'I did that for you,' responds the leprechaun, 'and might I ask how your money is holding out?'

'Well, now that you mention it, every time I put my hand in my pocket, I pull out a $100 bill,' he replies.

The leprechaun smiles and says, 'I did that for you. And might I ask how is your sex life?'

Now the golfer looks at him a little shyly and says, 'Well, maybe once or twice a week.'

Floored, the leprechaun stammers, 'Once or twice a week?'

The golfer looks at him sheepishly and says, 'Well, that's not too bad for a Catholic priest in a small parish.'

blondes

cop it

It's rough being a blonde. For some reason the blonde female, almost exclusively, comes in for a hell of a lot of crap. You may notice, you purveyors of e-mail joke books, that the 'Blondes' chapter this time is smaller than in past years.

Perhaps the 'blonde joke' is at last exhausted, or maybe blondes are no longer seen as being all that dizzy. Maybe they'll start on redheads next — Pauline Hanson alone is worth a few laughs — so, as she attempts to make the New South Wales parliament, expect some decent ones from the Aussie wags.

PUZZLED EXPRESSION >>>

A barman is sitting behind the bar on a typical day, when the door bursts open and in come four exuberant blondes. They come up to the bar, order five bottles of champagne and 10 glasses, take their order over and sit down at a large table. The corks are popped, the glasses are filled, and they begin toasting and chanting, '51 days, 51 days, 51 days!'

Soon, three more blondes arrive, take up their drinks and the chanting grows. '51 days, 51 days, 51 days!'

Two more blondes show up and soon their voices are joined in raising the roof. '51 days, 51 days, 51 days!'

Finally, the tenth blonde comes in with a picture under her arm. She walks over to the table, sets the picture in the middle and the table erupts. Up jump the others, they begin dancing around the table, exchanging high-fives, all the while chanting, '51 days, 51 days, 51 days!'

The barman can't contain his curiosity any longer, so he walks over to the table. There in the centre is a beautifully framed child's jigsaw puzzle of the Cookie Monster.

When the frenzy dies down a little bit, the barman asks one of the blondes, 'What's all the chanting and celebration about?'

The blonde who brought in the picture pipes up, 'Everyone thinks that blondes are dumb and they make fun of us. So, we decided to set the record straight. Ten of us got together, bought that puzzle and put it together … the side of the box said two to four years, but we put it together in 51 days!'

PHEW, THAT WAS CLOSE! >>>

Three girls, who all worked in the same office, noticed the boss left work early. One day the girls decided that, when the boss left, they would leave right behind her. After all, she never called or came back to work, so how would she know they went home early?

The brunette was thrilled to be home early. She did a little gardening, spent time playing with her son, and went to bed early.

The redhead was elated to be able to get in a quick workout at the spa before meeting a dinner date.

The blonde was happy to get home early and surprise her

husband, but when she got to her bedroom, she heard a muffled noise from inside.

Slowly and quietly, she cracked open the door and was mortified to see her husband in bed with her lady boss! Gently she closed the door and crept out of her house.

The next day, at their coffee break, the brunette and redhead planned to leave early again, and they asked the blonde if she was going to go with them.

'No way,' the blonde exclaimed. 'I almost got caught yesterday.'

 ## GOTTO LOTTO BOTTLE >>>

A blonde finds herself in serious trouble. Her business has gone bust and she's in dire financial straits. She's so desperate that she decides to ask God for help. She begins to pray: 'God, please help me. I've lost my business and if I don't get some money, I'm going to lose my house as well, please let me win Lotto.'

Lotto night comes, and somebody else wins it. She again prays, 'God, please let me win the Lotto! I've lost my business, my house and I'm going to lose my car as well.'

Lotto night comes and she still has no luck.

Once again, she prays, 'My God, why have you forsaken me? I've lost my business, my house, and my car. My children are starving. I don't often ask you for help, and I have always been a good servant to you. PLEASE let me win the Lotto just this once so I can get my life back in order.'

Suddenly there is a blinding flash of light as the heavens open. The blonde is overwhelmed by the voice of God himself, saying, 'Sweetheart, work with me on this — buy a ticket.'

 ## DENTS OR DENSE >>>

A blonde is driving home and she gets caught in a really bad hailstorm. The hailstones are as big as tennis balls and she ends up with her car covered with large dents. So the next day she takes her car to the panelbeater.

The panelbeater, seeing she is blonde, decides to have a little fun. He tells her just to go home and blow into the exhaust pipe, really hard, and all the dents will just pop out.

The blonde drives home, gets out of the car, gets down on her hands and knees and starts blowing into the exhaust pipe. Nothing happens. So she blows a little harder, and still nothing happens.

Meanwhile, her flatmate, also a blonde, comes home and asks, 'What in the world are you doing?'

The blonde car-owner tells her how the repairman had instructed her to blow into the exhaust pipe in order to get all the hail dents to pop out.

Her blonde flatmate rolls her eyes and says, 'Hell-oooo! Don't you think you should roll up the windows first!'

✉ SEE YOU LATER ALLIGATOR >>>

A young blonde was on holiday in the depths of Louisiana. She wanted a pair of genuine alligator shoes, but was very reluctant to pay the high prices the vendors were asking.

After becoming very frustrated with the 'no haggle' attitude of one of the shopkeepers, the blonde shouted, 'Maybe I'll just go out and catch me my own alligator so I can get a pair of shoes at a reasonable price!'

The shopkeeper said, 'By all means, be my guest. Maybe you'll get lucky and catch a big one!' Determined, the blonde turned and headed for the swamps, set on catching herself an alligator.

Later in the day, the shopkeeper was driving home when he saw the young blonde waist-deep in water, shotgun in hand. Just then, he sees a huge three-metre alligator swimming quickly towards her. She takes aim, kills the creature and with a great deal of effort hauls it onto the swamp bank.

Lying nearby were several more of the dead creatures. The shopkeeper watches in amazement. Just then, the blonde flips the alligator on its back and, frustrated, shouts out, 'Damn it, this one isn't wearing any shoes either!'

✉ DOWN IN THE VALLEYS >>>

Two tourists were driving through Wales. As they were approaching Llanfairpwllgwngyllgogerychwyrndrobwllllantysiliogogogoch, they started arguing about the pronunciation of the town's name.

They argued back and forth until they stopped for lunch in the village. As they stood at the counter, one tourist asked the blonde employee, 'Before we order, could you please settle an argument for us? Would you please pronounce where we are … very slowly?'

The blonde leaned over the counter and said, 'Burrrrrrr, gerrrrrr, Kiiiiiing.'

BLONDE'S CIGGIE BREAK >>>

A blonde is talking to her friends when one of them asks her why she has a tampon behind her ear?

The blonde says, 'Shit! Then where did I put my cigarette?'

VIRUS ALERT >>>

If you receive an e-mail entitled 'Bedtimes', delete it IMMEDIATELY. Do not open it. Apparently this one is pretty nasty. It will not only erase everything on your hard drive, but it will also delete anything on floppy disks within six metres of your computer.

It demagnetises the strips on all your credit cards. It reprogrammes your ATM access code, screws up the tracking on your VCR, and uses subspace field harmonics to scratch any CDs you attempt to play. It will programme the auto dial on your phone so that you can call only 0900 numbers. This virus will also mix antifreeze with water in your fish tank.

It will cause your toilet to flush while you are showering. It will drink ALL your beer.

FOR GOD'S SAKE, ARE YOU LISTENING?

It will leave dirty underwear on the coffee table when you are expecting company. It will replace your shampoo with Nair and your Nair with Rogaine.

If the 'Bedtimes' message is opened in a Windows 95 or 98 environment, it will leave the toilet seat up and leave your hairdryer plugged in dangerously close to a bath filled with water. It will not only remove the forbidden tags from your mattresses and pillows, it will also refill your skim milk with whole milk.

WARN AS MANY PEOPLE AS YOU CAN.

If you don't send this to 5000 people in 20 seconds, you'll fart so hard that your right leg will spasm and shoot straight out in front of you, sending sparks that will ignite the person nearest you.

Send this to everyone you know.

If you are blonde, this is a joke!

 ## MAILBOX MIX-UP >>>

A man was in his front garden mowing grass when his attractive blonde female neighbour came out of her house and went straight to her letterbox. She opened it then slammed it shut and stormed back inside the house.

A little later she came out of her house again, went to the letterbox and again opened it and slammed it shut. Angrily, back into the house she went.

As the man was getting ready to edge the lawn, she came out again, marched to the letterbox, opened it and then slammed it closed harder than ever.

Puzzled by her actions the man asked her, 'Is something wrong?'

To which she replied, 'There certainly is. My stupid computer keeps saying, "You've got mail".'

WOMAN FROM MIDDLE EARTH >>>

A married couple were asleep when the phone rang at two in the morning. The wife, a blonde, picked up the phone, listened a moment and said, 'How should I know, that's 200km from here!' and hung up.

The husband said, 'Who was that?'

The wife said, 'I don't know; some woman wanting to know if the coast is clear.'

 ## MIRROR, MIRROR >>>

Two blondes are walking down the street. One notices a compact on the footpath and leans down to pick it up. She opens it, looks in the mirror and says, 'Hmm, this person looks familiar.'

The second blonde says, 'Here, let me see!' So the first blonde hands her the compact.

The second one looks in the mirror and says, 'You dummy, it's me!'

CHEATS NEVER PROSPER >>>

A blonde suspects her boyfriend of cheating on her, so she goes out and buys a gun. She goes to his apartment unexpectedly and when she opens the door she finds him in the arms of a redhead.

Well, the blonde is really angry. She opens her purse to take out the gun, and as she does so, she is overcome with grief. She takes the gun and puts it to her head.

The boyfriend yells, 'No, honey, don't do it.'

The blonde replies, 'Shut up, you're next!'

A BRAINY ONE >>>

An Australian blonde is bragging about her knowledge of state capitals. She proudly says, 'Go ahead, ask me, I know all of them.'

A friend says, 'OK, what's the capital of NSW?'

The blonde replies, 'Oh, that's easy, "N".'

ARE YOU SURE? >>>

What did the blonde ask her doctor when he told her she was pregnant?

'Is it mine?'

TREE-MENDOUS >>>

A blonde had just totalled her car in a horrific accident. Miraculously, she managed to pry herself from the wreckage without a scratch and was applying fresh lipstick when a cop arrived.

'My God!' the cop exclaimed. 'Your car looks like an accordion that was stomped on by an elephant. Are you OK?'

'Yes, officer, I'm just fine,' the blonde chirped.

'Well, how in the world did this happen?' the officer asked as he surveyed the wrecked car.

'Officer, it was the strangest thing!' the blonde began. 'I was driving along this road when from out of nowhere this tree pops up in front of me. So I swerved to the right, and there was another tree! I swerved to the left and there was another tree! I swerved to the right and there was another tree! I swerved to the left and there was …'

'But,' the officer said, cutting her off, 'there isn't a tree on this road for 50 kilometres. That was your air freshener swinging back and forth.'

✉ BLONDE TRAVELLING SALESWOMAN >>>

A blonde travelling saleswoman is talking to her psychologist complaining about business.

'You know I am on the road a lot and my clients are complaining that they can never reach me.'

'Don't you have a phone in your car?'

'That was too expensive, so I did the next best thing. I put a letterbox in my car.'

'Mm, and how does that work?'

'Well, I haven't got any mail yet.'

'And why do you think that is?'

The blonde says, 'Well, I suppose that when I'm travelling around like I do, my postcode keeps changing.'

the

boozers

> Alcohol is dear to many of our hearts, as it is to the subjects populating this chapter. Thankfully, gone are the days of six o'clock closing that afflicted New Zealand until 1967. Now we can enjoy a drink at our leisure and feel dreadfully sorry for the soaks of our parents' generation who knocked off work at 5pm and had an hour's drinking before the last bus, train or ferry got you home.

> Many's a tale of the drinker taking just too long to drain that last jug, running down the wharf to catch that last ferry to Devonport and his dinner on the table on the dot of 6.30, making a jump for the rapidly departing boat and landing in the dirty harbour. Try explaining that to the fifties wifey with the burnt sausages?

> Of course, the British had terrible drinking hours until the early nineties, thanks to those Carlisle munitions workers getting on the plonk too much when making bombs in 1915.
> Thankfully, the powers that be realise we are all grown up now, and can be trusted to know when we've had too much... well, most of us, anyway.

✉ DEAR ALCOHOL >>>

I thought I'd take a minute to discuss some troubling factors with you. First and foremost, let me tell you that I'm a huge fan of yours … your many sides and dimensions are mind-boggling (different than beer-goggling, which I'll touch upon shortly).

Yes, my friend, you always seem to be there when needed, the perfect post-work cocktail, a beer with the game, a stress-reliever at lunchtime … and you're even around in the holidays, hidden inside chocolates, you warm us when we're stuck in the midst of endless family gatherings. Yet lately, I've been wondering about your intentions.

You see, I want to believe that you have my best interests at heart, but I feel that your influence has led to unwise consequences, briefed below for your review:

1. Phone calls. While I agree with you that communication is important, I question the suggestion that any conversation of substance or necessity occurs at 5am.
2. Eating. Now, you know I love a good meal and, although cooking is far from my speciality, why you suggested that I eat a kebab with chilli sauce coupled with a pot noodle and some stale crisps (washed down with chocolate Nesquik and topped off with a Kit Kat) is beyond me. Eclectic eater I am, but I

think you went a bit too far this time.

3. Clumsiness. Unless you're subtly trying to tell me I need to do yoga to increase my balance, I see NO need to hammer the issue home by causing me to fall down the stairs. Completely unnecessary. Similarly, it should never take me more than 30 seconds to get the front-door key into the lock.

4. Photos. This is a blessing in disguise, as it can often clarify the last point below, but the following costumes are henceforth banned from being placed on my head in public: Indian wigs, sombreros, bow-ties, boxers, upside-down cups, balloon animals, traffic cones, bras.

5. Beer goggles. If I think I may know him/her from somewhere, I most likely do not. PLEASE do not request that I go over and see if in fact, I do actually know that person. This is similar to the old 'Hey, you're in my class' syndrome circa 1996 and should henceforth be rendered illegal.

6. Coupled with this is the phrase 'Let's shag'. While I may be thinking this, please reinstate the brain-to-mouth block that would keep this thought from being a statement, especially in public and when the person in question is as ugly as sin.

7. Further, the subsequent hangovers have GOT to stop. Now, I know a little penance for our previous evening's debauchery may be in order, but the 2pm hangover immobility whilst bleeding to death through the eyes is completely unacceptable. I ask that if the proper steps are proactively taken on my part (i.e. water, vitamin B, bread products, aspirin) prior to going to bed/passing out face-down on the kitchen floor with a bag of popcorn, the hangover should be quite minimal and in no way interfere with my daily Saturday or Sunday — or any day, for that matter — activities. Come on now, it's only fair — you do your part, I'll do mine.

Alcohol, I have enjoyed our relationship for some years now, and want to ensure that we remain on good terms. You've been the invoker of great stories, the provocation of much laughter, and the needed companion when we just don't know what to do with the extra money in our pockets. In order to continue this relationship, I ask that you carefully review my grievances above and address them immediately.

I will look for an answer no later than Thursday at 5pm (pre-

Happy Hour) on your possible solutions and hopefully we can continue this fruitful partnership. Thank you for your prompt attention to these matters.

Sincerely,
Your Biggest Fan

✉ ALCOHOL — AN INTELLECTUAL DISCUSSION >>>

Norm and Cliff are sitting at the bar and discussing alcohol, and beer in particular. Cliff has a theory he calls the Buffalo Theory …
'Well, you see, Norm, it's like this … a herd of buffalo can only move as fast as the slowest buffalo. And when the herd is hunted, it is the slowest and weakest ones at the back that are killed first. This natural selection is good for the herd as a whole, because the general speed and health of the whole group keeps improving by the regular killing of the weakest member.

'In much the same way, the human brain can only operate as fast as the slowest brain cells. Now, as we know, excessive intake of alcohol kills brain cells. But naturally, it attacks the slowest and weakest brain cells first. In this way, regular consumption of beer eliminates the weaker brain cells, making the brain a faster and more efficient machine. And that, Norm, that is why you always feel smarter after a few beers.'

Well, if you put it like that …

✉ LOST BAGGAGE >>>

An Irishman, who had a little too much to drink, is driving home from the city one night and, of course, his car is weaving violently all over the road.

A cop pulls him over. 'So,' says the cop to the driver, 'where have ya been?'

'Why, I've been to the pub, of course,' slurs the drunk.

'Well,' says the cop, 'it looks like you've had quite a few to drink this evening.'

'I did all right,' the drunk says with a smile.

'Did you know,' says the cop, standing straight and folding his arms across his chest, 'that a few intersections back, your wife fell out of your car?'

'Oh, thank heavens,' sighs the drunk. 'For a minute there, I thought I'd gone deaf.'

 SPEECH IMPREDIMENT >>>

Things that are difficult to say when you're drunk:
- Indubitably
- Innovative
- Preliminary
- Proliferation
- Cinnamon

Things that are very difficult to say when you're drunk:
- Specificity
- British Constitution
- Passive-aggressive disorder
- Loquacious Transubstantiate

Things that are downright impossible to say when you're drunk:
- Thanks, but I don't want to have sex.
- Nope, no more booze for me.
- Sorry, but you're not really my type.
- Good evening officer, isn't it lovely out tonight?
- Oh, I just couldn't. No one wants to hear me sing.

CAUGHT SHORT >>>

A drunk staggers into a Catholic church, enters a confessional booth, sits down but says nothing. The priest coughs a few times to get his attention but the drunk just sits there. Finally, the priest pounds three times on the wall.

The drunk mumbles, 'It's no use knockin', there's no paper on this side either.'

(the boozers)

Police are warning all male clubbers, partygoers and unsuspecting pub regulars to be more alert and cautious when getting a drink offer from a woman. There is a date-rape drug going around called 'beer' and it is generally in liquid form. The drug is now being used by female sexual predators at parties to convince their male victims to have sex with them.

The shocking statistic is that 'beer' is available virtually anywhere! All girls have to do is persuade a guy to consume a few units of 'beer' and simply ask the guy home for no-strings-attached sex. Men are literally rendered helpless against such attacks. After several 'beers' men will often succumb to desires to perform sex acts on horrific-looking women whom they would never normally be attracted to.

Men often awaken after being given 'beer' with only hazy memories of exactly what has happened to them the night before, just a vague feeling that something bad has occurred. At other times these unfortunate men might be stung for their life's worth in a familiar scam known as 'a relationship'. Apparently men are easier victims for this scam after the 'beer' has been administered and they have already been sexually attacked.

If you should fall victim to this insidious drug and the predatory women administering it, there are male support groups with venues in every town where you can discuss the details of your shocking encounter in an open and frank manner with a bunch of similarly affected, like-minded guys.

For the nearest support group, look up 'Hotels & Taverns' in the Yellow Pages.

✉ WOOLIES' BLADDER >>>

Brenda O'Malley is home making dinner, as usual, when Tim Finnegan arrives at her door. 'Brenda, may I come in?' he asks. 'I've somethin' to tell ya.'

'Of course you can come in; you're always welcome, Tim. But where's my husband?'

'That's what I'm here to be tellin' ya, Brenda. There was an accident down at the Guinness Brewery …'

'Oh, God no!' cries Brenda. 'Please don't tell me …'

'I must, Brenda. Your husband Seamus is dead and gone. I'm sorry.'

Finally, she looks up at Tim. 'How did it happen, Tim?' she asks.

'It was terrible, Brenda. He fell into a vat of Guinness Stout and drowned.'

'Oh my dear Jesus! But you must tell me true, Tim. Did he at least go quickly?'

'Well, no Brenda … no. Fact is, he got out three times to pee.'

 MORAL OF THE STORY >>>

The teacher gave her class an assignment. The children had to get their parents to tell them a story with a moral in it.

The next day, Kathy said, 'My father's a farmer, and we have a lot of egg-laying hens. One time we were taking eggs to market in a box on the front seat of the truck, when we hit a bump and a lot of them broke and made a mess.'

'So, what's the moral of the story?' asked the teacher.

'Don't put all your eggs in one basket.'

Another child, Lucy, told her story. 'Our family are farmers too. But we raise chickens for the meat market. We had 16 eggs one time, but when they hatched, we only got 10 live chicks. And the moral to this story is: Don't count your chickens until they hatch.'

'That was fine,' said the teacher. 'Now, Johnny, do you have a story too?'

'Yes. My daddy told me about my Aunt Karen. She was a flight engineer in Desert Storm in Iraq, and her plane got hit. She had to bail out over enemy territory. All she had was a bottle of whisky, a machine gun, and a machete. She drank the whisky on the way down so the bottle wouldn't break. Then she landed in the middle of 100 enemy troops. She killed 70 with the machine gun until she ran out of bullets. She hacked 20 more with the machete until the blade broke. And she killed the last 10 with her bare hands.'

'Good heavens!' exclaimed the horrified teacher. 'What kind of moral did your daddy tell you was in this terrible story?'

'Don't mess with Aunt Karen when she's been drinking.'

✉ A SMALL PROBLEM >>>

Two dwarfs go into a bar, get drunk and pick up two prostitutes. They take them to their separate hotel rooms. The first dwarf, however, is unable to get an erection.

His depression is made worse by the fact that, from the next room, he hears his little friend shouting out cries of 'Here I come again ... ONE, TWO, THREE ... UUH!' all night long.

In the morning, the second dwarf asks the first, 'How did it go?'

The first mutters, 'It was so embarrassing. I simply couldn't get an erection.'

The second dwarf shook his head. 'You think that's embarrassing? I couldn't even get on the bed ...'

✉ SAUSAGE MEAT! >>>

Mick and Pat fancied a pint or two but didn't have a lot of money. Altogether they had a staggering 50 cents between them.

Mick said, 'Hang on, I've got an idea.' He went next door to the butcher's shop and came out with one large sausage.

Pat: 'Are you crazy? Now we haven't got any money left at all.'

Mick: 'Don't worry, just follow me.' They went into the next pub, where he immediately ordered two pints and two large vodka and tonics.

Pat: 'Now you have lost it! Do you know how much trouble we will be in? We haven't got any money!'

Mick: 'Don't worry, I've got a plan. Cheers.' So they had their drinks.

Mick: 'OK, I will now stick the sausage through my zip and you'll go on your knees and put it in your mouth.

Said and done. The landlord noticed it, went berserk and threw them out.

They continued this, pub after pub after pub after pub, getting more and more drunk — all free.

At the tenth pub Pat said, 'Mate, I don't think I can continue this any longer. I'm pissed and my knees are killing me!'

Mick: 'How do you think I feel? I lost the sausage in the third pub.'

✉ FLAPPING ABOUT >>>

The Reverend John Flapps was the pastor of a small town. One day he was walking down the High Street when he noticed a young lady of his congregation sitting in a pub drinking beer. The reverend wasn't happy. He walked through the open door of the pub and sat down next to the woman. 'Miss Fitzgerald,' he said sternly, 'this is no place for a member of my congregation. Why don't you let me take you home?'

'Sure,' she said with a slur, obviously very drunk. When Miss Fitzgerald stood up from the bar, she began to weave back and forth.

The reverend realised that she'd had far too much to drink and grabbed her arms to steady her. When he did, they both lost their balance and tumbled to the floor. After rolling around for a few moments, the reverend wound up on top of Miss Fitzgerald, her skirt hiked up to her waist.

The pub landlord looked over and said, 'Oi, mate, we won't have any of that carry-on in this pub.'

The reverend looked up at the landlord and said, 'But you don't understand, I'm Pastor Flapps.'

The landlord nodded and said, 'Oh well, if you're that far in, you might as well finish.'

✉ THE SOUTHERN MAN >>>

A bloke from Dunedin buys a round of drinks (Speight's, of course) for all in the bar because, he announces, his wife has just produced a typical Dunedin baby boy weighing 25 pounds.

Congratulations shower him from all around, and many exclamations of 'WOW!' are heard. A woman faints due to sympathy pains.

Two weeks later, the man returns to the bar. The barman says, 'Say, you're the father of the typical Dunedin baby that weighed 25 pounds at birth. How much does he weigh now?'

The proud father answers, '17 pounds.'

The barman is puzzled, 'Why? What happened? He already weighed 25 pounds at birth.'

The father takes a slow swig from his Speight's beer, wipes his lips on his shirt sleeve, leans towards the barman and proudly says, 'Had him circumcised.'

The barman says, in true southern fashion, 'Good on ya mate!'

✉ GOOD CRAIK >>>

An Irishman, an Englishman and a Scotsman were sitting in a bar in Sydney. The view was fantastic, the beer excellent and the food exceptional.

'But,' said the Scotsman, 'I still prefer the pubs back home. In Glasgow there's a little bar called McTavish's. Now the landlord there goes out of his way for the locals, so much so that when you buy four drinks he will buy the fifth drink for you.'

'Well,' said the Englishman, 'at my local, the Red Lion, the barman there will buy you your third drink after you buy the first two.'

'Ahhh that's nothing,' said the Irishman. 'Back home in Dublin there's Ryan's Bar. Now the moment you set foot in the place they'll buy you a drink, then another, all the drinks you like. Then when you've had enough drinks they'll take you upstairs and see that you get laid. All on the house.'

The Englishman and Scotsman immediately pour scorn on the Irishman's claims, but he swears every word is true.

'Well,' said the Englishman, 'did this actually happen to you?'

'Not myself, personally, no,' said the Irishman. 'But it did happen to my sister.'

✉ MILES MORE PISSED >>>

Three Irishmen, Paddy, Sean and Seamus, were stumbling home from the pub late one night and found themselves on the road which led past the old graveyard.

'Come have a look over here,' says Paddy. 'It's Michael O'Grady's grave, God bless his soul. He lived to the ripe old age of 87.'

'That's nothing,' says Sean. 'Here's one named Patrick O'Tool. It says here that he was 95 when he died.'

Just then, Seamus yells out, 'Good God, here's a fella that got to be 145!'

'What was his name?' asks Paddy.

Seamus stumbles around a bit, awkwardly lights a match to see what else is written on the stone marker, and exclaims, 'Miles from Dublin.'

HANGOVER GRADINGS >>>

* One-star hangover

No pain. No real feeling of illness. You slept in your own bed and when you woke up there were no traffic cones in there with you. You are still able to function relatively well on the energy stored up from all those vodka Redbulls. However, you can drink 10 bottles of water and still feel as parched as the Sahara. Even vegetarians are craving a cheeseburger and a side of fries.

** Two-star hangover

No pain, but something is definitely amiss. You may look OK but you have the attention span and mental capacity of an office stapler. The coffee you hug to try and remain focused is only exacerbating your rumbling gut, which is craving a full English breakfast. Although you have a nice demeanour about the office, you are costing your employer valuable money because all you really can handle is some light filing, followed by aimlessly surfing the net and writing junk e-mails.

*** Three-star hangover

Slight headache. Stomach feels crap. You are definitely a space cadet and not so productive. Any time a girl or lad walks by you gag because her perfume/aftershave reminds you of the random gin shots you did with your alcoholic friends after the bouncer kicked you out at 1.45am. Life would be better right now if you were in your bed with a dozen doughnuts and a litre of Coke watching daytime TV. You've had four cups of coffee, four litres of water, two sausage rolls and a litre of Diet Coke but you haven't peed once.

**** Four-star hangover

You have lost the will to live. Your head is throbbing and you can't speak too quickly or else you might spew. Your boss has already lambasted you for being late and has given you a lecture for reeking of booze. You are wearing nice clothes, but you smell of socks, and you can't hide the fact that you either missed an oh-so crucial spot shaving … or it looks like you put your make-up on while riding the dodgems (depending on your gender). Your teeth have their own individual jumpers. Your eyes look like one big vein and your hairstyle makes you look like a reject from the primary school class photo circa 1956/66/76. You would give a week's pay for one of the following: home-time, a burger and somewhere to be alone or a time machine so you could go back and NOT have gone out the night before. You scare small children in the street just by walking past them.

***** Five-star hangover

You have a second heartbeat in your head, which is actually annoying the employee who sits across from you. Vodka vapour is seeping out of every pore and making you dizzy. You still have toothpaste crust in the corners of your mouth from brushing your teeth. Your body has lost the ability to generate saliva, so your tongue is suffocating you. You'd cry but that would take the last of the moisture left in your body. Death seems like a pretty good option right now. Your boss doesn't even get mad at you and your co-workers think that your dog just died because you look so pathetic. You should have called in sick because, let's face it, all you can manage to do is breathe … very gently.

****** Six-star hangover

You arrive home and climb into bed. Sleep comes instantly, as you were fighting it all the way home in the taxi. You get about two hours' sleep until the noises inside your head wake you up. You notice that your bed has been cleared for take-off and is flying relentlessly around the room. No matter what you do now, you're going to chuck. You stumble out of bed and now find that your room is a yacht under full sail. After walking along the skirting boards on alternating walls knocking off all the pictures, you find the toilet. If you are lucky you will remember to lift the lid before you spontaneously explode and wake the whole house up with your impersonation of walrus mating calls. You sit there on the floor in your undies, cuddling the only friend in the world you have left (the toilet), randomly continuing to make the walrus noises, spitting, and farting. Help usually comes at this stage, even if it is short-lived. Tears stream down your face and your abdomen hurts. Help now turns into abuse and he/she usually goes back to bed leaving you there in the dark. With your stomach totally empty, your spontaneous eruptions have died back to 15-minute intervals, but your body won't relent. You are convinced that you are starting to turn yourself inside out and swear that you saw your tonsils projectile out your mouth on the last occasion. It is now dawn and you pass your disgusted partner getting up for the day as you try to climb into bed. She/he abuses you again for trying to get into bed with lumpy bits of dried vomit in your hair. You reluctantly accept their advice and have a shower in exchange for them driving you to the hospital. Work is not an option.

 ## BLOW UP THE BAG PADDY >>>

Late one Friday in Dublin, a policeman spotted a man driving very erratically. He pulled the man over and asked him if he had been drinking that evening.

'Aye, so I have. 'Tis Friday, you know, so me and the lads stopped by the pub where we had six or seven pints of the black stuff. And then there was something called Happy Hour and they served these mar-gar-itos, which were quite good.

'And then I had to drive me friend Mike home and o' course I had to go inside for a couple of Guinesses — I couldn't be rude, ye know. Then I stopped on the way home to get another bottle for later.'

The man fumbled around in his coat until he located his bottle of whisky, which he held up for inspection.

The policeman sighed and said, 'Sir, I'm afraid I'll need you to step out of the car and take a breathalyser test.'

'Why? Don't ye believe me?'

animal

kingdom

> Animals make great subjects for jokes. For a start, they aren't going to get offended, are they? Some jokes are new takes on the old, but the new ones are a welcome change from the 'elephant-in-the-fridge' variety, that have unashamedly appeared on these pages in the earlier editions.

> Bears seem to be the favourite this time and that's fair enough, because we're sure most of us have been in close proximity to a teddy bear at some stage in our lives and they are so cuddly.

✉ BEARING UP ON THE NEXT LIFE >>>

In this life I'm a woman. In my next life, I'd like to come back as a bear. When you're a bear, you get to hibernate. You do nothing but sleep for six months. I could deal with that. Before you hibernate, you're supposed to eat yourself stupid. I could deal with that, too. When you're a girl bear, you birth your children (who are the size of walnuts) while you're sleeping, and wake to partially grown, cute cuddly cubs. I could definitely deal with that. If you're a mama bear, everyone knows you mean business. You swat anyone who bothers your cubs. If your cubs get out of line, you swat them too. I could deal with that. If you're a bear, your mate EXPECTS you to wake up growling. He EXPECTS that you will have hairy legs and excess body fat. Yup … I'm gonna be a bear!!

✉ DOGS, OUR BEST MATES >>>

Why they aren't like a member of the opposite sex:

- The later you are, the more excited they are to see you.
- Dogs will forgive you for playing with other dogs.
- If a dog is gorgeous, other dogs don't hate it.
- Dogs don't notice if you call them by another dog's name.
- A dog's disposition stays the same all month long.
- Dogs like it if you leave a lot of things on the floor.
- A dog's parents never visit.
- Dogs do not hate their bodies.
- Dogs agree you have to raise your voice to get your point across.
- Dogs do their snooping outside rather than in your wallet or desk.
- Dogs seldom outlive you.
- Dogs can't talk.
- Dogs enjoy petting in public.
- You never have to wait for a dog; they're ready to go 24 hours a day.
- Dogs find you amusing when you're drunk.
- Dogs like to go hunting.
- Another man will seldom steal your dog.

- If you bring another dog home, your dog will happily play with both of you.
- A dog will not wake you up at night to ask, 'If I died would you get another dog?'
- If you pretend to be blind, your dog can stay in your hotel room for free.
- If a dog has babies, you can put an ad in the paper and give them away.
- A dog will let you put a studded collar on it without calling you a pervert.
- A dog won't force you to get a new car.
- If a dog smells another dog on you, it doesn't get mad, it just thinks it's interesting.
- On a car trip, your dog never insists on putting on the heater.
- Dogs don't let magazine articles guide their lives.
- When your dog gets old, you can have it put to sleep.
- Dogs like to ride in the back of a pick-up truck.
- Dogs are not allowed in Myers or David Jones.
- If a dog leaves, it won't take half your stuff.

✉ NO SILVER LINING >>>

The Lone Ranger was ambushed and captured by an Indian war party. The Indian Chief proclaims, 'So, you are the great Lone Ranger. In honour of the Harvest Festival, you will be executed in three days. But, before I kill you, I will grant you three requests. What is your first request?'

'I'd like to speak to my horse,' says the Lone Ranger. The chief nods and Silver is brought before the Lone Ranger, who whispers in Silver's ear, and the horse gallops away. Later that evening, Silver returns with a beautiful blonde woman on his back.

As the Indian Chief watches, the blonde enters the Lone Ranger's tent and spends the night. The next morning the Indian Chief admits he's impressed.

'You have a very fine and loyal horse, but I will still kill you in two days. What is your second request?' The Lone Ranger again asks to speak to his horse. Silver is brought to him, and he again whispers in the horse's ear.

As before, Silver takes off across the plains and disappears over the horizon. Later that evening, to the Chief's surprise, Silver again returns, this time with a voluptuous brunette, even more attractive than the blonde. She enters the Lone Ranger's tent and spends the night.

The following morning the Indian Chief again says he is impressed. 'You are indeed a man of many talents, but I will still kill you tomorrow. What is your last request?'

'I'd like to speak to my horse … alone.' The Chief is curious, but he agrees, and Silver is brought to the Lone Ranger's tent. Once they're alone, the Lone Ranger grabs Silver by both ears, looks him square in the eye and says, very slowly and loudly …

'Listen carefully now for the last time. I said 'BRING POSSE!'

 DID YOU KNOW? >>>

The average cost of rehabilitating a seal after the Exxon Valdez oil spill in Alaska was $80,000. At a special ceremony, two of the most expensively saved animals were being released back into the wild amid cheers and applause from onlookers. A minute later, in full view, a killer whale ate them both.

Two animal rights protesters were in action at the cruelty of sending pigs to a slaughterhouse in Bonn, Germany. Suddenly, all 2000 pigs broke loose and escaped through a broken fence, stampeding madly. The two hopeless protesters were trampled to death.

BREWSTER'S BIG REWARD >>>

Zebediah was in the fertilised egg business. He had several hundred young layers, called pullets, and eight or 10 roosters, whose job was to fertilise the eggs. Zeb kept records, and any rooster that didn't perform well went into the soup pot and was replaced.

That took an awful lot of Zeb's time, so he got a set of tiny bells and attached them to his roosters. Each bell had a different tone so that Zeb could tell, from a distance, which rooster was performing. Now he could sit on the porch and fill out an efficiency report simply by listening to the bells.

Zeb's favourite rooster was old Brewster. A very fine specimen he was too, but on this particular morning Zeb noticed that Brewster's bell wasn't ringing at all. Zeb went to investigate. The other roosters were chasing pullets, bells a ringin'. The pullets, hearing the roosters coming, would run for cover.

But to Zeb's amazement, Brewster had his bell in his beak so it couldn't ring. He'd sneak up on a pullet, do his job and head for another one. Zeb was so proud of Brewster he entered him in the County Fair. Brewster was a sensation. The judges not only awarded him The No Bell Piece Prize, but also The Pullet-Surprise.

✉ HARE TODAY GONE TOMORROW >>>

A man was driving along the highway and saw a hare hopping across the middle of the road. He swerved to avoid hitting the animal, but unfortunately it jumped in front of the car and was hit.

The driver, being a sensitive man as well as an animal lover, pulled over to the side of the road, and got out to see what had become of the animal. Much to his dismay, the hare was dead.

The driver felt so awful, he began to cry. A woman driving down the highway saw the man crying at the side of the road and pulled over. She stepped out of her car and asked the man what was wrong.

'I feel terrible,' he explained, 'I accidentally hit this hare and killed it.'

The woman told the man not to worry. She knew what to do. She went to her car and took out a spray can. She walked over to the limp, dead hare, and sprayed the contents of the can onto it.

Miraculously, the hare came to life, jumped up, waved its paw at the two humans and hopped down the road. Fifty metres away the hare stopped, turned around, waved and hopped down the road, another 50 metres, turned, waved and hopped another 50 metres.

The man was astonished. He couldn't figure out what substance could be in the woman's spray can! He ran over to the woman and asked, 'What is in your spray can? What did you spray on that hare?'

The woman turned the can around so that the man could read the label. It said: 'Hair spray. Restores life to dead hair. Adds permanent wave.'

GO FOR IT MAMA >>>

It's a sunny morning in the Big Forest, and the Bear family is just waking up. Baby Bear goes downstairs and sits in his small chair at the table, and looks into his small bowl. It is empty. Who's been eating my porridge?!' he squeaks.

Papa Bear arrives at the big table and sits in his big chair. He looks into his big bowl, and it is also empty. 'Who's been eating my porridge?' he roars.

Mama Bear puts her head through the serving hatch from the kitchen and yells, 'For God's sake, how many times do we have to go through this?'

'It was Mama Bear who got up first, it was Mama Bear who woke up everyone in the house, it was Mama Bear who made the coffee, it was Mama Bear who unloaded the dishwasher from last night and put everything away, it was Mama Bear who went out in the cold early morning air to fetch the newspaper, it was Mama Bear who set the table, it was Mama Bear who put the cat out, cleaned the litter box, and filled the cat's water and food dish. And now that you've decided to drag your arses downstairs and grace Mama Bear's kitchen with your grumpy presence, listen good, 'cause I'm only going to say this one more time … I HAVEN'T MADE THE DAMN PORRIDGE YET!'

BILL GATES' BEST MATE? >>>

An IT executive in Silicon Valley sees a sign in front of a house that says 'Talking Dog for Sale'. He rings the bell and the owner tells him the dog is in the backyard. The man goes into the backyard and sees a mutt sitting there. 'Are you a talking dog?' he asks.

'Yes, that's me,' the mutt replies.

'So, what's your story?'

The old hound looks up and says, 'Well, my original owner discovered my gift and auctioned me off in a private bid. I was bought by none other than Bill Gates. In no time he had me sent anonymously to each of his competitors as a present. Soon I was sitting in private meetings with Larry Ellison, Scott McNealy and other IT innovators, because no one figured a dog would be eavesdropping. After a week or so I would run away back to Bill and tell him what I heard.

I was one of his most valuable employees eight years running. I couldn't tell you how many IT innovations I am responsible for. But, the continuous 'show up on a doorstep then run away a week later' really tired me out, and I knew I wasn't getting any younger and I wanted to settle down.

So I signed up for a job at the Seattle airport to do some undercover security work, mostly wandering near suspicious characters and listening in. I uncovered some big crime syndicates … and was awarded a batch of medals. I had a wife, a lot of puppies, and now I'm just retired.'

The guy is amazed, this dog is better than a new dotcom scheme. He goes into the house and asks the owner what he wants for the dog. 'Ten bucks and he's yours,' the owner says.

'But this dog is amazing!' the guy exclaims. 'Why on Earth are you selling him and why so cheap?'

'He's such a liar,' the owner says. 'He didn't do any of that stuff.'

 ## SILLY QUESTION >>>

A camel and an elephant meet. The elephant asks the camel, 'Why do you have your breasts on your back?'

The camel, clearly irritated, replies, 'What a silly question from someone who has a dick on his face.'

 ## THE BEAR, RABBIT AND FROG >>>

One day in the great forest a magical frog was walking down to a waterhole. This forest was so big that the frog had never seen another animal in all his life. By chance, today a bear was chasing after a rabbit to have for dinner.

The frog called for the two to stop. The frog said, 'Because you are the only two animals I have seen, I will grant you both three wishes. Bear, you go first.'

The bear thought for a minute, and being the male he was, said, 'I wish for all the bears in this forest, besides me, to be female.'

For his wish, the rabbit asked for a crash helmet, and

immediately put it on. The bear was amazed at the stupidity of the rabbit, wasting his wish like that.

It was the bear's second turn for a wish: 'Well, I wish that all the bears in the next forest were female as well.'

The rabbit asked for a motorbike and immediately hopped on it and gunned the engine. The bear was shocked that the rabbit was asking for these stupid things when, after all, he could have asked for money and bought the motorbike.

For the last wish the bear thought for a while and then said, 'I wish that all the bears in the world, besides me, were female.'

The rabbit grinned, gunned the engine, and said, 'I wish that THIS bear was gay.'

✉ HOW MANY DOGS DOES IT TAKE TO CHANGE A LIGHT BULB? >>>

Afghan: Light bulb? What light bulb?

Golden retriever: The sun is shining, the day is young, we've got our whole lives ahead of us, and you're worrying about a burned-out light bulb?

Border collie: Just one. And I'll replace any wiring that's not up to date.

Dachshund: I can't reach the stupid light!

Toy poodle: What? Where? I'll get it, no you get it, no I got it! Look! The border collie did it! Look! A bug!

Rottweiler: Make me!

Shi-tzu: Puh-leeez, dahling. I have servants for that kind of thing.

Labrador: Oh, me, me! Pleeeeeeaze let me change the light bulb! Can I? Can I? Huh? Huh? Can I?

Malamute: Let the border collie do it. You can feed me while she's busy.

Cocker spaniel: Why change it? I can still pee on the carpet in the dark.

Doberman pinscher: While it's dark, I'm going to sleep on the couch.

Mastiff: Mastiffs are not afraid of the dark.

Beagle: Light bulb? Light bulb? That thing I ate was a light bulb?

A guy is browsing in a pet shop and sees a parrot sitting on a little perch. It doesn't have any feet or legs. The guy says aloud, 'Jeesh, I wonder what happened to this parrot?'

The parrot says, 'I was born this way. I'm a defective parrot.'

'Holy shit,' the guy replies. 'You actually understood and answered me.'

'I got every word,' says the parrot. 'I happen to be a highly intelligent, thoroughly educated bird.'

'Oh yeah?' the guy asks. 'Then answer this … how do you hang onto your perch without any feet?'

'Well,' the parrot says, 'this is very embarrassing but seeing as you asked … I wrap my "willie" around this wooden bar like a little hook. You can't see it because of my feathers.'

'Wow,' says the guy. 'You really can understand and speak English, can't you?'

'Actually, I speak both Spanish and English and I can converse with reasonable competence on almost any topic: politics, religion, sports, physics, philosophy. I'm especially good at ornithology. You really ought to buy me. I'd be a great companion.'

The guy looks at the $200 price tag. 'Sorry, but I just can't afford that.'

'Psssssst,' says the parrot. 'I'm defective, so the truth is, nobody wants me cause I don't have any feet. You probably can get me for $20. Just make the guy an offer.'

The guy offers $20 and walks out with the parrot. Weeks go by. The parrot is sensational. He has a great sense of humour, he's interesting, he's a pal, he understands everything, he sympathises and he's insightful. The guy is delighted.

One day he comes home from work and the parrot says, 'Psssssssssssst' and motions him over with one wing. 'I don't know if I should tell you this or not, but it's about your wife and the postman.'

'What are you talking about?,' asks the guy.

'When the postman delivered today, your wife greeted him at the door in a sheer black nightie and kissed him passionately.'

'WHAT?' the guy asks incredulously. 'THEN what happened?'

'Well, then the postman came into the house and lifted up her nightie and began petting her all over,' reported the parrot.

'My God!' he exclaims. 'Then what?'

'Then he lifted up her nightie, got down on his knees and began to kiss her all over, starting with her breasts and slowly going down.'

'WELL?!' demands the frantic guy. 'THEN WHAT HAPPENED?'

'Damned if I know, I got a hard-on and fell off my perch.'

 ## CAN YOU BEAR IT?

A bear walks into a bar in Billings, Montana, and sits down. He bangs on the bar with his paw and demands a beer.

The barman approaches and says, 'We don't serve beer to bears in bars in Billings.'

The bear, becoming angry, demands again that he be served a beer.

The barman tells him again, more forcefully, 'We don't serve beer to belligerent bears in bars in Billings.'

The bear, very angry now, says, 'If you don't serve me a beer, I'm going to eat that lady sitting at the end of the bar.'

The barman says, 'Sorry, we don't serve beer to belligerent, bully bears in bars in Billings.'

The bear goes to the end of the bar, and, as promised, eats the woman. He comes back to his seat and again demands a beer.

The barman states, 'Sorry, we don't serve beer to belligerent, bully bears in bars in Billings who are on drugs.'

The bear says, 'I'm NOT on drugs.'

The barman says, 'You are now. That was a "bar bitch you ate".'

 ## BURGLAR BILL GETS A FRIGHT >>>

A burglar broke into a house one night. He shone his flashlight around, looking for valuables, and when he picked up a CD player to place in his sack, a strange, disembodied voice echoed from the dark saying, 'Jesus is watching you.' He nearly jumped out of his skin, clicked his flashlight off and froze.

When he heard nothing more, he shook his head, clicked the light back on and began searching for more valuables.

Just as he pulled the stereo out to disconnect the wires, clear as a bell he heard, 'Jesus is watching you.'

Freaked out, he shone his light around frantically, looking for the source of the voice. Finally, in the corner of the room, his flashlight beam came to rest on a parrot.

'Did you say that?' he hissed at the parrot.

'Yep,' the parrot confessed, 'I'm just trying to warn you.'

The burglar relaxed. 'Warn me, huh? Who the hell are you?'

'Moses,' replied the bird.

'Moses?' the burglar laughed. 'What kind of stupid people would name a parrot Moses?'

'Probably the same kind of people that would name a Rottweiler Jesus,' the bird answered.

 COCKROACH HORRORS >>>

A man was sitting at home one evening, when the doorbell rang. When he answered the door, a six-foot-tall cockroach was standing there. The cockroach immediately punched him between the eyes and scampered off.

The next evening, the man was sitting at home when the doorbell rang again. When he answered the door, the cockroach was there again. This time, it punched him, kicked him in the bollocks and karate-chopped him before running away.

The third evening, the man was sitting at home when the doorbell rang. When he answered the door, the cockroach was there yet again. It leapt at him and stabbed him several times before running off. The gravely injured man managed to crawl to the telephone and summon an ambulance. He was rushed to intensive care, where they saved his life.

The next morning, the doctor was doing his rounds. He asked the man what happened, so the man explained about the six-foot cockroach's attacks, culminating in the near-fatal stabbing.

The doctor thought for a moment and said, 'Yes, there IS a nasty bug going around.'

 CONFUSED TRUCKIE >>>

A truck breaks down on the Auckland motorway with a cargo of live monkeys on board, bound for Auckland Zoo. They need to be

(animal kingdom)

delivered by 9am and the driver fears he will get the sack if they don't get there on time.

He decides to try and thumb a lift for his monkeys and eventually a truck driver from the Waikato pulls over. 'Where they going?' asks the Waikato bloke.

'Do us a favour mate and take these to Auckland Zoo for me,' says the driver, 'and here's 200 bucks for your troubles.'

'Good on ya mate,' says the Waikato fella, loads the monkeys onto his truck and gets on his way.

The Auckland truckie goes about trying to fix his vehicle and is there for a good few hours when he notices the Waikato man coming back down the motorway, still with all the chimps on board.

Panicking, he flags him down again. 'What are you playing at?' he fumes, 'I told you to take them to Auckland Zoo!'

'I did,' says the bemused fella, 'but there's still 150 bucks left so now we're going to the Rainbow's End amusement park.'

✉ GOING APE! >>>

It's a beautiful, warm spring morning and a man and his girlfriend are spending the day at the zoo. She's wearing a cute, loose-fitting, pink spring dress, sleeveless with straps. He's wearing jeans and a T-shirt.

The zoo is not very busy. As they walk through the ape and gorilla section, they pass in front of a very large hairy gorilla. Noticing the girl, the gorilla goes crazy. He jumps up on the bars, and holding on with one hand (and two feet), he grunts and pounds his chest with his free hand.

He is obviously excited at the pretty lady in the dress. The boyfriend, noticing the excitement, thinks this is funny. He suggests that his girl teases the poor ape some more. The man suggests she pucker her lips, wiggle her bottom at him, and play along.

She does, and Mr Gorilla gets even more excited, making noises that would wake the dead. Then the man suggests that she let the straps fall to show a little more skin and cleavage. She does, and Mr Gorilla is about to tear the bars off his cage. 'Now try lifting your dress up to your thighs and sort of fan it at him,' he says.

This drives the gorilla absolutely crazy and now he's doing flips.

The man then grabs his girl, rips open the door to the cage, flings her in with the gorilla and slams the cage door shut. 'Now, tell HIM you've got a headache!'

✉ BLIND PARACHUTIST >>>

A blind man was describing his favourite sport — parachuting. When asked how this was accomplished, he said that things were all done for him.

'I am placed in the door and told when to jump. My hand is placed on my release ring for me, and out I go.'

'But how do you know when you are going to land?' he was asked.

'I have a very keen sense of smell and I can smell the trees and grass when I am 100 metres from the ground,' he answered.

'But how do you know when to lift your legs for the final arrival on the ground?' he was asked.

He quickly answered, 'Oh, the dog's leash goes slack.'

the good,
the bad
and the
ugly

> All hell has broken loose in Iraq and we admit the pictures we see daily of innocents lying injured or dead certainly don't bring on the need for a laugh. All of this chapter, a lot of which takes the piss out of George W and Saddam Hussein, was penned in the months leading up to Bush's unheeded 48-hour warning to the Iraqi leader.

So they lampoon the jousting leading up to the first shot, which in the light of what's happened since the war began, can at least bring the odd wry chuckle, if not exactly belly laughs. The jokes pertaining to the then pending

> war are shamelessly biased against Bush (and Hussein), but then people who were pro-Bush and by definition, pro-war, were hardly likely to come up with anything remotely funny before the hostilities began.

> We hope that by the time you read this, the war is over and the losers have not yet begun to seek revenge.

✉ JOHNNY GIVES THE AUSSIE SLANT >>>

The hard man of the Coalition of the Willing, John Winston Howard, has put Saddam Hussein on notice, declaring in Washington this week that it's time for Iraq to get 'fair dinkum'.

This is a full transcript of the Prime Minister's announcement before the world's media explaining the Australian position:

'The people of Australia are neither dills nor drongos. It should by now be obvious that Saddam Hussein reckons we're both and, frankly, I've had a gutsful.

'That quality bloke from the UN, Hans Blix, has on several occasions now rocked up in Baghdad for a squizz, only to be stuffed around by a blue-chip bullshit artist who insists that, apart from a couple of two-penny bangers and a Catherine wheel, his arsenal of weapons amounts to three-fifths of stuff-all.

'To you, Saddam, I say: "Get your hand off it." This isn't bush week. We didn't come down in the last shower, and will muck in for one almighty stink unless you pull your finger out and stop taking the freedom-loving world for a ride.

'The President was asked whether Australia is part of the coalition of the willing. My oath we are. We're as willing as buggery. As billy-o. We're as willing as all get-out.

'That said, we are not yet dead-set for a stoush, and still believe that an honest yarn can sort out this barney — but only if Saddam is true blue about it.

'We see little point, however, in adopting the shirt-lifting position taken by some of the continentals.

'Tony Blair has been beaut, even if the average Pom on the street remains iffy. But France and Germany are an absolute cot-case, a hopeless bloody rabble. This is hardly surprising, as both nations have well and truly got the runs on the board in the showpony stakes.

'Many of you will be familiar with my colleague Alexander Downer and his doctrine of the busted-arse countries. Today I expand that doctrine to include another category — the up-themselves purse-swinging states of Western Europe.

'The Frogs, with their history of having a bob each way, only to bludge their way out of strife, and the Krauts, who brought us the maddest bastard and biggest dust-up of the twentieth century, but come the raw prawn in the face of a comparable global shemozzle.

'To the Europeans I say — fair suck of the sav. Unless you lift your game — and quick smart — you will be found standing, dacked, before world opinion.

'In the coming donnybrook, I would also stress that we have absolutely no worries with the Muslim peoples of the world. My government has been bagged by bolshies for hopping into queue-jumpers — some reckon I pinched my third spell in the bush capital by giving them heaps — but they're a bloody marvellous mob and I would be more than happy to blow the froth off a couple with any of them should they shack up next door, provided they've had their bona fides sussed by our pen-pushers.

'Any war will be about a fair go for the people of Iraq who have had the mockers put on them for far too long by this rolled-gold, 24-carat nong who, cunning as a shithouse rat, has tried to con the world while acting like a low mongrel towards his own citizens and a raving fruitcake throughout the region.

'Time is running out, Saddam. Comply with the UN's demands and everything will be tickety-boo. Keep piss-farting around and we'll be in like Flynn. And you, Saddam, will be cactus.

'To those domestic whiners and whingers who accuse me of cranking it too hard too early — particularly Simon Crean and his pinko mates, who have given the seppo dippos the irrits by having a red-hot go at their President — I warn that you are playing right into the hands of a man who is demonstrably as mad as a cut snake.

'I trust this clarifies the Australian position. I would now like to invite the President back to the embassy for a phlegm-cutter. I understand he is no longer massively on the turps and may not be on for a proper session. In these troubled times, however, we should allow ourselves a couple of sly ones. I thank youse all.'

Glossary

Fair dinkum: honest, genuine.
Dill: rather idiotic person.
Drongo: one who is intellectually challenged.
Had a gutsful: has crossed the threshold of tolerance.
Quality bloke: fine fellow.
Rocked up: arrived.
Squizz: observed.
Stuffed around: to have one's time wasted; obstructed.
Bullshit artist: one of dubious verbal honesty.
Two-penny banger: a small percussive firework.
Catherine wheel: a magnesium-based firework on a stick designed to spin around.
Three-fifths of stuff-all: nothing.
Get your hand off it: please desist in partaking in all forms of onanism; stop kidding oneself.
Bush week: period when farmers and other yokels might come to town; a period of universal relaxation.
Didn't come down in the last shower: not utterly naïve.
Muck in: willing to participate in a difficult task.
Almighty stink: significant quarrel.
Pull your finger out [of your rectum]: desist in mindless delay.
My oath: upon my word.
Willing as buggery: rather keen.
Billy-o: a superlative; extremely.
All get-out: another superlative; most assuredly.
Dead-set: absolutely.
Stoush: a fight.
Honest yarn: engage in earnest dialogue.
Barney: a fight.
True blue: genuine.
Shirt-lifting: exhibitionist.
Beaut: exemplary.
Pom: individual of English origin.

Iffy: questionable.

Cot-case: hopeless; finished.

Runs on the board: credibility or past predilection.

Showpony stakes: scale of exhibitionist and self-indulgent behaviour.

Busted-arse country [one which has the arse out of its trousers]: less-developed country.

Purse-swinging: demonstrating overt homosexuality.

Frogs: individuals of French origin.

Bob each way: to place a bet on a win or a place; to hedge one's position.

Bludge: attempt to gain something for nothing.

Kraut: individual of German origin.

Dust-up: a fight.

Come the raw prawn: behave disingenuously.

Shemozzle: a mess.

Fair suck of the sav [saveloy]: a decent chance; a reference to sharing food from a fast-food outlet.

Dacked: to have one's underwear removed rapidly in public.

Donnybrook: a fight.

No worries: relaxed attitude towards.

Bagged: criticised.

Bolshies: Bolsheviks.

Hopping into: criticising.

Queue-jumper: illegal asylum seeker.

Pinched: obtained through less than honest means.

Third spell in the bush capital: secured a third term of office as Head of Government.

Give them heaps: extreme criticism.

Blow the froth off a couple: drink several beers in a convivial atmosphere.

Shack up: move into a house.

Sussed: examine carefully.

Pen-pusher: appropriate bureaucratic authority.

Fair go: demonstrably equitable opportunity.

Had the mockers put on them: victimised most perniciously.

Rolled gold, 24-carat nong: individual of questionable integrity.

Cunning as a shithouse rat: one possessed of an extremely devious nature.

Low mongrel: one who has behaved reprehensibly.

(the good, the bad and the ugly)

Pinko: communist raving fruitcake; of questionable sanity.
Tickety-boo: pleasant condition.
Piss-farting around: wasting time.
In like Flynn: moving rapidly to a position of advantage (ref: Errol Flynn, Aussie actor famous for rapid seductions).
Cactus [cactus profundus]: mock Latin phrase for in a moribund condition.
Cranking it too hard: excessive effort to achieve.
Mate: friend.
Seppo dippo: American Embassy Official (ref: seppo = septic = septic tank= Yank = American. Dippo = diplomat).
Irrits: the irritable shits; consternation.
Red-hot go: violent verbal attack.
Mad as a cut snake: excessively aggravated.
Phlegm-cutter: a beer.
Massively on the turps: consistent and excessive consumption of alcohol (turps = turpentine = spirituous liquors).
On for a proper session: planning to indulge in a bout of binge drinking.
Couple of sly ones: several surreptitiously consumed beers.

✉ WHOOPS, A MORON >>>

A woman bought a new Lexus. Cost a bundle. Two days later, she brought it back, complaining that the radio was not working. 'Madam,' said the sales manager, 'the audio system in this car is completely automatic. All you need to do is tell it what you want to listen to, and you will hear exactly that!'

She drove out, somewhat amazed and a little confused. She looked at the radio and said, 'Nelson.'

The radio responded, 'Ricky or Willie?' She was astounded.

If she wanted Beethoven, that's what she got. If she wanted Nat King Cole, she got it. She was stopped at a traffic light enjoying 'On the Road Again' when the light turned green and she pulled out. Suddenly an enormous 4WD, coming from the street she was crossing, sped toward her, obviously not paying attention to the light. She swerved and narrowly missed a collision.

'Idiot!' she yelled and, from the radio: 'Ladies and gentlemen, the President of the United States.'

Terry Jones (of *Monty Python* fame) in the *Observer*,
26 January 2003

I'm really excited by George Bush's latest reason for bombing Iraq:
he's running out of patience. And so am I! For some time now I've
been really pissed off with Mr Johnson, who lives a couple of doors
down the street.

Well, him and Mr Patel, who runs the health-food shop. They
both give me queer looks and I'm sure Mr Johnson is planning
something nasty for me, but so far I haven't been able to discover
what. I've been round to his place a few times to see what he's up
to, but he's got everything well hidden. That's how devious he is.

As for Mr Patel, don't ask me how I know, I just know — from
very good sources — that he is, in reality, a mass murderer. I have
leafleted the street telling them that if we don't act first, he'll pick
us off one by one.

Some of my neighbours say that if I've got proof, why don't I go
to the police? But that's simply ridiculous. The police will say that
they need evidence of a crime with which to charge my neighbours.
They'll come up with endless red tape and quibbling about the
rights and wrongs of a pre-emptive strike and all the while Mr
Johnson will be finalising his plans to do terrible things to me,
while Mr Patel will be secretly murdering people. Since I'm the only
one in the street with a decent range of automatic firearms, I
reckon it's up to me to keep the peace. But until recently that's been
a little difficult.

Now, however, George W Bush has made it clear that all I need to
do is run out of patience, and then I can wade in and do whatever I
want!

That's why I want to blow up Mr Johnson's garage and kill his
wife and children. Strike first! That'll teach him a lesson. Then
he'll leave us in peace and stop peering at me in that totally
unacceptable way. Mr Bush makes it clear that all he needs to know
before bombing Iraq is that Saddam is a really nasty man and that
he has weapons of mass destruction — even if no one can find
them. I'm certain I've just as much justification for killing Mr
Johnson's wife and children as Mr Bush has for bombing Iraq.

Mr Johnson and Mr Patel are just the tip of the iceberg. There are

dozens of other people in the street who I don't like and who —
quite frankly — look at me in odd ways. No one will be really safe
until I've wiped them all out. My wife says I might be going too far
but I tell her I'm simply using the same logic as the President of
the United States. That shuts her up. Like Mr Bush, I've run out of
patience, and if that's a good enough reason for the President, it's
good enough for me.

I'm going to give the whole street two weeks — no, 10 days —
to come out in the open and hand over all aliens and
interplanetary hijackers, galactic outlaws and interstellar terrorist
masterminds, and if they don't hand them over nicely and say
'Thank you', I'm going to bomb the entire street to kingdom come.
It's just as sane as what George W Bush is proposing and, in
contrast to what he's intending, my policy will destroy only one
street.

 BUSH WARFARE >>>

Kofi Annan, the Secretary General of the United Nations, was deep
in discussion with George W Bush about the impending invasion of
Iraq.

'Tell me George,' says Kofi, 'what makes you so certain that Iraq
and Saddam Hussein have weapons of mass destruction?'

'Oh, we know Kofi,' says George.

'But how can you be so absolutely certain?' Kofi continues.
'Remember, if this war starts it's going to lead to hundreds if not
thousands of deaths and they could be innocent deaths if you are
not sure there are weapons of mass destruction in Iraq. Are you sure
you're certain?'

'Oh, we're certain alright,' says George, 'and we have copies of
the invoices to prove it.'

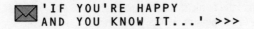
If You're Happy And You Know It Bomb Iraq

If you cannot find Osama, bomb Iraq
If the markets are a drama, bomb Iraq
If the terrorists are frisky
Pakistan is looking shifty
North Korea is too risky
Bomb Iraq.

If we have no allies with us, bomb Iraq
If we think that someone's dissed us, bomb Iraq
So to hell with the inspections
Let's look tough for the elections
Close your mind and take directions
Bomb Iraq.

It's pre-emptive non-aggression, bomb Iraq
To prevent this mass destruction, bomb Iraq
They've got weapons we can't see
And that's all the proof we need
If they're not there, they must be
Bomb Iraq.

If you never were elected, bomb Iraq
If your mood is quite dejected, bomb Iraq
If you think Saddam's gone mad
With the weapons that he had
And he tried to kill your dad
Bomb Iraq.

If corporate fraud is growin', bomb Iraq
If your ties to it are showin', bomb Iraq
If your politics are sleazy
And hiding that ain't easy
And your manhood's getting queasy
Bomb Iraq.

Fall in line and follow orders, bomb Iraq
For our might knows not our borders, bomb Iraq
Disagree? We'll call it treason
Let's make war not love this season
Even if we have no reason
Bomb Iraq.

 ## QUOTE OF THE YEAR >>>

Nominated for Quote of the Year is the statement made by Texas
Congressman Dick Armey when asked, 'If you had been in President
Clinton's place would you have resigned?'

Armey's reply: 'If I had been in the president's place I would not
have gotten the chance to resign. I would have been lying in a pool
of my own blood, looking up, and listening to my wife ask, "How
do you reload this son of a bitch?"'

 ## SEARCHING SURGEONS >>>

Five surgeons are discussing who makes the best patients to operate
on but, like economists, they can never agree on anything.

The first surgeon says, 'I like to see accountants on my operating
table, because when you open them up, everything inside is
numbered.'

The second responds, 'Yeah, but you should try electricians!
Everything inside them is colour-coded.'

The third surgeon says, 'No, I really think librarians are the best;
everything inside them is in alphabetical order.'

The fourth surgeon chimes in, 'You know, I like construction
workers … those guys always understand when you have a few
parts left over at the end, and when the job takes longer than you
said it would.'

But the fifth surgeon shut them all up when he observed: 'You're
all wrong. Politicians are the easiest to operate on. There's no guts,
no heart, no balls, no brains and no spine, and the head and the
arse are interchangeable.'

VALENTINE FOR OSAMA >>>

Little Melissa comes home from school and tells her father that they learned about the history of Valentine's Day in class that day.

She says, 'You know that Valentine's Day is in honour of a Christian saint and our family is Jewish …' She then asks, 'So will God get mad at me for giving someone a valentine?'

Melissa's father thinks a bit, then says, 'That's a nice thing to do, I don't think God would get mad at all. Who do you want to give a valentine to?'

'Osama bin Laden,' she says.

'Really? Why Osama bin Laden?' her father asks in shock.

'Well,' she says, 'I thought that if one little Jewish girl in America could have enough love to give Osama a valentine, he might start to think that maybe we're not all bad, and maybe he would start loving people a little bit. And if other kids saw what I did and sent valentines to Osama, maybe he'd be able to love even more. And then he'd start going all over the place to tell everyone how much he loved them and how he didn't hate anyone any more.'

Her father's heart swells and he looks at his daughter with new-found pride. 'Melissa, that's the most wonderful thing I've ever heard.'

'I know,' Melissa says, 'and once that gets him out in the open, the Marines could blow the shit out of him.'

JOHN'S ANSWER >>>

An Aussie bloke, on his way home from work, came to a complete halt in a traffic jam. Nothing was moving. He notices a police officer walking back and forth between the lines of cars.

'Officer, what's the problem?' the man asks.

'John Howard is just so depressed about moving with Janette back to Lane Cove that he stopped his motorcade in the middle of the freeway and he's threatening to douse himself in petrol and set himself on fire,' said the copper.

'He says his family hates him and he doesn't have the money to pay for the new house renovations. We're taking up a collection for him.'

the good, the bad and the ugly

'Oh really? How much have you got so far?' said the driver.

'About three hundred litres, but a lot of people are still siphoning.'

 GEORGE W'S A VERY CONFUSED MAN >>>

We take you now to the Oval Office …

George: 'Condi! [Condileesa Rice] Nice to see you. What's happening?'
Condi: 'Sir, I have the report here about the new leader of China.'
George: 'Great. Lay it on me.'
Condi: 'Hu is the new leader of China.'
George: 'That's what I want to know.'
Condi: 'That's what I'm telling you.'
George: 'That's what I'm asking you. Who is the new leader of China?'
Condi: 'Yes.'
George: 'I mean the fellow's name.'
Condi: 'Hu.'
George: 'The guy in China.'
Condi: 'Hu.'
George: 'The new leader of China.'
Condi: 'Hu.'
George: 'The Chinaman!'
Condi: 'Hu is leading China.'
George: 'Now whaddya asking me for?'
Condi: 'I'm telling you Hu is leading China.'
George: 'Well, I'm asking you. Who is leading China?'
Condi: 'That's the man's name.'
George: 'That's who's name?'
Condi: 'Yes.'
George: 'Will you or will you not tell me the name of the new leader of China?'
Condi: 'Yes, sir.'
George: 'Yassir? Yassir Arafat is in China? I thought he was in the Middle East.'
Condi: 'That's correct.'
George: 'Then who is in China?'

Condi: 'Yes, sir.'

George: 'Yassir is in China?'

Condi: 'No, sir.'

George: 'Then who is?'

Condi: 'Yes, sir.'

George: 'Yassir?'

Condi: 'No, sir.'

George: 'Look, Condi. I need to know the name of the new leader of China. Get me the Secretary General of the UN on the phone.'

Condi: 'Kofi?'

George: 'No, thanks.'

Condi: 'You want Kofi?'

George: 'No.'

Condi: 'You don't want Kofi.'

George: 'No. But now that you mention it, I could use a glass of milk. And then get me the UN.'

Condi: 'Yes, sir.'

George: 'Not Yassir! The guy at the UN.'

Condi: 'Kofi?'

George: 'Milk! Will you please make the call?'

Condi: 'And call who?'

George: 'Who is the guy at the UN?'

Condi: 'Hu is the guy in China.'

George: 'Will you stay out of China?!'

Condi: 'Yes, sir.'

George: 'And stay out of the Middle East! Just get me the guy at the UN.'

Condi: 'Kofi.'

George: 'All right! With cream and two sugars. Now get on the phone.'

(Condi picks up the phone.)

Condi: 'Rice here.'

George: 'Rice? Good idea. And a couple of egg rolls, too. Maybe we should send some to the guy in China. And the Middle East. Can you get Chinese food in the Middle East?'

✉ SURVEY SHAMOZZLE >>>

Dear UN General Assembly members,

Last month, a worldwide survey was conducted by the United Nations. The only question asked was: 'Would you please give your most honest opinion about solutions to the food shortage in the rest of the world?'

The survey was a HUGE failure because … in Africa they did not know what 'food' meant; in Western Europe they did not know what 'shortage' meant; in Eastern Europe they did not know what 'opinion' meant; in the Middle East they did not know what 'solution' meant; in South America they did not know what 'please' meant and in the United States they did not know what 'the rest of the world' meant.

Regards,
Kofi Annan

✉ MR PRESIDENT TALKS HIMSELF INTO TROUBLE >>>

President George W Bush is visiting an elementary school, and he visits one of the classes.

They are in the middle of a discussion related to words and their meanings. The teacher asks the President if he would like to lead the class in the discussion of the word 'tragedy'. So the illustrious leader asks the class for an example of a 'tragedy'.

One little boy stands up and offers, 'If my best friend, who lives next door, is playing in the street and a car comes along and runs him over, that would be a tragedy.'

'No', says Mr Bush, 'that would be an ACCIDENT.'

A little girl raises her hand: 'If a school bus carrying 50 children drove off a cliff, killing everyone involved, that would be a tragedy.'

'I'm afraid not,' explains Mr President. 'That's what we would call a GREAT LOSS.'

The room goes silent. No other children volunteer. President Bush searches the room. 'Isn't there someone here who can give me an example of a tragedy?'

Finally, way in the back of the room, a small boy raises his hand. In a quiet voice he says, 'If Air Force One, carrying Mr Bush, were struck by a missile and blown up to smithereens by a terrorist like Osama bin Laden, that would be a tragedy.'

'Fantastic,' exclaims Bush, 'that's right. And can you tell me WHY that would be a TRAGEDY?'

'Well,' says the boy, 'because it wouldn't be an accident, and it certainly wouldn't be a great loss.'

POLITICS IN A CONDOM >>>

A prominent ad agency has suggested that the Liberal Party of Australia change its logo to something resembling the Olympic rings, using intertwined coloured condoms instead. The reasoning is that it more clearly reflects the Government's political stance. A condom stands up to inflation, halts production, destroys the next generation, protects a bunch of pricks and gives you a sense of security while you're actually being screwed. It just doesn't get more accurate than that.

MORON-FILLED GOVERNMENTS >>>

A major research institution has recently announced the discovery of the heaviest element yet known to science. This new element has been tentatively named 'governmentium'. Governmentium has one neutron, 12 assistant neutrons, 75 deputy neutrons, and 112 assistant deputy neutrons, giving it an atomic mass of 200.

These 200 particles are held together by forces called morons, which are surrounded by vast quantities of lepton-like particles called peons. Since governmentium has no electrons, it is inert. However, it can be detected as it impedes every reaction with which it comes into contact. A minute amount of governmentium causes one reaction to take over four days to complete when it would normally take less than a second.

Governmentium has a normal half-life of three years; it does not decay but instead undergoes a reorganisation in which a portion of the assistant neutrons and deputy neutrons exchange places. In fact, governmentium's mass will actually increase over time, since each reorganisation causes some morons to become neutrons, forming isodopes. This characteristic of moron-promotion leads some scientists to speculate that governmentium is formed whenever morons reach a certain quantity in concentration. This hypothetical quantity is referred to as: 'Critical Morass'.

You will know it when you see it ...

✉ BILL'S THE MAIN MAN >>>

A man takes the day off work and decides to go out golfing. He is on the second hole when he notices a frog sitting next to the green.

He thinks nothing of it and is about to shoot when he hears, 'Ribbit nine iron.' The man looks around and doesn't see anyone. Again, he hears, 'Ribbit nine iron.'

He looks at the frog and decides to prove the frog wrong, puts the club away, and grabs a nine iron. Boom! He hits it 25 centimetres from the cup. He is shocked.

He says to the frog, 'Wow that's amazing. You must be a lucky frog, eh?'

The frog replies, 'Ribbit lucky frog.'

The man decides to take the frog with him to the next hole. 'What do you think frog?' the man asks.

'Ribbit three wood.' The guy takes out a three wood and, boom! Hole in one. The man is befuddled and doesn't know what to say.

By the end of the day, the man has played the best game of golf in his life and asks the frog, 'OK, where to next?'

The frog replies, 'Ribbit Las Vegas.'

They go to Las Vegas and the guy says, 'OK frog, now what?'

The frog says, 'Ribbit roulette.'

Upon approaching the roulette table, the man asks, 'What do you think I should bet?'

The frog replies, 'Ribbit $3000, black six.'

Now, this is a million-to-one shot to win, but after the golf game the man figures what the heck. Boom! Tons of cash comes sliding back across the table. The man takes his winnings and buys the best room in the hotel.

He sits the frog down and says, 'Frog, I don't know how to repay you. You've won me all this money and I am forever grateful.'

The frog replies, 'Ribbit kiss me.' He figures why not, since after all the frog did for him, he deserves it. With a kiss, the frog turns into a gorgeous 15-year-old girl.

'And that, your honour, is how the girl ended up in my room. So help me God or my name is not William Jefferson Clinton.'

✉ GEORGE W, THE CLEVEREST PRESIDENT! >>>

An aeroplane was about to crash with five people on board but only four parachutes. The first passenger said, 'I am Kobe Bryant, the best NBA basketball player. The Lakers need me; I can't afford to die.' So he took the first pack and left the plane.

The second passenger, Hillary Clinton, said, 'I am the wife of the former US President, a NY State Senator and a potential future president.' So she took the second pack and jumped out of the plane.

The third passenger, George W Bush, said, 'I'm the President of the United States of America. I have great responsibility being the leader of a super-power nation and I am the cleverest President in American history, so America's people won't let me die.' So he grabbed the pack next to him and jumped out of the plane.

The fourth passenger, the Pope, said to the fifth passenger, a 10-year-old schoolgirl, 'I am old and frail and don't have many years left, and as a Catholic I will sacrifice my life and let you have the last parachute.'

The girl said, 'It's OK, there is a parachute left for you. America's cleverest President has taken my school-bag.'

✉ JAYSUS, MARY AND JOSEPH >>>

Saddam Hussein was sitting in his office wondering whom to invade next, when his telephone rang.

'Hallo, Mr Hussein?' a heavily accented voice said. 'Dis is Paddy, down at the Harp and Fiddle Pub in County Sligo, Ireland, so it is. Oy'm ringin' to inform you dat we are officially declaring war on you!'

'Well, Paddy, this is indeed important news! How big is your army?'

'Roit now …' said Paddy, after a moment's calculation, 'dere's meself, me cousin Sean, me next-door neighbour Seamus and the entire darts team from the pub. Dat makes eight … an' me dog.'

Saddam paused. 'I must tell you Paddy, that I have one million men in my army waiting to move on my command.'

'Jaysus, now!' said Paddy. 'Oi'll have to ring you back.'

Sure enough, the next day Paddy called again.

'Mr Hussein, the war is still on! We've managed to acquire some infantry equipment.'

'And what equipment would that be, Paddy?' Saddam asked.

'Well now, we have two combines, a D9 bulldozer and Murphy's farm tractor.'

Saddam sighed. 'I must tell you Paddy, that I have 16,000 tanks and 14,000 armoured personnel carriers. Also I've increased my army to 1.5 million since we last spoke.'

'Saints preserve us!' said Paddy. 'I'll have to get back to you.'

Sure enough, Paddy rang the next day. 'Mr Hussein, the war is still on! We have managed to get ourselves airborne! We've modified Harrigan's ultra-light crop sprayer with a couple of shotguns in the cockpit and four boys from the Shamrock Pub have joined us as well.'

Saddam was silent for a minute and then cleared his throat. 'I must tell you Paddy, that I have 1000 bombers and 2000 fighter planes. My military complex is surrounded by laser-guided, surface-to-air missile sites. And since we last spoke I've increased my army to TWO MILLION!'

'Jaysus, Mary and Joseph!' said Paddy. 'I'll have to ring you back.'

Sure enough, Paddy called the next day. 'Top of the mornin', Mr Hussein! I am sorry to tell you that we have had to call off the war.'

'I'm sorry to hear that,' said Saddam. 'Why the sudden change of heart?'

'Well,' said Paddy, 'we've all had a long chat over a few pints of the Guinness, and we don't tink dere's any feckin' way we can feed two million prisoners.'

Snow White, Muhammad Ali and Saddam Hussein all visit the magic mirror. The magic mirror on the wall confirms their greatest wish. Snow White is indeed the fairest of them all, Ali is the greatest of them all and Saddam is the biggest bastard of them all.

They leave the hall of the magic mirror quite pleased with themselves, until Snow White has a thought and turns to the others. 'That's all very well,' she says, 'but I want a second opinion.' The others agree, so they decide to do a bit of research to find who would be more qualified than the magic mirror.

After asking around, they hear of a wise man in a cabin in the mountains.

After tramping for a few days in the mountains, they find the cabin of the wise man, tucked away in a forest under a mountain.

Snow White knocks on the door, and is welcomed by a big bearded man, the Wise Man of the Mountains. She goes in and sits down. 'What can I do for you?' asks the wise man.

'Can you tell me please,' she asks, 'am I truly the fairest in the land?'

'Yes, my dear,' says the wise old man, 'you are the fairest, and indeed, the most beautiful.'

She leaves beaming widely, happy in the knowledge that she is the fairest in the land. Next, Ali bangs on the door and is let in. Without bothering to sit down, he bellows, 'Yo! Tell me square, old man. Am I the greatest or what?'

Smiling, the wise man says, 'Ali, there is none greater. I doubt there will ever be one greater than you.' Ali slaps the old man on the back and leaves with a big grin on his face.

Finally, Saddam enters without knocking. Outside, the other two can only hear murmurs, a cry of dismay, then silence. The door slowly opens and out comes Saddam with a puzzled expression on his face. 'Who's Russell Coutts?' he says.

IN MEMORY OF PIGGY MULDOON >>>

In the 1970s and early 1980s, Rob Muldoon — or Piggy Muldoon to the general populace — ruled the roost in New Zealand politics in a ruthless and often nasty manner. He was admired by a great many, or enough to get him and his National Party elected in 1975 and ruling until he called an ill-judged snap election in 1984, allegedly under the influence of the gin bottle, and got soundly beaten by David Lange's Labour Party.

Muldoon had influence, and some time in the late 1970s he was dining at a popular Wellington restaurant with friends when a man went up to him and, apologising profusely, wondered if he could ask the Prime Minister a favour. Muldoon was intrigued and told the man to ask away.

'Well, it's like this, Mr Muldoon,' the man said. 'I am a small businessman trying to get into the big league and I am dining with a prospective client that could go a long way to me realising my dream of making it big.

'Now I have been a National voter all my life and have admired you. You have the tough style I like and don't take any nonsense. You're also a great believer in small business and have been an inspiration.'

Muldoon was basking in this little man's praise but, mindful of the company he was entertaining, decided to cut him short and demand what favour the man required of him.

'Well,' the man said rather nervously, 'I was hoping that some time tonight you could come by my table, stop and say hello like an old friend, ask me how business is and generally be friendly. I know my dinner guest would be most impressed and it would probably help me with my negotiations. By the way, my name is Tom and we're just over there near the men's toilets.'

Muldoon was amused by the man's candour and said yes he would come by his table and impress the dinner guest.

Some time later, Muldoon went to the toilets and on his way back to his table he stopped at the man's table and said, 'Hello Tom, I haven't seen you for ages. How's business?'

To this the man looked at Muldoon and said, 'F*** off, Piggy, can't you see I'm busy?'

 OUT TO LUNCH >>>

George Bush and Dick Cheney are enjoying a celebration lunch at a fancy Washington restaurant. Their waitress approaches the table to take their order. She is young and very attractive. She asks Cheney what he wants.

He replies, 'I'll have the heart-healthy salad.'

'Very good, sir,' she replies. Turning to Bush she asks, 'And what do you want, Mr President?'

Bush answers, 'How about a quickie?'

Taken aback, the waitress slaps him and says, 'I'm shocked and disappointed in you. I thought you were bringing in a new administration that was committed to high principles and morality. I'm sorry I voted for you.' With that, the waitress departed in a huff.

Cheney leans over to Bush, and says, 'Mr President, I believe that's pronounced "quiche".'

✉ TOP 21 ANAGRAMS FOR OSAMA BIN LADEN >>>

21. Sane Oilman Bad
20. I bona leadsman
19. Nasal Nomad Be I
18. Be a Slain Nomad
17. A bend lama son
16. Albania's Demon
15. A lesbian nomad
14. Alias 'Boned Man'
13. So I anal bad men
12. And I blame a son
11. No Asian bedlam
10. I.D.: Mean Anal S.O.B.
9. I, a sad nobleman
8. A slain abdomen
7. I'm so banal, Edna
6. I model bananas
5. A mob, insane lad
4. Is a lone, bad man
3. Do a samba, Lenin
2. I'm Dole bananas
1. Abandon e-mails

the good, the bad and the ugly

BUSLOAD OF LIES >>>

A busload of politicians were driving down a country road when, all of a sudden, the bus ran off the road, and crashed into a tree in an old farmer's field. The old farmer, after seeing what had happened, went over to investigate. He then proceeded to dig a hole to bury the politicians.

A few days later the local sheriff came out, saw the crashed bus, and asked the old farmer where all the politicians had gone.

The old farmer said he had buried them.

The sheriff asked the old farmer, 'Were they all dead?'

The old farmer replied, 'Well, some of them said they weren't, but you know how them politicians lie.'

 FROM THE MOUTHS OF... >>>

'Things are more like they are now than they have ever been.'
— President Gerald Ford

'My fellow astronauts …'
— Vice President Dan Quayle, beginning a speech at an Apollo 11 anniversary celebration

'Capital punishment is our society's recognition of the sanctity of human life.'
— Orrin Hatch, Senator from Utah, explaining his support of the death penalty

'China is a big country, inhabited by many Chinese.'
— Charles de Gaulle, ex-French President

'I stand by all the misstatements.'
— Dan Quayle, defending himself against criticism for making verbal gaffes

'Gerald Ford was a Communist.'
— Ronald Reagan in a speech. He later indicated he meant to say 'Congressman'.

'Outside of the killings, Washington DC has one of the lowest crime rates in the country.'
— Mayor Marion Barry, Washington DC

'We found the term "killing" too broad.'
— State Department spokesperson on why the word 'killing' was replaced with 'unlawful or arbitrary deprivation of life' in its human rights reports for 1984–5

'This is a great day for France!'
— President Richard Nixon while attending Charles de Gaulle's funeral

'This is the worst disaster in California since I was elected.'
— California Governor Pat Brown, discussing a local flood

'The exports include thumbscrews and cattle prods, just routine items for the police.'
— US Commerce Department spokesman on a regulation allowing the export of various products abroad

'What he does on his own time is up to him.'
— Harlon Copeland, Sheriff of Bexar County, Texas, when one of his deputies was caught exposing himself to a child

'Facts are stupid things.'
— Ronald Reagan, misquoting John Adams in a speech to the Republican convention

'Let me tell you my thoughts about tax relief. When your economy is kind of ooching along, it's important to let people have more of their own money.'
— George W. Bush, 4 Oct 2002

'We need an energy bill that encourages consumption.'
— George W. Bush, 23 Sept 2002

**If You're Invited to a Dinner Party at His Secret Afghan Lair
by Alan Meiss**

1. Point out the lice in his beard to make him feel self-conscious.
2. Pause for a moment, listen carefully, and say, 'Doesn't that sound a lot like a B-52?'
3. Ask him if he's looking forward to replacing Hitler as Satan's favourite chew toy in the lowest inferno of Hell.
4. Tell him all about your great vacation to Saudi Arabia, where you went absolutely everywhere and did everything, just stomped all over the place.
5. Use his satellite phone to call the time and weather line in Buenos Aires and leave it off the hook.
6. Tell him how much less you paid for your Kalashnikov rifle.
7. Now that you know the address of his secret cave hideout, fill out magazine subscription cards for him for the *Wine Spectator* and *Penthouse*. But do not, under any circumstances, send him *Popular Mechanics*.
8. Order him ten pizzas with extra ham topping.
9. Correct him when he ends a sentence with a preposition.
10. Ask whether the Taliban gets cable, because you haven't seen *Sex and the City* for weeks.
11. Yank the end of his turban really hard to make him spin around like a top.
12. Switch all the CD cases in his CD collection, so that when he reaches for Michael Bolton, he'll actually get the Oak Ridge Boys.
13. Mine his bathroom.
14. Use your dinner fork for your salad, and, if questioned by your host, mutter something about 'spots'.
15. Leave business cards for the Israeli Mossad in his Rolodex.
16. Take pictures of all his wives and post them on www.amihotornot.com.
17. Ask him if he wears boxers or briefs. Check. Take pictures. Again, post these on www.amihotornot.com.
18. Give him a 'Hot Chicks of Palestine' calendar.

19. Ask him if paradise is different for each person, and whether in your own paradise you'll get to kick his ass every day for eternity.
20. Reset his VCR and leave it blinking 12:00.
21. Refer to him as 'Osama-osama-fee-fi-fo-fama bin Laden'.
22. Ask whether suicide bombers have to pay union dues.
23. Tell him it's lovely what he's done with his cave, but that it'd look much nicer covered with huge, smoking craters.
24. At dinner, imply that the Northern Alliance has much prettier place settings.
25. Claim you once saw him at a Hooter's in Muncie wearing a yarmulke.
26. Ask him if he wouldn't mind if you opened the door and shined your laser pointer on his forehead for a few minutes.
27. Tell him that this is the worst pyjama party you've ever attended.
28. Ask for some pork rinds and a good brew to wash them down.
29. Mix up his Rubik's cube.
30. Ask him if he provides his employees with a retirement plan.
31. Compliment him on all his poppies outside, but mention that a few day lilies would be a nice accent.
32. Run your finger along his credenza, and say, 'tsk, tsk' if there's dust.
33. Ask whether the Taliban is hoping to be bombed ahead into the Stone Age, or perhaps the Iron Age if enough shell casings survive.
34. Explain that America is a land of freedom and opportunity, filled with people of every race, religion, and background, including millions of women strong enough to knock the crap out of him.
35. Claim that they serve much better felafel at the public executions in Sudan.
36. Ask him if he's pursuing the Lesser Jihad, the Greater Jihad, or the 'Completely Whacked Out of his Freaking Gourd' Jihad.
37. Swirl your drink thoughtfully and mention, 'Just think, in a few weeks you might fit in this glass!'
38. Check to see if Saddam is on his speed-dial list.
39. They have to wait a few years to see current television shows in Afghanistan, so give away the secret of who's having a baby on *Friends*.

the good, the bad and the ugly

40. Warn him that you're 'in a New York state of mind'.
41. Mention that his wives look quite fetching in their burkas, and ask whether they've ever thought of modelling.
42. Ask him, 'Say, where do you keep all those Stinger missiles?' just in case he'll be caught off guard and answer correctly.
43. Give him a 'noogie' or a 'wedgie'. If there's actually still a flush toilet left in Afghanistan, give him a 'swirlie'.
44. Ask to borrow his hedge trimmer and never give it back.
45. Play a game of Monopoly with him. Make him play the thimble. See if he charges interest. Claim that his properties are your 'holy lands' and blow up his hotels.
46. Fish out the secret toy surprises in all his cereal boxes.
47. Offer to take him 'clubbing' in Tel Aviv with your friends Saul and Ivan.
48. Ask him which Ninja Turtle is his favourite.
49. Give him your cellphone as a gift and ask him to leave it on for a few days so your friends can call and say hi.
50. When you leave, wave and say, 'Shalom!'

✉ WHAT A GAS >>>

George W was to represent the United States of America on a highly formal, orchestrated 'state visit' to Great Britain. Air Force One stopped at a bright red carpet along which the President strode to join Queen Elizabeth II in a beautiful, ornate 17th-century coach hitched to 6 enormous matched white horses.

The coach proceeded through the streets en route to Buckingham Palace with the President and the Queen alternating between exchanging pleasantries and waving each out their respective windows to the cheering throngs.

At one point, the right rear horse produced a thunderous, cataclysmic fart that reverberated through the air and rattled the doors of the coach. Presidents and Queens are, first and foremost, human beings. Their first reaction was to focus their attentions outside their respective windows, and behave as if nothing extraordinary had happened.

The President was the first to realise that ignoring what had happened was ridiculous. 'Queen Elizabeth, please accept my regrets ... I'm sure you understand that there are some things that even the President of the United States cannot control.'

'Mr. Bush, please don't give the matter another thought. Why, if you hadn't said something, I would have thought it was one of the horses.'

 GEORGE W'S CAMPAIGN SLOGANS >>>

- I'll turn capital punishment into a new game show!
- I promise to get cocaine off our streets: 1 kilo at a time.
- I'll finish what Bill started — the interns.
- Like father, like son. You liked my dad, right?
- I promise no sex scandal: just look at me.
- New penal plan: I won't use mine!
- Read my lips: Al Gore sucks.
- George W Bush: No hang-ups. Just hangovers.
- Vote for Bush and against Common Sense.

 TEA WITH THE QUEEN >>>

While visiting England, George Bush is invited to tea with the Queen. He asks her what her leadership philosophy is. She says that it is to surround herself with intelligent people.

Bush asks how she knows if they're intelligent.

'I do so by asking them the right questions,' says the Queen. 'Allow me to demonstrate.'

Bush watches as the Queen phones Tony Blair and says, 'Mr Prime Minister, please answer this question: your mother has a child, and your father has a child, and this child is not your brother or sister. Who is it?'

Tony Blair responds, 'It's me, ma'am.'

'Correct. Thank you and goodbye, sir,' says the Queen. She hangs up and says, 'Did you get that, Mr Bush?'

Bush nods: 'Yes ma'am. Thanks a lot. I'll definitely be using that!'

Bush, upon returning to Washington, decides he'd better put the Chairman of the Senate Foreign Relations Committee to the test. Bush summons Jesse Helms to the White House and says, 'Senator Helms, I wonder if you can answer a question for me.'

'Why, of course, sir. What's on your mind?'

Bush poses the question: 'Uhh, your mother has a child, and your father has a child, and this child is not your brother or your sister. Who is it?'

Helms hems and haws and finally asks, 'Can I think about it and get back to you?'

Bush agrees, and Helms leaves. He immediately calls a meeting of other senior Republican senators, and they puzzle over the question for several hours, but nobody can come up with an answer. Finally, in desperation, Helms calls Colin Powell at the State Department and explains his problem.

'Now lookee here, son, your mother has a child, and your father has a child, and this child is not your brother or your sister. Who is it?'

Powell answers immediately, 'It's me, of course.'

Much relieved, Helms rushes back to the White House, finds George Bush, and exclaims, 'I know the answer, sir! I know who it is! It's Colin Powell!'

And Bush replies in disgust, 'Wrong, you dumb sh*t, it's Tony Blair!'